Schooling New Media

Schooling New Media

Music, Language, and Technology in Children's Culture

Tyler Bickford

OXFORD
UNIVERSITY PRESS

OXFORD
UNIVERSITY PRESS

Oxford University Press is a department of the University of Oxford. It furthers the University's objective of excellence in research, scholarship, and education by publishing worldwide. Oxford is a registered trade mark of Oxford University Press in the UK and certain other countries.

Published in the United States of America by Oxford University Press
198 Madison Avenue, New York, NY 10016, United States of America.

Library of Congress Cataloging-in-Publication Data
Names: Bickford, Tyler.
Title: Schooling new media : music, language, and technology in children's culture / Tyler Bickford.
Description: New York, NY : Oxford University Press, [2017] |
Includes bibliographical references and index.
Identifiers: LCCN 2016045105 (print) | LCCN 2016048178 (ebook) |
ISBN 9780190654146 (hardcover : alk. paper) | ISBN 9780190654153 (pbk. : alk. paper) |
ISBN 9780190654184 (oxford scholarly online : alk. paper) |
ISBN 9780190654160 (Updf) | ISBN 9780190654177 (Epub)
Subjects: LCSH: Music and children. | Education, Elementary. | Digital media—Social aspects. | Digital music players—Social aspects.
Classification: LCC ML83 .B53 2017 (print) | LCC ML83 (ebook) | DDC 372.87—dc23
LC record available at https://lccn.loc.gov/2016045105

CONTENTS

ACKNOWLEDGMENTS

This book would not have been possible without the participation, friendship, support, advice, encouragement, and help of many people. I am most indebted to the kids at Heartsboro Central School (HCS), who made me welcome in their community and treated me like a friend. Spending a year teaching, talking, playing, laughing, arguing, and listening with them stands out as one of the great experiences of my life. I learned an enormous amount from them, only a tiny fraction of which is included in this book, but I sincerely hope that my efforts at thinking through how they make communities with one another reflects at least some small bit of the actual substance of their lives. I wish I could thank them by name, because they deserve all the credit. Teachers, parents, staff, and administrators at HCS also welcomed me, treated me as a friend and colleague, and found ways for me to be useful. They made this research possible and enjoyable, and they made me feel like I could contribute to their school's mission.

I began this project as a graduate student at Columbia University. My advisor, Aaron Fox, gave me the space to put together an unusual project and trusted me to make it work. Susan Boynton, Thomas Porcello, Patricia Shehan Campbell, and Jackie Marsh provided crucial advice, guidance, and mentorship. An extraordinary community of graduate students at Columbia provided feedback, encouragement, friendship, and professionalization, including Lauren Ninoshvili, Anna Stirr, Toby King, Niko Higgins, Simón Calle, Ryan Skinner, David Novak, Ryan Dohoney, Amanda Minks, Matt Sakakeeny, Tim Mangin, Marceline Saibu, Karen Hiles, and Andrew Eggert. Maria Sonevytsky, especially, has been a dear partner and friend since we started in this business. And this book simply would not exist without Farzaneh Hemmasi's generous and timely interventions over the last several years. I am lucky and very grateful to have such a brilliant and supportive writing partner.

Helpful feedback, encouragement, support, and advice also came from Jennifer Woodruff, Susan Young, Charlie Keil, Heather Horst, Kathy Marsh, Bambi Schieffelin, Andrea Emberly, Micah Gilmer, Paula Levin,

Bambi Chapin, Anna Beresin, Josh Pilzer, Ruti Talmor, and Kate Isard. I finished this book at the University of Pittsburgh, where I am deeply grateful to Courtney Weikle-Mills and Marah Gubar for their mentorship, encouragement, and friendship, and for welcoming me into the childhood studies community at Pitt. Brian Beaton and Rachel Mundy have been dear friends. Many colleagues have generously given advice, friendship, assistance, guidance, and support, including Don Bialostosky, Gayle Rogers, Nancy Glazener, Jen Waldron, Jonathan Arac, Troy Boone, Neepa Majumdar, Jean Carr, Amanda Godley, Adriana Helbig, Jessica Isaac, Joe Kluchurosky, and Jesse-Burton Nicholson. Suzanne Ryan at Oxford University Press has been a helpful guide and advocate through the process of publishing my first book.

I am grateful to Daniel Neilson, Ian Bickford, and Lincoln Bickford for their friendship and intellectual camaraderie over many years. Barbara Bickford and Ross Bickford have been great sources of support, encouragement, and care, and I owe them much more than I can say. My deepest thanks are to my partner, Sherilyn Saporito, who has supported me and this project (emotionally and financially) for a very long time and with great patience and enthusiasm. Her thoughts about school and teaching have been as influential on my thinking here as anyone's. Also, Lorelai Bickford Saporito is really great, and teaches me new things every day about intimacy and expressivity.

Research for this book was supported financially by a graduate fellowship at Columbia University that allowed me to work remotely while doing fieldwork in 2007–2008. The Richard D. and Mary Jane Edwards Endowed Publication Fund at the University of Pittsburgh provided resources to support publication expenses. Writing this book was also supported by my reduced teaching responsibilities at Pitt, thanks to the commitment of colleagues and administrators who value research and publication of work like this. My limited course load is also made possible by my colleagues who work on nontenurable, part-time, and contingent contracts and as graduate employees, whose teaching fills in directly for my course reductions. For what it is worth, I offer these colleagues not my gratitude but my solidarity, and I pledge to continue to work toward a future in which our labor counts equally.

Portions of *Schooling New Media* previously appeared as "Tinkering and Tethering in the Material Culture of Children's MP3 Players," in *The Oxford Handbook of Children's Musical Cultures*, edited by Patricia Shehan Campbell and Trevor Wiggins, pp. 527–42 (Oxford University Press, 2013), and as "Earbuds Are Good for Sharing: Children's Headphones as Social Media at a Vermont School," in *The Oxford Handbook of Mobile Music Studies*, vol. 1, edited by Jason Stanyek and Sumanth Gopinath, pp. 335–55

(Oxford University Press, 2014). Both are reproduced by permission of Oxford University Press. Lyrics in chapter 5 were reprinted by permission of Hal Leonard Corporation:

The Bad Touch

Words and Music by James Franks

Schooling New Media

Introduction

This book is about the encounter between entertainment and education in the everyday lives of children at a small elementary school I call Heartsboro Central School, the center of life in a small rural community in Vermont. The expressive ecology of school, through which the roles of child and adult, teacher and student, and friend and peer are constituted, is built out of productive tensions between entertainment and education, and between consumption and learning. Popular music, media, and literacy provide key repertoires that structure interaction and expression in school, and this book considers how these repertoires provide resources for individual action that structure the complex social dynamics of school.

The core of this study is a close examination of the role of portable digital music devices—iPods and MP3 players—in kids' social lives at school. Music listening practices, commonly viewed as simply receptive, can and should be understood as distinctly *expressive* and as a prominent element of a wider ecology of expressive practices that includes talk, verbal poetics, literacy, gesture, and touch, among other modalities. Music listening is expressive in school primarily as a subtle repertoire for articulating interpersonal relationships and accumulating social capital, more than it is an expression of taste and cultural capital.

The small-scale interactions in which kids put emerging technologies and mass-mediated music to use in everyday school environments reveal the interconnections of education and media in the everyday lives of children. Media, especially popular entertainment media, is often neglected in both scholarly and popular discourses about schooling. Similarly, children's media consumption is commonly understood without reference to the schools in which kids spend large portions of their lives. But in children's lives such a separation is much less clear. Certainly adults resist the intrusion of media into pedagogical spaces, and the texts of popular music for children can often seem entirely unrelated, or even opposed, to school-based educational goals. But practices or texts from education and entertainment make reference to one another precisely through exclusion and opposition. In children's everyday school lives, education and entertainment become powerful resources through which powerful institutions—governmentally chartered schools, transnational media corporations, and the modern "institution" of childhood itself—are positioned in relation to one another as part of a larger system of meaning and social organization. An analytical separation between schooling and consumerism is fundamentally unsustainable, but not simply because increasingly commercialized and privatized schooling simply reproduces consumerism. Rather, *childhood* is the mediating term than brings these fields into relation, because children are the subjects and objects of both schooling and consumer media. Despite distinct histories and institutional structures, schooling, media, and childhood are mutually constituted fields of meaning and power, and children's lives today cannot be understood outside of a framework that includes at least these three terms.

This perspective is revealing, not simply on theoretical grounds but also for what it tells us about historical and cultural developments in childhood in the contemporary United States. Childhood seems increasingly to be articulated—by children themselves, in media representations, and in adult discourse—in terms of *solidarity* among children. Such solidarity is made possible because of the positioning of children as unequal participants in the powerful institutions of school and media. Children's media consumption practices in school provide unique insights into this dynamic through which children's "peer culture" is articulated as an expression of solidarity, with implications for the wider politics of education and consumerism.

Heartsboro

In 2007 the town I call "Heartsboro" in southern Vermont had a population of fewer than eight hundred people.[1] Children in pre-kindergarten through eighth grade (ages three to fourteen) attended Heartsboro Central School (HCS). While I was in residence as a full-time researcher during the 2007–2008 school year, HCS had fewer than seventy kindergarten to eighth-grade students, so classes were paired—first with second grade, third with fourth, fifth with sixth, seventh with eighth—and still the largest class had only seventeen students. Heartsboro does not have a high school, so older kids were bused to high schools in neighboring towns.

HCS was the center of Heartsboro's social life. It was the largest institution in the town, its building contained the town office and administration, and its gym/auditorium was where social events, fundraisers, select board meetings, and annual "town hall meetings" (the classic New England political institution) were held. Heartsboro has a small downtown that is built somewhat densely. About half of the population lived in town, and the other half in houses on the surrounding hills and mountains. The kids who lived in town spent time out of school playing together, but kids from up in the hills could be isolated by the long drive to get anywhere. As in many communities, the school created opportunities for social interaction and participation for kids as well as adults who, coming to pick up or drop off their children, found opportunities to interact with other adults that would not otherwise arise. With a small student body and a wide range of ages, the social life of HCS may have been more inclusive than at larger schools. Friendships between fifth and eighth graders were common, for example, if only because the pool of possible friends one's own age was so small. Older girls often helped care for younger children, sometimes holding kindergarteners on their laps during school-wide assemblies, or taking responsibility for supervising children with special needs during the lunch period. To adults at HCS, this mixing of ages was not always positive, as they sometimes blamed social difficulties among elementary-age students on their imitation of older kids' behaviors. In general, HCS had a population small enough to allow familiarity with each individual, but large enough that students of a range of age were represented, forming multiple relationships, networks, and affiliations around age, gender, family, and other factors.

There was a strong sense of community in Heartsboro. Many families went back locally several generations, and cousins and siblings from a few large extended families accounted for a substantial portion of the student body at HCS. Town hall meetings were well-attended, and half a dozen Italian surnames were shared among several multi-generation Heartsboro families. Many students were from families with low incomes. In 2007 all of the students were white, though in other years there were one or two students of color enrolled.[2]

Historically Heartsboro's economy was dominated by small manufacturing and some tourism, but by 2007 little local industry remained. A chair factory and ski slope had both closed in the last generation. Thus Heartsboro had been a microcosm of a dramatic regional process of deindustrialization in the northeastern United States (cf. Kirsch 1998). Many of the parents of HCS's students, therefore, found themselves commuting long distances to work each morning.[3] The nearest grocery store was a thirty-minute drive away, and in the winter the roads through the mountains could be treacherous. Despite a strong investment in local identity and community, regional travel outside Heartsboro was still a major part of the lives of its inhabitants.

Rural New England has long been subject to contestations of place and class in the competing economic pulls of tourism, industry, and agriculture (D. Brown 1995; Conforti 2001; Gittell and Colgan 2004; Harrison 2006). Heartsboro exists on the rural periphery of three small cities, each of which has been powerfully affected in the last generation by the nationwide deindustrialization of the United States (Kirsch 1998; Kotval and Mullin 1997). Heartsboro's historically rural identity was decentered by its growing dependence on surrounding urban centers for jobs and daily amenities like grocery stores, medical services, and entertainment. Residents joked that the town is "forty minutes from everywhere" via often-treacherous mountain roads. Regional development emphasized "high art" cultural tourism, and the area now hosts several museums, performing arts venues, and theater festivals (e.g., Graham 2005). The service and hospitality industries that revolved around these institutions provided most of the jobs for Heartsboro's residents.[4] In the decade prior to my research several individuals with administrative positions in arts institutions had moved their families to Heartsboro and enrolled their children in the village's well-regarded primary school. Increasingly, political and economic positions were framed as aesthetic or "cultural" orientations, so "taste" was discursively focused in the region's power relations (Bourdieu 1984; Hennion 2004).[5]

Heartsboro was framed by its own residents as provincial, or at least isolated. While I was proposing this project, many adults expressed surprise that I would consider Heartsboro a relevant site to study children's media practices. As one teacher put it, HCS kids "can't be very representative of American children," and they "don't know a lot about the rest of the world." Certain teachers also made dismissive (if usually affectionate) comments about Heartsboro residents as "goombas" and "swamp yankees"—pointing to the various ethnic and cultural identifications available (Italian American, multigenerational New England Anglo-Saxon) but also highlighting shared rural and working-class identifications. Kids, too, participated in this discourse of provincialism. One complained that she wished she lived someplace "with a mall" and "where you can walk to see your friends" (which, at least for those who live in the surrounding hills rather than the small downtown, was not possible). One student with strong connections to friends in neighboring communities said of his local peers, "these kids never know anything outside of Heartsboro." Kids commonly labeled recent transplants "flatlanders" and those from neighboring Massachusetts "Mass-holes."[6]

This self-portrayal of Heartsboro as outside-the-mainstream, peripheral, or rustically "other" (Cloke and Little 1997) and its representation as small, out-of-the-way, and rural colored the participation of Heartsboro children in US public culture as consumers and audiences. Many HCS students prioritized recreational activities and consumer interests associated in the United States with white, rural, working-class culture, like hunting, snowmobiling, riding ATVs, and viewing NASCAR races. Mass media in diverse contexts are used by producers and consumers to articulate translocal—national, regional, and global—social identities (Abu-Lughod 2001; Mankekar 1999; Postill 2006), and mass-media identifications have been shown to be important markers of "fitting in as a New American" for many children of immigrants to the United States (Minks 1999:86). For many Heartsboro children, rurality is a marker of a particular status in the United States, and constructing musical identifications drawn from the mass media can allow rural children to claim a cosmopolitan identity in a deterritorialized world (Appadurai 1996).

By 2007 only a few teachers at HCS were from Heartsboro. Several commuted as much as an hour from Bennington or across the borders in New Hampshire and Massachusetts. In fact, this represented a drastic and abrupt shift. A cohort of teachers and administrators from Heartsboro and neighboring towns who had worked at HCS continuously for the previous thirty years had either retired the year before or were planning to retire after the 2007–2008 school year. The few years before and after my research marked a major transition for the school and its relation to the community. New teachers and administrators were less patient with the "way things have always been," which created some tensions with students (who were decidedly conservative about school traditions) and the community. At the same time new staff could be forces for positive change. For example, a few recent hires noted the lack of a regular guidance counselor and became advocates for including such a position (with mixed success). The language of opposition to outsiders or mild resentment toward teachers who commuted from out of town may have partly reflected long-term historical changes in which the town became much more dependent on regional economic and cultural forces than it was when local manufacturing, timber, and tourism supported a stronger local economy.

Studying Heartsboro kids

I was first introduced to Heartsboro in 2002, when I spent a year as the music teacher at HCS. I returned in 2007 to do the research for this book. I spent the entire 2007–2008 school year doing full-time fieldwork at Heartsboro Central School. With few exceptions I was at HCS all day every day from September to June. This project was tailored to account for the particular challenges and promises of doing research in schools and with children (Christensen and James 2000; Gilmore and Glatthorn 1982), mindful that schools structure interaction, authority, and social identity in unique ways (Becker 1972; Mehan 1979; Pelissier 1991). I spent my days following kids around school, hanging out, talking, and playing during free time, and sitting with kids or at the back of the classroom during classes. I would ask students after (or while) observing an interesting practice to explain things I might have missed or misunderstood, but I made it clear that they should feel no obligation to answer my questions. Sometimes I sat back and observed, but mostly I engaged with them actively. We talked, played, and hung out together, we exchanged views, and sometimes we disagreed or argued. I repeatedly emphasized that anything the kids did or said would remain strictly anonymous, and in particular that I would never use my authority as an adult to discipline them or get them in "trouble" with teachers or parents.

Data collection for the study consisted of observations of children's vocal-expressive practices and interactions in class and out, and participation in free-time talk, playground games, and daily classroom activities. I took notes constantly, and I made audio and video recordings of children's sociable talk and performances, especially before school, at lunchtime, and at recess. I interviewed every third- to eighth-grade student about media use, school values, and social life, and I recorded informal question-and-answer interactions with kids in all grades. I interviewed students alone or, more commonly, in pairs, according to their preference. The interviews were held in a room connected to the school library, which was usually the only available space in the small school building, with the door open. In most cases I would pull kids out of quiet reading, or similar periods during the day, with the permission of their teachers. I also led regular open-ended discussion groups in which children would talk about music and videos brought in by them or accessed on the Internet. I would spend a week or two following one class, sitting in on all their lessons and accompanying them to art, gym, and library classes, recess, and lunch. (I spent the vast majority of my time sitting in class with students, since that is how they spent the majority of their time.) I focused especially on the third- and fourth-, fifth- and sixth-, and seventh- and eighth-grade classes, though I also spent significant time with the first- and second-grade class. After a week or two I would switch to another class. Before school, at lunch, and at recess, when students had more freedom to arrange their own groups, I tried to spend several days or a week with one group, and then circulate to another. When I sensed or was told by a group of students that they did not want me to sit with them at lunch or stand with them at recess, I would always respect that. The "high-status" girls I discuss in chapter 2 commonly did not want me to join them during free time, so I rarely did. They were still willing to participate in formal interviews, and sometimes I would join them if invited by one of their friends, but I tried not to push the issue. I had close relationships with some kids and more distant relationships with others. The kids who appear the most frequently in these pages were likely to be the most actively engaged in musical activities and discourses. But in the course of the research I made a conscious effort not to focus my attention on any one group or individual. A number of kids with whom I had close personal relationships do not appear as much here, because their interests or activities were less directly related to my research topics.

I tried to be as transparent and open as possible about my work. I explained my project to everyone at the start of the year, emphasizing my interest in children's musical interests and activities. I reintroduced the project and explained my interests and goals again when I pulled kids for interviews or group discussions. At these later meetings, I would point to particular activities that I was focusing on, such as sharing headphones, and explain why I found them interesting. When kids asked why, if I was just interested in music, I accompanied them to their other classes, I would discuss with them how music and music-related topics came up in a wide range of situations including their classes and why that was interesting to me. I wrote constantly and visibly in my notebook. Kids would often ask me, "Did you write that down?" I did not let kids see my written notes, out of respect for other kids' privacy, but I willingly talked to them about what I included in my notes. Sometimes they would ask me not to make note of something, and I would comply. I also used an audio recorder multiple times every day, setting it in the center of the lunch table, for example, and I allowed kids to handle the device, play with it, and record themselves and each other when they wished. When I took still photographs and video, I explained what I was doing, and again I let the students use the devices themselves when they asked. Still it was easy for the kids to take me for granted as a normal part of their environment. Once, well into the year, I explained to the fifth- and sixth-grade class the word "ethnomusicology," breaking down the morphology of "ethno-," "music," and "-ology" into "the study of music in culture," and sixth grader Courtney exclaimed, partly in surprise and partly in recognition, "Wait, you're doing that to us?!"

HCS commonly had trouble staffing their music, art, and physical education classes, which were all one-day-a-week positions.[7] By November HCS still had not filled the music teacher position, a job I had held five years earlier in 2002. The principal asked me to consider taking the position, since I had experience and was already on site five days a week. I was concerned about the implications for my research, but I agreed to take on the position, partly as a way to contribute to a pressing need at the school.

I made sure to clearly communicate to the administration and students that I would prioritize my non-authoritative relationships with kids over behavior management or discipline, and that I would not be responsible for assessment or grades, preserving a commitment to confidentiality and reciprocity at the frequent expense of maintaining an orderly or effective classroom. That such neutrality was necessary, and that power relations were understood as confrontational, at least by kids, was apparent in the reference one seventh-grade boy made to me as a "civilian" (i.e., non-combatant) while explaining to another student that I would not "put his name in the book," or officially record and punish some act of troublemaking. Surprisingly, to me, despite taking on a position of formal authority, this institutional role helped legitimate and solidify my continuous presence at HCS for both kids and adults, and very much facilitated my research when I was not teaching. I was now "the music teacher," which made a lot more sense to everyone than "researcher," even if only a fraction of my time was spent teaching music classes.[8]

As the part-time music teacher, I participated in regular staff meetings and collaborated with teachers and the principal to design curricula, discuss social and behavior problems, and develop extracurricular performance opportunities. In my music classes I had students conduct research about popular musicians, the music industry, and media channels for advertising and distributing music. These projects were tailored to meet Vermont music education standards, but they also elicited substantial discourse about popular media that provided useful data for my research. In all, I combined interviews, discussion groups, and classroom projects with multiple strategies for observing and recording children's naturally occurring talk, expression, and interaction to provide diverse types of material for analysis.

I walked a fine line as an adult with social and institutional responsibilities and a researcher interested in understanding kids' lives and not limiting their forms of expression. I encouraged kids to call me whatever was most comfortable, so I was Tyler to some and Mr. Bickford to others. Eventually many kids settled on Bicky—a comfortably informal nickname but still not so familiar as my first name—and later, in the absurd and kind of mean humor of middle-school kids, a few converted that to Icky Vicky (a character from the cartoon show *Fairly Odd Parents*), and then to Kyle (in reference to a short, bald performer in the comedy rock band Tenacious D). I answered to all of these. To make sure I stayed within the bounds of "appropriate" interactions with the kids, I strictly avoided contributing to discussions about drugs or sex or other illicit topics, though they came up regularly in kids' conversations. But I also had an obligation to my research and to the kids not to actively suppress these common discourses the way a teacher might. Such topics would often slip away as quickly as they arose, but if kids were engaged in extended conversation that I did not think I should participate in, I would exit quietly or turn to join an adjacent conversation. (I consider issues of "appropriateness" at length in chapter 5.)

I argue in this book that we should understand the roles of adult and child as intrinsically political: that is, as a historically constituted class relation between groups whose unequal or hierarchical relation to one another is structured into their very constitution as recognizable social categories in ways that intersect meaningfully with other historically constituted relations like race, gender, and economic class. Such a perspective raises serious challenges for adults doing research with or about children. I am a white man of considerable physical presence from a middle-class family of public school teachers. In 2007 I was twenty-six years old and working on a PhD at an Ivy League university. I have long-standing family and professional ties to the region surrounding Heartsboro, but I am not a native Vermonter, or even New Englander. I was younger than many of the teachers at HCS, which may have made me more approachable to HCS students. But my geographical and educational background were much more distant. I did not share kids' rural investments—for example, I've never hunted or shot a gun, which was very unusual to them. While many planned to attend college (and did, in the years since), few aspired to post-graduate work, or had a sense that it was an option. Kids vocally complained to me about my vocabulary, and I often struggled to rephrase sentences with simpler language. I write in chapter 5 about how easy it was to fall into normative teacher-student roles even with kids who I had especially friendly and comfortable relationships. As a man I may have had certain privileged access to boys' activities, but there were certainly situations where groups of boys asked me not to inquire into the details of their activities—including a secret club of middle-school boys based on Erin Hunter's *Warriors* books (Hunter 2003). I would argue with them about calling each other "gay" and calling women "bitches," which is a characteristic feature of school masculinity in the United States (e.g., Pascoe 2007). And I did not share many of their interests or experience in sports or outdoor activities. My gender probably created some explicit barriers with some of the older girls, for whom opposite-sex relationships were highly charged (which I discuss further in chapter 2). I was a friendly resource for certain kids with smaller or less intimate social networks to express themselves and feel comfortable. In different ways, each of these subject positions situated me in complex web of relations to the kids at HCS that made this particular book possible, while closing off other possible accounts.

I don't claim to have achieved any particularly special access to children's secret lives or private knowledge. It is easy to read ethnographic descriptions of non-dominant groups through a sort of colonial logic of discovery and revelation. That is not my intent. Most of the information in this book is based simply on observations and conversations about topics of only marginal interest to most people but of strong interest to me and to many kids at HCS. I was always respectful, but I did not go out of my way to be deferential. I frequently argued with them, often playfully and sometimes seriously—which is to say, I tried hard to be myself, and arguing comes naturally to me. It is a way that I know to learn about other people and to show respect and engagement for their ideas. Also, I genuinely liked most of them and I had a lot of fun that year, which was probably helpful. Beyond that, to the best of my understanding any information that might have been available to me but not to other adults was the product of my constant presence as a familiar, mostly non-authoritative figure with no disciplinary role and with few connections into their social networks beyond school.

A body of important methodologically and theoretically powerful work has been produced in the last two decades exploring the challenges of research with children, particularly around the problem of power hierarchies between child subjects and adult researchers, and the desire to involve and empower children as central participants in research design, rather than merely as research subjects (for example, Pole, Mizen, and Bolton 1999; O'Kane 2000; Woodhead and Faulkner 2000; Christensen 2004; Gallacher and Gallagher 2008; K. Marsh 2009; Holland and Hillman 2010; Cheney 2011; Emberly 2013; Raffety 2015). This work might be seen as a useful rejoinder to Jacqueline Rose's (1984) influential argument for the "impossibility" of knowledge about children because the category "child" is always a product of adult interests, ideologies, desire, and fantasy (see also Lesnik-Oberstein 2011; and, for a helpful reply, Nodelman 1997). Marah Gubar (2013, 2016) has responded productively to Rose's critique by offering provisional refinements to the category "child" that make it more nimble, nuanced, and useful. As helpful as such refinements are in clarifying and focusing our terms and concepts, I still follow Rose in acknowledging that the problem of intersubjective knowledge of other people, especially of people in social groups that are politically subordinated to one's own, is a fundamental epistemological limit to knowledge, and that efforts to overcome such challenges risk merely reproducing the hierarchies that produce distance and difference in the first place. The body of methodologically innovative childhood studies research cited above might be seen in the tradition of "writing culture" critique in anthropology (Clifford and Marcus 1986), which advocated not for doing away with anthropological knowledge but instead for recognizing the contingent and, especially, political nature of all knowledge production and representation, motivating a generation of scholars to pursue new modes of ethical, politically engaged, and reflexive study. Childhood studies shows that theoretically sophisticated, reflexive, and self-critical efforts to bridge social distance through participation, reciprocity, and mutual obligation can be intellectually and politically worthwhile, if also provisional, partial, and never ethically "innocent." That is, interacting with, learning from, developing relationships with, and accepting responsibilities to particular people—not merely theorizing better—is the beginning of knowledge and the basis of good research about people. Actually engaging directly with people who hold the historically contingent and culturally constructed social status "child" does not resolve profound philosophical problems, but it does confront them. Intersubjective knowledge becomes, in a sense, a material problem of social practice, more than an abstract question of theory.

I tried to be aware of and sensitive to these dynamics in my own research, and I did my best to negotiate them in the design of the study, in the contingencies of everyday fieldwork, and in my efforts to represent HCS kids in writing—which is not to say that I was always successful. My research questions were and are idiosyncratic, and I did not consult HCS kids in the design of the study. They would have posed very different questions were I to have taken that step. But they probably also would have rejected the project out of hand as not worth their time or effort (which strikes me as fair). I argue in chapters 3 and 5 that discourse *about* music is opposed in some fundamental ways to what made music valuable to HCS kids, which is that it was largely a non-discursive, embodied, and intimately social practice. To the extent that any research project would entail objectifying music as a topic of discourse, it would contradict some of those values. Still some of the most interesting findings in this book, and the ones for which I am the most grateful to the kids at HCS, are the result of moments where they resisted or rejected my interests or interpretations. In that sense much of the knowledge here was produced dialogically, through engagement and interaction. I did my best to be consistently respectful, honest, and transparent about my work, and to follow the ethical principles of human subjects research (respect for persons, beneficence, and justice). Once I tried to talk a group of fifth and sixth graders through a presentation about them that I had given at a conference (Bickford 2008). They enjoyed scrutinizing the pseudonyms I had chosen (only then did it occur to me to let them choose their own, which some did) and hearing themselves described in anecdotes, but they found little to engage them in my arguments—no "dialogic editing" here (Feld 1990). Mostly during my research we hung out and talked together, and I reflected on and wrote about their actions and interactions. In the end, as with much anthropological fieldwork, they gave me a lot more (a career!) than I gave them.

Music, technology, and new media poetics

The period of my fieldwork at HCS coincided with remarkable expansion in the children's music industry (Bickford 2012). In 2006 the soundtrack to the Disney Channel musical movie *High School Musical* was an explosive success and became the top-selling album for the entire year. One week early in 2006, the top three spots on the Billboard album sales charts were occupied by children's records. Paving the way for the success of *High School Musical*, the independent label Razor & Tie had several years of remarkable success marketing collections of Top 40 pop songs re-recorded for pre-adolescent "tweens," under the brand Kidz Bop, including multiple top-ten records. In 2006 and 2007 Disney expanded on the success of *High School Musical* by introducing Hannah Montana (Miley Cyrus) and then the Jonas Brothers. Since 2006 recordings with children as their primary audience consistently rank at the top of the sales charts, in direct competition with mainstream, adult pop artists.

At HCS, kids' musical tastes ranged widely, from such "tween" music acts, which were very popular, to Top 40 pop, rock, hip-hop, and R&B, to more obscure recordings of hardcore metal or hip-hop passed down from older siblings or friends, and even to popular music from the 1970s and 1980s, which many were introduced to by their parents. Country music was not specifically privileged in most kids' musical preferences, despite the associations with white, rural, working-class culture that it shares with other interests that were more common at HCS, like hunting and NASCAR racing. In general, music was important to children's peer culture at HCS, a frequent topic of conversation and debate. Children listened to music whenever they could get away with it, using the MP3 players that more and more of them carried around (and which school authorities increasingly viewed with suspicion) or sneaking views of music videos on websites they found to bypass the Internet content filters on the school's recently installed computers.

MP3 players were by far the most widely used media devices at school. Many HCS students also owned portable gaming devices—the Nintendo DS was the most common—and most were interested in and desired cell phones, but two factors limited the presence of phones at school. First, as elementary- and middle-school students, this population was relatively young to have their own mobile phones, whose monthly service costs represented a much larger investment than the one-time purchase of an MP3 player or gaming device. Second, Heartsboro is geographically isolated and had no cell phone towers at the time, so even the few students who did have phones used them primarily for their built-in cameras, since they did not get any signal and they did not subscribe to music services. One girl received a satellite radio receiver at Christmas that doubled as an MP3 player, but it seemed to work only intermittently. I expect that MP3 players were likewise prominent in other populations of schoolchildren of similar ages in 2007–2008, but Heartsboro's rural isolation may have tipped the balance somewhat against wireless telecommunication devices.

Christmas of 2007 was a watershed for personal music player ownership at Heartsboro. Throughout the fall semester, kids without MP3 players had talked constantly about desiring one and fawned over their friends' devices. By Christmas the products had become so available and affordable that in January a majority of kids in third grade and above returned to school with one. This mirrors a process nationally: in 2004, twelve percent of eight- to ten-year-olds and twenty percent of eleven- to fourteen-year-olds owned MP3 players (Roberts, Foehr, and Rideout 2005:13), while by 2009 the figures for those groups were sixty-one percent and eighty percent, respectively (Rideout, Foehr, and Roberts 2010:10). The parallel with the expansion of children's music sales during these years should be clear: the middle of the decade represented a distinct turning point for children's media and entertainment overall. Research suggesting that media consumption varies by age and gender conforms broadly with my observations at HCS, as well (Rideout, Foehr, and Roberts 2010:37), though to a large extent the meaning of these practices seemed to overlap for kids of different ages and genders.

MP3 players clearly participated in hierarchies of brand value. For instance, kids rarely referred to their non-iPod devices by brand name. Instead the labels that circulated were "iPod" and "MP3" (often without the modifying "player").[9] They distinguished categorically between "MP3s" and Apple-branded "iPods," explicitly and vehemently rejecting any suggestion I might make that iPods were a subset of the category "MP3 player." Owners of iPods would commonly answer "no" to the question, "do you own an MP3 player?"[10]

These hierarchies and negotiations of brand value were apparent in a playful competition one morning before school in June, when I sat at breakfast with eighth grader Daisy, fifth grader Cally, and several of their friends. Cally bragged, "I got this necklace for twenty-five dollars at the flea market!"

Daisy replied as though Cally's comment were a challenge: "Oh yeah, well I got this necklace for free from my aunt!"

Cally took up the game: "Well I have a locket."

Daisy lifted her ankle over the table, "I have these flip flops."

"I have *Adidas* flip flops."

"Well mine have polka dots—you can't beat that."

Cally came back with a trump card: "I have this MP3 player."

Daisy smiled. "Well you gotta play fair." But then her smile widened and she reached over and grabbed the iPod Shuffle Melissa had clipped to her sweatshirt. "I have an *iPod*!"—expressing the clear hierarchy of iPods over any old MP3 player.

"But that's Melissa's."

Daisy turned to Melissa, "Give me your iPod for the day. Say it." Melissa mumbled her consent.

"Okay, see, it's mine!" And with that clear statement of possession, Daisy won and the competition was over. Cally could not beat an iPod, and had no response.

Status competition was far from the only way that ownership and use of digital music devices participated in social relationships at HCS. Perhaps the most common way kids at HCS listened to music was to share their earbuds with one another—one for me, one for you—so that each kid had a speaker in only one ear. Sharing was a clear expression of existing friendship and provided opportunities for establishing new friendships. Listening together presented everyday physical challenges. Walking together while sharing earbuds involved careful coordination of two bodies, and friends would spend time practicing especially difficult tasks like walking through doors together. In larger groups, pairs of friends would listen with one ear as they participated in the dense overlap of talk, touch, and gesture that characterized their unmonitored peer interactions. Wires literally tethered kids to one another, and headphone cables suspended from ear to ear traced out the intersecting nodes of social networks stratified by overlapping hierarchies of age, gender, kinship, friendship, status, and taste. By sharing earbuds kids activated and delineated these relationships, excluding some children from listening even while expanding access for others who might be limited by parental resources or restrictions. Compact little objects—much like toys—MP3 players were ever-present throughout the school day, slipped into pockets, and handled until worn. MP3 players bundled with headphone cables circulated among lockers, desks, pockets, and backpacks. Wires threaded under clothing and tangled across crowded lunchroom tables. Hanging from a shoulder or shirt collar, maxed-out earbuds strained to liven up group spaces with portable, lo-fi background music. In class, students listened surreptitiously to earbuds concealed in sleeves and under the hoods of sweatshirts.

The structure of kids' media use coincided with and shared many features with the structure of their talk and expression. Media consumption and talk both shared an emphasis on dense, layered, and interactive sociability. Audio and oral channels of communication were first and foremost charged with an intimate indexicality that pointed to the relationships between individuals in interaction. Whether linkage, contest, solidarity, or negotiation, the channels of communication and the relationships those channels indexed seemed more important than the content. Just as MP3 players neatly fit into existing material practices with toys, sound effects and poetic tropes from games and TV built nicely on existing childish repertoires of hoots, howls, growls, and trills that signaled pleasure or frustration to peers and adults.

Groups of students would cultivate poetic or musical phrases as social refrains. During the fall middle-school boys sang to themselves "dunna nunna nunna," to the "dungeon" theme from Nintendo's *Mario Bros.* video games. Gradually this was incorporated into talk, so one boy demanded another's lunchtime treat by singing "gimme gimme gimme" (figure I.1). Another kid sang quietly to himself while playing solitaire during an after school program, "monkey monkey monkey," to the same melody, adding a layer of "silliness" with the non-sequitur animal reference.

One day at lunch a few fourth-grade girls started talking about Webkinz, a brand of stuffed toys with a kid-friendly "virtual world" website tie-in (see e.g., Black 2010; J. Marsh 2010). As a token of friendship and a test of trust, one whispered her password to the others. But then they repeated it too loudly—"S-Q-R-3-4!"—and she feared it was compromised. So she chimed in, even louder, with a slightly altered string of letters and numbers: "No that's not it. It's S-3-R-Q-1!"[11] The neighboring boys heard this and repeated it, immediately catching on that this game of "remember the password" was motivated by poetic contest, and began themselves to call out letters and numbers, challenging each other to repeat them back. Soon the table was full of a dozen or so kids talking over one another, repeating and altering complex strings of letters and numbers in a poetic competition linking spelling, numeracy, and childish memory games with the lived tension between adult exhortations to online privacy and youthful conventions of gossip and sharing.

Figure I.1: *Mario Bros.* dungeon theme.

Underneath all this, the cable from one girl's music device snaked across the table, linking her with a friend whose memory she was challenging. Like the headphone cables that passed from ear to ear, these sociable media poetics were used to actively negotiate relationships, trust, power, and status, and also to foreground the backchannel, highlighting connectivity, sociability, and linkage.

Such peer practices took on particular significance in the institutional context where these interactions occurred. Claiming a rhyme she says she found on the social networking site Myspace as "my saying," seventh grader Jenn would impishly greet her teachers with, "Howdy ho, Ranger Joe?" (a phrase that kids online seem to have borrowed from the 1990s television show *Full House* and turned into an inside joke). This mischievous borrowing from the Internet put teachers in a difficult position. If a teacher challenged her for disrespect, she'd object that, "It's just what I say"—a harmless motto or catchphrase. In contrast to kids' unsupervised interactions in the halls, lunchroom, and playground, in the classroom teachers emphasized individual over interactional competencies. They instructed students in essayist genres of writing (exposition, narrative, personal essay), in the visual formatting of paragraphs and the rules of sentence construction, and in named "problem solving strategies." These lessons followed a set of goals and procedures laid out in the school's local "literacy action plan" and in the district's math curriculum, which in turn implemented standards outlined by the state, in partial response to federal guidelines and funding priorities. Teachers formalized and regulated the ways questions were asked and answered, the one-at-a-time structures of classroom talk, and "respectful" modes for students to address teachers and each other. The writing and speaking practices taught in the classroom competed with the chaotic vocalizations that bubbled up from kids, which were certainly inappropriate, and in their undirected, playful, non-sensical aspects, also "inarticulate," as I will argue in chapter 5.

A core argument of this book is that music listening and other media reception practices are in many cases themselves *expressive* practices, equivalent to speech, writing, singing, and other more conventionally expressive modes, and analyzable using linguistic methods. Expressive-poetic practices like those outlined here are often about media or in intertextual relation to media. But even the narrow act of listening to headphones can be distinctly expressive, a form of active communication to others, and not simply, or even primarily, about expressions of taste or cultural affiliation through practices like song selection. I outline this perspective in chapters 2 to 5, and I work through the comparison of music listening to expressive speech in detail in chapter 5.

Studying popular music and popular music audiences

The broad theoretical results of this study, about the place of childhood within institutions of education and entertainment, emerged out of my desire for ethnographic understanding of the experience of popular music audiences. That goal quickly leads to a question of feasibility: how do you investigate popular music consumption in context, when the contexts of music's consumption are so often distributed and hidden within personal and private spaces? The research site, then, is deeply connected with theoretical questions about the status of individuals in society.

Studying popular music and media audiences with ethnographic depth is a significant challenge. Maureen Mahon writes in an aside to her study of the Black Rock Coalition that, "it is relatively easy to identify and get access to potential research subjects who are media consumers. Indeed, most media studies by anthropologists focus on audiences and consumption rather than production" (2004:281n1). But this is not so simple. Media producers can be surrounded by gatekeepers, and their cultural, economic, and institutional status may make it easier for them to decline requests from academic researchers. While the doors to producers' offices may often be closed, researchers can at least determine which doors to knock on in the first place. Media producers are consolidated geographically and institutionally. By contrast, audiences are dispersed, to the point that research with ethnographic detail can seem almost impossible. The doors to audiences' homes are also closed to researchers, and homes are not publicly accessible in the way that corporate offices are. Notably, ethnomusicological studies of popular music focus much more on musicians than audiences or media executives, and musicians fit into the category of "producers" rather than "audiences." Mahon's own research on the Black Rock Coalition is a case in point: the coalition provides an institutional structure through which Mahon is able to access musicians of interest to her. And for researchers interested in audiences, formal institutions like "fan clubs" can be useful (e.g., Pecknold 2007; Yano 2002), as are the informal institutions of "subcultural" affiliations (Hebdige 1979). But insofar as they select for individuals with uncommon interest in a particular artist or genre, these institutions do not necessarily provide access to the more widespread experiences of mass audiences.

Audiences increasingly engage with music and entertainment media in informal, everyday, and relatively ubiquitous ways on the Internet, with social media, and with mobile devices, and researchers are increasingly turning to Internet practices for fine-grained data about everyday life (Bird 2003; Boellstorff 2008; Baym and Ledbetter 2009; Coleman 2010; K. Miller 2012; Suhr 2012). But despite their growing ubiquity, social media have serious limitations as social data: their guise of universality conceals important selection effects, including important phenomena such as media refusal; despite ubiquitous mobile computing, vast portions of people's lives still take place outside social media's reach; and the data social media make available have already been flattened and rationalized to conform to the database structures of their platforms (Tufekci 2014; Portwood-Stacer 2012; boyd 2007; Grimes and Feenberg 2009). And in the United States, federal privacy regulations make it nearly impossible to conduct online research about children younger than thirteen (Montgomery 2007; boyd et al. 2011). My findings suggest that many of the most significant social practices that directly involve digital devices are nonetheless never captured as information in databases. This may be somewhat less true as smartphones replace standalone music devices, but it points to important caveats.

Canonical private everyday sites of music consumption and performance—the car radio during the morning commute, singing in the shower—are likely to remain closed to ethnographic field research, even in a world of ubiquitous mobile computing. Focus groups, surveys, and interviews of randomly sampled individuals are useful tools, but anthropologists know that they produce different sorts of data than long-term participant observation does. None of this should be understood as critical of the studies cited above, each of which has had significant influence on my thinking and the research reported here. But these studies circle around my questions about the dispersed everyday experience of music for casual listeners, a question that is partly personal.

My own interest in music has always been decidedly casual, and I have never experienced a long-term commitment to a role as performer, fan, or critic. Still, music has a profound role in my life, despite the fact that I rarely listen to it or perform it. That apparently contradictory experience, of music mattering immensely, but not enough to focus significant time or effort on, is what motivated me to pursue ethnomusicological study. My own experience resonates with the interviews in the now-canonical *My Music* study (Crafts et al. 1993), but as rich as they are, those interviews have always seemed to me to outline the beginning, not the conclusion, of a research topic.[12] My goal has been to find some way to explore, in ethnographic detail and with attention to historical and social contexts, these experiences where music is powerfully important for participants but is not necessarily the central focus or driving motivation for their activities.

The inclusion of "ethnographic detail" in this requirement is not simply an artifact of my disciplinary training, but has substantive implications for the sorts of questions that can be asked and answered. The details of chapters 2 to 5 demonstrate that there are types of data that long-term, intensive, and qualitative research techniques produce that simply cannot be achieved through other means. I would not even know to ask about sharing earbuds, connecting MP3 players to kids' material culture, or locating portable music devices within the expressive ecology of school—practices that have great meaning for how we understand children's approaches to school and media—had I not witnessed the quiet prominence of these activities in the small everyday details of kids' lives at HCS. But "ethnography" brings its own set of assumptions about human experience, most notably that the activities or interpretations under investigation will be, at least to some extent, bounded in space and time. The element of ethnographic field research that binds its subjects to places by now has long been problematized by anthropologists interested in translocal practices (Gupta and Ferguson 1997), but disentangling the emplaced method of research from its implications about how humans organize themselves spatially remains difficult. Additionally, multisited ethnographies or other approaches to studying practices that are not bounded geographically can create their own tradeoffs, notably emphasizing practices whose interest is predetermined by the researcher—mediated communication, say, or travel, or trade—rather than locating particular practices holistically within the overall context of people's lives.

In a sense, my concern about studies of popular music is the same: they run the risk of asserting the importance of music in participants' lives, simply because that is the topic under investigation, rather than investigating as an important and primary question *whether* music is important. Thus, for completely understandable reasons, people for whom music matters are privileged in music scholarship, but the empirical possibility that music might be unimportant to people should be just as relevant to music scholars as the reverse. This is not to suggest that we should ignore spaces and communities that are organized specifically around music. Clearly such spaces have much to tell us about music and about society (Small 1998), and even about practices of circulation and performance that transcend spatial bounds (Novak 2013). And some spaces may not be explicitly organized around music, but music is inescapably central to their sociality. The honky tonk at the center of Aaron Fox's (2004) study is an interesting case. The fact that Ann's Other Place is a venue for live music may not determine the centrality of country music talk, performance, and listening to its sociality, so much as the intimate mediations of music, language, and expression in the social life of its clientele give meaning and importance to the live performances. If we imagine Ann's Other Place as a location *not* organized primarily around music, then the importance of music in its sociality is even more remarkable. Recent work in studies of music and violence, such as Suzanne Cusick's (2006, 2008) investigations of music as torture in US detention camps and Martin Daughtry's (2015) account of music and sound in wartime Iraq, provide an especially pointed illustration of this point. Daughtry's study, by taking as its starting point a situation—American military service members and Iraqi civilians during the US war in Iraq—that is not primarily musical, opens up profoundly new perspectives on the role of music and sound in human experience. Daughtry identifies specific ways that music takes on special significance in that context, but he also situates music within a broader ecology of wartime sound practices, allowing him to note even the ways that war can specifically *de*value music and musicians, exposing circumstances in which "music's *powerlessness* or inefficacy" (2015:259)—or, for Cusick, music's destructive potential—are as important for our understanding of music's social role as scenarios in which it is powerful or moving. This is the sort of perspective I would like to take toward elementary and middle school as a site for ethnomusicological research. If we start with institutions, communities, or spaces whose initial constitution has nothing to do with music, then the constant presence of musical practices in the everyday life of such institutions—to the extent that even the fundamental activities of the institution such as literacy education are implicated in this constant bubbling up of particular orientations toward music—*then* the role of music in everyday life, in relations of power and authority, can reveal itself more clearly and more realistically, which can only strengthen and expand the scope and stakes of music studies.

When we attend to "non-musical" spaces, we can begin to see the forms in which music circulates in everyday life less as fully realized texts or performances than as fragments, snippets, tropes, allusions, half-remembered quotations, puns, improvisations, and momentary performances of the sort of ephemeral and apparently inconsequential "silly objects" that cultural theorist Lauren Berlant calls the "waste materials of everyday communication" (1997:12). We can start to see better how music and other forms of media and entertainment are integrated into the everyday language and expression that anthropologists and linguists identify as central to large-scale social reproduction and power relationships (e.g., Rampton 2006). The separateness of musical performance has the effect of marginalizing it from the everyday microinteractional tactics that make up people's continual negotiations of power and identity. But if we de-privilege music as a separate space of aesthetic enjoyment and see it in its fragmentary everyday circulation and performance, we can see much better how it participates, and even has a privileged role, in everyday interactions and communications that produce and reproduce social identities and relationships. This project, therefore, began with a desire to better understand the experience of popular music audiences, and became, of necessity, a study of the institutions—school, media, and childhood—in which music takes on meaning in everyday life.

Some notes on terms and categories

Throughout this book I use the term "childish" advisedly. I am sensitive to Adora Svitak's argument that "the traits the word 'childish' addresses are seen so often in adults that we should abolish this age-discriminatory word when it comes to criticizing behavior associated with irresponsibility and irrational thinking" (2010). But to describe without criticism things identified by children and adults as marked for childhood, I find the adjective "childish" preferable to the genitive "children's," which is more common in childhood studies. To my ear, "children's" carries a suggestion of independently claimed ownership, and this celebratory valence potentially obscures how children negotiate the boundaries of their lives with adults and others. On the other hand, it would be impossible to scrub the term "childish" of senses of triviality, irrationality, or irresponsibility, and I am not sure a more neutral term would be preferable. For example "childlike" suggests neutral description or even valorization that are just as ideological, if less openly so, as "childish." If anything the value judgments implicit in "childish" might be useful, insofar as they highlight the fact that children and childhood remain marginalized and disputed categories, which helps to avoid whitewashing the actual discourses and genealogies that come with notions of childhood or childishness.

Further, the negative meanings of "childish" are implicit in the noun "child" itself. Children of all ages certainly bristle under the suggestions of immaturity and innocence that the word "child" carries. Children in the United States are much more likely to identify as "kids," and the word seems to be preferred by adults as well to describe their offspring or students. "Child" seems to be loaded with so much ideological friction that it gets stuck in speakers' mouths. The preference for "kid" by kids and adults suggests a logic of labeling and identity that strikes me as characteristic, or at least suggestive, of debates about language and "identity politics"—an argument I will pursue in some detail in the next chapter. Moreover, the boundaries of "child" are controversial at best (are thirteen-year-olds "children"?), whereas the boundaries of "kid" are broad and ever expanding.

Therefore I try to use "kid" to denote the children in this study, and "child" as a formal theoretical term with particular histories and currency in academic usage. This book seeks to explore how affiliations to categories like "childhood," "kid," or "childish" take place in actual people's lives, but that means that I do not place strict boundaries on those categories. Much of the material analyzed in the later chapters comes from eleven- to thirteen-year-olds, which tracks closely with the marketing category "tween" (Cook and Kaiser 2004). But over the course of the project I conducted research with kids from four to fourteen years old. I justify this wide range in part out of convenience, but also because I think it corresponds to an actually occurring social formation that is observable every day at school and in the media. In many cases, of course, the category of "kids" is further subdivided by age, gender, race, ethnicity, and social status, so kids articulating solidarity with one another against particular adult authority will not necessarily identify with kids significantly younger than them. But that is why it is important to take a wide view, to see how peer solidarity practices play out similarly among peer groups of different ages. Age is one terrain in which social distinction is taking place, and the broad categories of "child" or "kid" are clearly constructed as part of a binary of opposition to something like "adults," so it matters less that there are subdivisions within either side of that binary. While some studies may start by defining their subjects precisely by age, it is not clear at all to me that chronological age is anything more than an arbitrary measure, and we should be much more interested in the lived experience of categories of identity.

Finally, I do not spend much time discussing adults at HCS in this book, which is not to suggest that adults are not important to the questions I ask. Adults at HCS had many opinions about the practices I discuss, which, because of their authority, had direct bearing on those practices. In staff meetings and conversations, for instance, teachers associated MP3 players with behavioral problems, and the year following my residence all portable electronic devices (MP3 players, video game devices, cell phones) were banned from use in school. But this fact should not imply an overdetermined model of school as structured simply by (adult) power and (child) resistance. For a cultural studies–primed audience, the banning of MP3 players can be an expected punchline or "aha" moment that crystallizes the complicated social practices I'm trying to explore into a simple and inescapable model of power. These caveats aside, I consider the banning of MP3 players in some more detail in the conclusion of this book. As an instance of adults reacting en bloc to students' practices, the banning suggests a solidarity in action among adults that is complementary to the childhood solidarity I trace throughout this book. Further, that it is adults reacting to children's practices, and not always vice versa, suggests clearly that children's cultural practices are frequently autonomous and independent—not simply responses to a dominant adult culture. But in order to privilege children's voices, and to avoid overstating the importance of individual adults' authority or discipline, in general I try to bracket adults out from my analysis. My mental image is for the adults in these pages to appear somewhat like the unspeaking and faceless adults in the cartoon television show *The Muppet Babies*, or perhaps the film adaptations of the *Peanuts* comics—present only when ethnographically relevant, and intentionally voiceless. I think this accurately reflects children's experience of their peer sociality as a space in which adults are largely absent (or present mostly in the background). From this perspective giving voice to adults would not only be unnecessary but even perhaps counterproductive.

Childhood

Finally, the earlier claim that childhood might be something greater than just chronological age merits further discussion, especially because this book is intended, in part, for an audience of scholars for whom "childhood" is less familiar as an analytical category. In the next chapter I provide an extended exploration of the importance of this view of childhood to institutional arrangements of schooling and education, but I take the opportunity here to diverge somewhat from the topical focus of this project to outline the broader philosophical and theoretical perspective on childhood that informs this book. I start from the premises of the "new social studies of childhood" (James, Prout, and Jenks 1998), which acknowledges children as actors in their communities and agents in the production of their roles and relationships. This model moves away from universalist, developmental models that depoliticize children and childhood while silencing children's own ideas and interests in what childhood is and should be. From this perspective, "childhood" is a socially constructed category of identity that intersects with gender, class, race, ethnicity, nationality, religion, disability, and sexuality (Prout and James 1997), and children are best understood as social actors who co-construct their roles and relationships in expressive interactions with peers and adults (Jacoby and Ochs 1995; Goodwin 2006).

Alan Prout and Allison James (1997) propose a social constructionist model of childhood that distinguishes biological immaturity from the specific social and cultural forms that childhood takes throughout history and around the world—by analogy to a distinction between (biological) sex and (social) gender. It may be that assumptions about the ontological integrity of biological immaturity invite a critique similar to that Butler (1990) directs at the sex-gender distinction, but for my purposes Prout and James's framework provides a strong enough basis to maintain that childhood, like gender, is the performative accomplishment of actual children (see also Austin, Dwyer, and Freebody 2003). Prout and James criticize psychological models of children's development that—under the guise of empiricism—propose normative scripts along which all children should progress, in which biologically determined infants are gradually socialized into cultural and autonomous adults. Such claims about universal patterns in childhood—and therefore human—progress distinctly resemble evolutionist models of cultural development and draw on a binary of nature versus culture that have been subject to powerful critique in other domains (Fabian 1983; Ortner 1972; see also Kromidas 2014). Nonetheless such developmental/evolutionist views of childhood continued to permeate ethnomusicological, folkloristic, and educational scholarship on children's expressive practices long after being rejected for other groups (Minks 2002; K. Marsh 2008). The assumption that children follow a single, universal script in their development automatically denies their capacity for culturally specific childhood traditions, histories, and subcultures. Furthermore, developmental models of childhood contribute to racist, sexist, and primitivist discourses by providing scientistic authority to perspectives that infantilize stigmatized groups and deny them full social membership (Stephens 1995; Field 2014), while refusing to value or even acknowledge the childhoods of children of color (Goff et al. 2014; Gill-Peterson 2015)

Objections that children eventually become adults, and so childhood is not like other categories of identification which are stable, permanent, and definitive, effectively reinscribe essentialist views of identity that scholars of race and gender have persuasively dismantled (Radano 2003; Butler 1990). Identities are not fixed, though they may have a phenomenal stability for many (Hall 1996). Neither are childhood identities fixed, but the apparent transience of childhood does not make childhood any less powerfully determining of children's social status and self-conception. Rather, "temporality" is precisely the discursive and ontological terrain on which childhood is constructed, as a period of rapid transition along a determined trajectory toward adulthood, toward the future, toward stable identities, toward full-fledged social participation, etc.—always *toward* (James and Prout 1997; J. Cole and Durham 2008b). The construction of childhood is one of constant displacement from the present to the future, a futurity that has powerful ideological implications for adult politics, defining and radically constraining visions of possible or good lives (Edelman 2004). Therefore one long-standing slogan of childhood scholars has been to demand that children be understood not simply as "becomings" but also as "beings" in their own right (Qvortrup 1994), because the hegemonic vision of childhood is so powerfully temporalizing it denies children any claim to present, rather than future, identities. Ironically, this move to understand children as "beings" inverts Stuart Hall's intervention that the formation of cultural identities should be understood as a "process of becoming rather than being" (1996:4). If other identity categories are fixed and essentialized as stable, transhistorical, and unchangeable, childhood is fixed, essentialized, and dehistoricized as an identity defined by constant change and always-emergent futurity.[13]

The corollary of the construction of childhood as emergent becoming is the privilege placed on "adulthood" as stable and unchanging (Blatterer 2007; Cook 2011; Johansson 2012). Such a position is purely ideological and does not stand up to scrutiny. Even if we grant that *rates* of change decrease, it is certainly the case that individuals occupy social roles differently during young adulthood, middle age, and old age, and the boundaries of adulthood change dramatically across history and geography (Mintz 2015). We should also be attentive to the ideological value placed on stable adulthood as a key element in the Western project of delineating a rational subject suitable for citizenship and economic autonomy. This subject is the sort of being who can "make promises" (Nietzsche 1989 [1887]:59), that is, present his or her identities and actions as stable, predictable, and accountable into the future. To convincingly produce adulthood as stable or unchanging—that is, to develop the ideological basis of contemporary Western society—requires the simultaneous identification of an "Other": the constantly changing and unpredictable child.

Therefore, childhood is admittedly unlike race, class, or gender, in that its processes of social differentiation are indexed specifically to time, but this is no different than pointing out that race and gender are distinct because (to simplify drastically) the one articulates to traits like skin color and population while the other to reproductive organs and sexuality. Applying the analytical term "identity" to these various categories highlights commonalities among them; to acknowledge childhood as a category of identity is to suggest these similarities with other more thoroughly studied such categories—*not* to obscure meaningful differences. Recognizing that just as race, gender, and class vary in relation to one another they also vary across the life course, we ought to include age within frameworks of intersectionality (McCall 2005): gender identities may shift significantly for individuals who become parents; mass criminalization and incarceration of African American men applies with particular force to adolescents and young men, just as valorized notions of childhood innocence are historically denied children of color; or the imputed *a*sexuality of children and the elderly highlights fundamental changes in individuals' sex and gender roles across the life course, with profound implications for their social status and well being, as demonstrated by issues of child sexual abuse or the social and therefore also sexual—isolation of elderly people in the contemporary United States.

Discourses of intimacy, domesticity, and privacy that characterize children are similar to discourses that exclude women from full public participation. The feminist critique that the family, home, and private life are fundamentally political (Nussbaum 2000) ipso facto applies to these aspects of childhood. That is, insofar as it is tied up with the family, itself a political and historical institution, childhood is inherently political and historical.[14] Similarly, political discourses that infantilize women, people of color, colonial subjects, or working-class people as childlike and therefore incapable or dependent necessarily inflect childhood with political meaning (Weikle-Mills 2013; Field 2014).

One useful approach for understanding childhood comes from theories of disability. Discourses of childhood and disability explicitly overlap in many ways, not least in their shared construction in terms of "temporality" (Kafer 2013). Disability is frequently articulated using the language of childhood development, so terms like "retardation" identify a pause in a course of cognitive and psychological development that "normal" children pass through. In critical discourses such linguistic slippage often explicitly conflates childhood and disability, as with Theodor Adorno's critique of musical "regression" in which listening subjects "are not child-like . . . but they are childish; their primitivism is not that of the undeveloped, but that of the forcibly retarded" (1991 [1938]:46–47). The presence or absence of "capacities" or "faculties" that are monitored and contested in disputes over disabled people's rights to public access or political enfranchisement are at least discursively positioned in parallel to the "aptitudes" and "achievements" that are measured in educational and psychological assessments of children (McDermott, Goldman, and Varenne 2006). That cognitive faculties are definitive of "personhood" and therefore of basic rights is a controversial but nonetheless commonplace claim (e.g., Singer 1994), and the view that cognitive ability (under the catchall "rationality") is the ideal test for "citizenship" extends back at least to Aristotle, and includes the "rational-critical" discourse that modern philosophers have identified as central to democratic life (Habermas 1989 [1962]). Arguments from activists and disability scholars suggest that the limits of disabled people's ability are not fixed and are constrained more by social contexts than physical impairments (Bérubé 2003; McDermott and Varenne 1995), while examples of "precocious" children similarly suggest that ability is not at all adequately indexed by age (Bickford 2016).

Pointing to all of these commonalities between various formations of marginal or stigmatized social identities, I am not so much interested in arguing that children, like women, people of color, or even disabled adults are unfairly excluded from the level of political participation that their actual capabilities would suggest for them, and that therefore the clear "solution" is to enfranchise them. To be clear, "minors" certainly have made political demands in the past (T. Cole 2010; Gordon 2009; Youth Liberation of Ann Arbor 1972), and the view that children and teenagers should have rights to self-determination and political participation is an important one with significant history and influence (Firestone 1970; J. Holt 1974;

see also, Hart and Atkins 2011; Rehfel 2011; Van Bueren 2011). For my purposes it is more important to affirm that childhood is philosophically difficult (Schapiro 1999), and that difficulty can be intellectually productive. Thinking through childhood in terms of politics and identity might contribute toward critiques of the priority given "rationality" and abstraction in political deliberation as the ultimate marker of full membership in a (political) community (Warner 1990), when, instead, necessity, dependence, and intimacy are often key values of human life and community (Nussbaum 2006). On the one hand, Nussbaum's critique of social contract theories of society and justice applies directly, if not explicitly, to children.[15] But I think there may be even more here. While it is beyond the scope of this book, I want to suggest the outlines of a critique that sees children not simply as specific problems for theories that seek progressively expanding political participation, in the way that mentally disabled people and nonhuman animals figure in Nussbaum's account as "frontiers" for political philosophy. The problem identified for contract theories of social justice involves the *exclusion* of women, people of color, disabled people, or nonhuman animals from social life, such that these individuals are simply invisible to the proposed regimes of social relations. But even within contract theories, children are not quite simply "excluded," hidden within the private sphere of the family that is somehow untouched by the social contract. Rather, children are a fundamental concern for such contractarian visions, even if only because of their future adulthood—note the importance of education to each of Locke, Rousseau, and Rawls. Courtney Weikle-Mills (2008), for example, has demonstrated the contradictory centrality of childhood to John Locke's contractarian political theory. The universality of childhood, therefore, does not neutralize it as a category of identity and social difference. Rather, the universal experience of childhood, and the ready acknowledgement of childhood by contract theorists as a period of dependency and nonparticipation, inscribes need, dependence, and care into the core of political theories that purport to bracket off such concerns.

Childhood, in this telling, is a constitutive Other to Western ideologies of an autonomous, rational, and equal subject. If liberal narratives see political participation progressively expanded to previously excluded groups such as women or people of color who can empirically demonstrate their fitness, while categorically unfit individuals such as the disabled or animals are simply excluded from the narrative altogether, children are both of these things: necessary participants in a social contract if only by their future status as adults, but categorically excluded from that participation at the same time.

The question again is around temporality. How much is it worth worrying about that exclusion if everyone "has" a childhood and will eventually be an adult? But that's exactly the point: children can't be argued away. The simple fact that all of our communities are chock full of children who are subject to public institutions (who can't be hidden behind the fiction of the family as a voluntary private institution) positions dependence and care as fundamental, primary values, *even within* contractarian views of society as ideally composed of voluntary, rational, independent participants. The point here is not to privilege childhood as an essential category of human dependence, but rather to see its irreducible dependence reflected in other "adult" roles and relationships, and to recognize the importance of necessity, dependence/interdependence, and intimacy in every aspect of social life. Such an approach would build on a long-standing line of argument from feminist, queer, and disability studies and activism (e.g., Federici 1975; Hochschild 2003 [1989]; Berlant and Warner 1998; Kittay and Feder 2002; McRuer 2006; Boris and Parreñas 2010; Poo 2015). Therefore, rather than relying on moral intuitions that excluded groups merit inclusion in our models of society as the motivation for challenging existing theories, I suggest that once we activate age as a meaningful category of social differentiation it quickly becomes clear that need, dependence, and inequality cannot even be written out of contract theories that try to base their account of social justice on voluntary and reciprocal relations among equals.

Ultimately I am interested less in sorting out these abstract analytical claims about childhood and political philosophy than in examining actually existing meanings of childhood in the lives of children and adults. That childhood might plausibly be understood through theories of politics and identity is only meaningful insofar as childhood actually is experienced as a political identity. Therefore, I look especially to instances where children perform or express relations of solidarity with other children *as children*—that is, situations where individuals articulate themselves as members of a group of children, rather than, or in addition to, say, as members of an ethnic group, or a gender identity, or a family unit, or a geographical affiliation. Thus, in chapter 1 I consider in detail how childhood in this sense has long been a central element in the constitution of schools, with strong and interesting connections to the ways that class, gender, and ethnicity are articulated in educational institutions. In the ethnographic focus of chapters 2 to 5, I attend in fine-grained detail to how children perform solidarity defined around age categories in their everyday interactions with language and media in school.

This book's organization

Chapter 1, "Intimate and Instrumental: An Expressive Practices Approach to Childhood in School," provides the core theoretical support for the book. Because this book makes interdisciplinary interventions into three fields that are not always in conversation—childhood studies, education studies, and music studies—this chapter makes crucial theoretical and conceptual interventions to support the arguments developed and sustained through the ethnographic core of the book. It argues that childhood is a central organizational focus of educational institutions, synthesizing approaches from linguistics, anthropology, folklore, and ethnomusicology. Building on an influential "expressive practices" approach that emphasizes the centrality of expressive language and communication in the social reproduction of class, gender, and ethnicity in schools, the chapter extends this model to include the social production of childhood roles and identities. It identifies "instrumentality" and "intimacy" as the key concepts for understanding how expressive practices are linked to social relationships. It then argues that the expressive practices of children's peer cultures are characteristically "intimate" in their linguistic features and social embeddedness, by contrast with the instrumental approaches to language and communication characterized by classroom routines and literacy education. This contrast between instrumental and intimate modes of interaction and expression provides an important basis for understanding children's practices around entertainment media and digital technologies in subsequent chapters. This chapter also presents an overview of research on children's expressive traditions, and develops key themes that are considered in relation to media and technology in later chapters.

Chapter 2, "Earbuds Are Good for Sharing," presents a detailed analysis of children's practices of sharing earbuds with friends and peers. Portable music technologies, in this telling, are prominently involved in mediating face-to-face relationships among schoolchildren, and the social links they articulate provide an intimate environment for interaction and connection that is largely closed to adults. These face-to-face interactions using digital audio technologies challenge theoretical perspectives from two fields: First, a prominent view of sound technologies as progressively isolating individuals from one another fails entirely to account for children's intimate and sociable practices. Second, while approaches to portable communication technologies increasingly do privilege communication among intimates, in their focus on communication at a distance they neglect the face-to-face connections in which these devices are embedded. Technology studies are also largely unconcerned with portable music listening as a central practice of "new media," accepting uncritically the view from music and sound studies that portable music is necessarily isolating. The opposite is true for children, and music devices, far from being exceptions to the hyperconnected social environments of new media, provide a perspective for locating those connections in materially and spatially grounded face-to-face relationships.

Chapter 3, "Tinkering and Tethering," considers MP3 players at HCS from a material culture perspective. This approach reveals that children emphasized the tangibility of their MP3 players as objects more than as devices for communication or data storage. Children's MP3 players have been thoroughly domesticated within an intimate and childish material culture already characterized by playful physical interaction and portable objects such as toys, trading cards, and dolls that can be shared, manipulated, and held close, and in a culture of embodied participation that emphasizes touch, physical closeness, and movement. Children's emphasis and interest in the materiality of their devices has implications for understanding their conceptions of sound, music, and circulation, and it decenters adult values of fidelity in sound recordings. It also provides an important link for understanding how MP3 players are incorporated as authentic elements in existing cultures of childhood, and thus inflected with the peer cultural solidarity that characterizes children's expressive culture in schools.

Chapter 4, "Intimate Media In and Out of the Classroom," considers how girls and boys view the conflict between media consumption and learning in class, focusing on uses of portable media in the classroom that take place mostly in secret. It compares listening practices in school and at home to bring the institutional structure of kids' listening practices into relief, and compares kids' use of portable video game devices with MP3 players to explore the gendering of kids' media consumption. The contrast between discourses of "multitasking" that are volunteered differently by boys and girls suggest that each group sees the fine-grained details of their media interactions as deeply tied up with their gendered social identities in school.

Chapter 5, "Inappropriate and Inarticulate," examines how interactions using music devices are part of a "childish" expressive tradition that is engaged primarily with the bureaucratic organization of language and communication in school. Music listening, despite being wordless, is an important part of children's intimate expressive repertoires. I propose understanding these modes of music listening through reference to two master tropes of intimate peer expression in school: inappropriateness and inarticulateness. I consider several examples where music listening practices make clear reference to the bureaucratic and authoritative context of school to argue that music consumption should not be understood as a phenomenon separate from schooling, but rather is intimately tied up with schooling. Identifying music listening as an element of these interactional and communicative frames grounds popular music listening and consumer culture in everyday expressive practices, and provides a key perspective for linking bureaucratic networks of educational institutions to the emerging public presence of children in commercial culture, through the small-scale, everyday activities of children in school.

The conclusion, "Kids' Rules," advocates for understanding music in terms of interpersonal relationships as much or more than as repertoires of texts with their own cultural meanings. Music should be considered in terms of Bourdieu's concept of "social capital" in addition to "cultural capital" as it is normally conceived. Children's in-school media use does not involve the intrusion of foreign consumer culture into education, but rather historically and culturally grounded traditions of peer cultural solidarity provide a context into which entertainment media practices fit naturally. A seeming opposition between education and consumer culture is in fact a constitutive dialectic, which helps explain the politicization of children's peer cultural practices in school. Consumer culture represents the extension of dynamics from school into the wider public sphere. The invasion of these practices into schools is only a return to original fields of conflict between children and adults.

CHAPTER 1

Intimate and Instrumental

An Expressive Practices Approach to Childhood in School

The fields of education research and childhood studies substantially overlap in their topics and would seem to be naturally aligned. Childhood research is often conducted in schools, and anthropologists and scholars of education frequently study children as they go about the situated activities of schooling. But, surprisingly, studies of childhood rarely make explicit the central role of educational discourses and practices in the production of childhood identities, and, similarly, anthropologists of education rarely address the ideologies about childhood and youth that are central to schools' missions and practices. Nonetheless, schools are an important site of the production of childhood roles and identities, and childhood is an idea that is central to the organization and constitution of educational institutions. The social institutions of schooling and childhood are mutually constituted. Each fundamentally depends on the other. Education research is incomplete without a critical perspective on childhood, and childhood research is incomplete without attention to the structuring force of educational institutions. To bridge these approaches, this chapter explores how models of the reproduction of social difference through school expressive practices can be usefully extended to understand how expressive practices in school also produce the identities of children and adults. Establishing the centrality of expressive practices to the social organization of school and the cultural construction of childhood helps to explain how practices like music listening and media consumption are important to children in their negotiation of the expressive life of educational institutions.

Ethnographic studies of class reproduction in high schools have identified processes through which contrasting and conflicting repertoires of expression and communication are centrally involved in social stratification. In their foundational works, Paul Willis, Douglas Foley, and Penelope Eckert separately identify a particular "instrumental" communicative style associated with schools—and associated by extension with bureaucratic, bourgeois, management, or "systems" communication broadly—that they link to "mental labor," "instrumental speech practices," and "school's corporate practice," respectively. Each author argues that people of color, working-class people, and otherwise stigmatized populations construct oppositional identities (and are constructed as marginal or stigmatized in institutional discourse) through their rejection of such bureaucratic communicative modes and adoption of some contrasting or alternate communicative styles that can be characterized as emphasizing social relationships and community. By linking these studies to formal linguistic and ethnomethodological studies of classroom question-answer interactional frameworks and "objectifications" of knowledge, we can identify an opposition between "contextualized" and "decontextualized" language (specifically turning on the relative indexicality of utterances) in school. This formalizes the suggestions of Willis, Foley, and Eckert and links their broad conclusions to the small-scale language practices of classroom settings. Grouping these parallel analyses together, I propose the terms "instrumental" and "intimate" to characterize the expressive practices that index bureaucratic culture on the one hand and oppositional cultures on the other.

Despite their explanatory power, these studies of social stratification through opposition to instrumental communicative modes in schools neglect a category of central importance to the social organization of schools: childhood. But ideas and practices related to childhood are central to schooling, and classroom question-answer frameworks specifically situate students in classrooms as children. Children and childhood bear many of the traits that produce groups as marginal in capitalist societies, particularly if we look to the expressive traditions that link children to one another. Exploring accounts of children's expressive practices in school suggests that they produce "childish" expressive communities in opposition to school's instrumental practices. Therefore the social construction of childhood in schools is best understood using the same framework of intimate and instrumental expressive contrasts that others have used to understand gender, class, and ethnic differentiations.

Expressive practices, schooling, and the social reproduction of inequality

As in any governmentally chartered institutional setting, in schools the everyday "tactics" of individual teachers and students encounter bureaucratic "strategies" (de Certeau 1984) for regulating and structuring social practices, producing educational institutions as complex sites of competition among both individuals and class segments. Anthropological studies of schooling and class stratification find in particular that class hierarchies reproduce themselves across generations as students from different family backgrounds orient differently to schools' bureaucratic goals (P. Willis 1981 [1977]; Foley 1990; Eckert 1989). Willis, Foley, and Eckert each identify students' expressive culture as a central site in producing their orientations toward schooling, linking broad markers of style like clothing and musical genres with fine-grained patterns of speech (Eckert 1996).

Paul Willis's account of a group of working-class "lads" at a 1970s English high school frames class struggle in school in terms of contrasting values of mental and manual labor, highlighting language and expressivity as the central elements of social differentiation as emergent and continually negotiated. While Willis emphasizes mental and manual *labor* in his analysis, he places expressivity at the center of that binary. Willis argues that class divisions are produced by the bureaucratic organization of school, and that through students' orientation toward the value of schooling—and especially the value of different modes of language use associated alternately with school and friendship—young people position themselves for different roles in the adult workplace. These orientations are produced primarily through values about forms of work, such that the "lads" in his study maintain "a deep seated skepticism about the value of qualifications [i.e., degrees] in relation to what might be sacrificed to get them: a sacrifice ultimately, not of simply dead time, but of a quality of action, involvement, and independence" (1981 [1977]:126). Willis writes that "mental work demands too much, and encroaches—just as the school does—too far upon those areas [especially sociable talk and joking] which are increasingly adopted as their own, as private and independent." Hence students' orientation to a particular communicative practice associated with school manifests as an orientation toward bureaucratic authority, as "mental labour henceforth always carries with it the threat of a demand for obedience and conformism. Resistance to mental work becomes resistance to authority as learnt in school" (1981 [1977]:103). In Willis's model, such small-scale processes of everyday skepticism and opposition to school culture ramifies into broader social structures: "The specific conjunction in contemporary capitalism of class antagonism and the educational paradigm turns education into control, (social) class resistance into educational refusal, and human difference into class division" (1981 [1977]:103).

Though Willis suggests that the lads actively choose their futures as manual laborers, he argues that this is not because they value manual labor as such. Rather, ironically, it might be said that the lads so value the independence of their mental practices—language, joking, trash talking, etc.—that they are unwilling to cede control of them to the authority of a bureaucratic school or white-collar workplace, preferring on principle to submit their bodies to the estrangements of labor. Thus, the specific terrain of conflict between working-class and bureaucratic cultures is not an opposition between mental and manual labor but between differing values *within* mental activity itself—particularly a willingness or not to commodify one's mental activities as estranged labor. These contrasting values of mental work manifest as stylistic differences between expressive repertoires, specifically the "pisstakes" or "kiddings" of both counter-school and shopfloor culture (1981 [1977]:55), and the abstraction and "considered language" of "the dominant bourgeois mode of signification" (1981 [1977]:124).

Douglas Foley's approach to similar questions about the social organization of schooling draws out in more detail the communicative and expressive characteristics of class struggle. In place of the deterministic Marxian class stratification that he sees in Willis's account,[1] Foley turns to Habermas (1984) for a model of capitalist culture that is characterized by particular communicative practices: "instrumental communication" and "technological rationality" that spill over from increasingly powerful bureaucracies into everyday life (a "systems" world that colonizes the "life-world"). Foley articulates Habermas's model through the lens of class culture, arguing that instrumental communication is not distributed homogeneously, but is a marker of class segmentation, so "instrumental speech practices, that is, the logic of capital, are more characteristic of the bourgeois/petty bourgeois class than of the proletariat" (1990:175). Foley's effort "to redefine class cultures as alienated communicative labor and qualitatively different types of speech practices" (1990:170) further reframes Willis's approach to emphasize expression and communication, while building on Willis's intimation that certain types of abstract language (alienated communicative labor) index bourgeois and bureaucratic subjectivities.

Foley grounds his adaptation of Habermas's instrumental communication in Erving Goffman's performance perspective, to construct a "'situational speech performance' concept of class cultures": "Dramaturgically, class groups are socialized to use distinct styles of speech. They select a speech style that fits the general social identity that 'normal' society bestows upon them and marks the performers' social status" (1990:179). Foley emphasizes the manipulations and concealment that Goffman's analysis reveals in everyday interactions, linking this to the pattern of instrumental communication in which "people increasingly treat each other like objects to be managed rather than free and equal expressive subjects" (1990:172).

In pursuit of a theory of "class cultures as situational speech performance of status groups" (1990:178), Foley outlines the characteristics of two expressive styles whose distribution structures the stratification of populations into hierarchically related class segments:

> Two generalized class roles are routinely enacted in reoccurring everyday situational speech performances . . . Standard, official speech is authoritative and proper. Proper, polite speech and etiquette can become a strategic weapon in their everyday communication. Such instrumental, manipulative speech practices help preserve the image of bourgeois class privilege as cultural models and as political leaders . . . Unofficial speech is often non-standard, informal, and lacking in politeness forms. Impolite speech becomes an unstrategic form of expressiveness that either meekly enacts the subordinate, stigmatized role of outsider or openly, hostilely rejects it. (1990:180)

Foley continues with this outline, providing structural/functionalist reasons for the historical emergence of these different styles:

> A more collective organizational context may create speech communities that are generally more context-bound or indexical in character . . . In the end, actors in more traditionalistic, context-bound speech communities judge themselves more by their deeds than by their public situational speech performances. In contrast, more anonymous communicative contexts such as modern suburban communities and corporate work groups are marked by intense individualism, competition, restricted information, and considerable impression management. In such market-like modern speech contexts, the split between public and private self is much greater than in more traditionalistic communities. Such relatively unindexical, ahistorical, anonymous communicative contexts give rise to the greater use of strategic, instrumental speech and impression management. As a result, people in such speech contexts develop greater communicative competencies in instrumental speech and impression management. (1990:184)

With this framework, Foley examines the school culture of working-class and middle-class white and Hispanic high-school students in a Texas town. He finds these styles map broadly onto social class (more so than ethnicity), and that the official language practices of schools produce the same sort of "unindexical, ahistorical" contexts and instrumental practices as other middle-class sites. Further, Foley finds that movement between these styles characterizes social mobility: "The more one is in, or wants to be in, the 'mainstream,' the more one uses instrumental communicative practices rhetorically to define and manage social reality" (1990:185). Conversely, like Willis, Foley frames the unwillingness of certain groups to conform to these instrumental practices as a reaction against the "cultural homogenization and administration" by which "a person's everyday discourse practices become reified," and through these oppositions communication is politicized: "the appropriation of people's communicative labor in the cultural sphere is a new level of dehumanization . . . A new reason for revolt emerges, therefore, with the growing theft of communicative labor" (1990:185).

Penelope Eckert and Sally McConnell-Ginet (1995) retheorize school communicative practices in terms of "communities of practice" (Lave and Wenger 1991). Like Willis and Foley, Eckert and McConnell-Ginet find that social differentiation among high-school students is constituted primarily through orientations to the "corporate practice" of school, through categories like "jock" and "burnout" (Eckert 1989) that strongly mark social class affiliations. For jocks, "social status is constructed as a function of institutional status, personal identities are intertwined with institutional identities, and social networks are intertwined with institutional networks" (Eckert and McConnell-Ginet 1995:473). For burnouts, on the other hand, "because they are bound for the work force immediately after high school, . . . the extracurricular sphere has no hold on them as qualification for future success; rather, it appears to them as a form of infantilization and as a hierarchy existing only for its own sake" (1995:474). This differentiated orientation to the school institution is recognizable in the opposition of Willis's lads to school "conformity" and their focus on future lives as manual laborers, and in the rejection by Hispanic and working-class Texas kids of Foley's account of the "instrumental" speech practices of school and school's extracurricular events.

But in contrast to Willis and Foley, Eckert and McConnell-Ginet's communities of practice approach emphasizes the emergent processes of affiliation and differentiations in everyday expressive practices, arguing that, "speech differences are not simply markers of category affiliation. They carry in themselves complex social meanings, like tough, cool, slutty, casual, or mean, and these meanings are part of the construction of categories like those labeled by female, male, jock, burnout" (1995:500). By noting the complex matrixes of meaning carried through speech practices, we begin to see how the same expressive repertoires that produce social class divisions have implications in the construction of overlapping categories of identity. Eckert and McConnell-Ginet focus on the simultaneous construction of gender identities with class affiliations in their analysis of two marked phonological shifts differentially distributed among the population of their subject school. They find that girls in both groups displayed more of the phonological shift than boys in their same group, and the most extreme variant was used by "burned-out burnout girls" (marking both their gender and their class identities) such that "whatever distinguishes jocks and burnouts also distinguishes boys and girls within those categories" (1995:502). This process of distinction happens in real time, as individuals imbue speech styles with meaning as they perform them: "In their extreme speech, then, the burned-out burnout girls are not simply using phonetic variants with a meaning already set . . . Rather, their very use of those variants produces a social meaning. They are simultaneously creating meaning for [the variant] and for being burned-out burnouts" (1995:503). By noting the emergent constructions in expressive speech of overlapping parameters of social difference, Eckert and McConnell-Ginet help to decouple the process of differentiation from the historical or ideological constitution of the groups that are its product, while retaining the critical force of Willis's and Foley's examinations of the institutional mediations of expressivity and power relation in schools.

Instrumental language: IRE, objectification, and essayist literacy

Willis, Foley, and Eckert strongly demonstrate that social class identities are produced through orientations toward and against a particular bureaucratic mode of expression found in schools. But their suggestions as to just what that expressive repertoire consists of are incomplete, so it is useful to examine school expression more closely. Linguistic studies of classrooms point to a set of discursive practices that persistently structure classroom interactions, in which we can recognize the detailed constitution of "abstract" and "instrumental" communication. These are (1) initiation, response, evaluation (IRE) frameworks for interaction, (2) objectification and componentiality as orientations to knowledge, and (3) "essayist" literacy. Contestations and negotiations over these frameworks in interactions between teachers and students reveal the constant tensions and attention to power and social organization by classroom participants.

Classroom activities appear to be conventionally organized by interactions that take the form of "initiation, response, evaluation (or feedback)"—in which the teacher initiates an interaction, often with a question to which she or he anticipates the correct answer (Mehan 1986), selects a student to respond, and evaluates the response. While IRE is clearly structured in terms of adult/school authority over both knowledge and the structure of talk, accounts of IRE still identify the necessity of children's assent and participation for the framework to succeed (Mehan 1979). So despite the clear top-down structure, the conventionality and scriptedness of IRE is always partial. Flattening out social differences between children,

IRE frameworks position adults and children into roles of teachers and students, and through the segmentation and regulation of classroom discourse IRE frameworks are oriented toward facts as discrete and toward knowledge as componential—embedding ideas about what can or should be learned as well as what types of people teach and learn. Because of the wide dissemination of research, teachers are often aware of the ubiquity of these routines, and many educators make significant efforts to develop alternative classroom interaction frameworks that are less hierarchical and more student-centered. Still, even in many conscientiously progressive classrooms, teacher-initiated IRE routines can be a common feature, or may appear in some lessons and not others (Austin, Dwyer, and Freebody 2003:23). To be clear, IRE is not good or bad, it is simply a recognizable feature of many, but not all, classroom interactional routines, which has interesting implications for the roles and relationships of teachers and students.

Accompanying IRE interactions is an orientation toward knowledge as a set of componential "facts" that are authoritative and separated from their contexts. Massoud and Kuipers, writing about various processes of "objectification," note that "classrooms in general tend to be places where knowledge is broken down into digestible chunks, often packaged and repackaged into different forms in relation to the different subjective perspectives of the students" (2008:214). In this framework, objectification is a social and semiotic process, such that "part of the power of objectification comes by its capacity to obscure its own indexical creativity, and to make it appear that it is only encapsulating and representing what is already there, when in fact it is creating something new" (2008:218). More than simply an ideology about abstract knowledge, componentiality depends on participation frameworks like IRE that orient to facts as discrete objects, and pedagogy is geared as much to interactional competence in these frames as to acquisition of specific curricular knowledge: "Close attention is given in classroom talk to what counts as knowledge and what is required in the way of reasoning and presentation of an answer . . . So while the propositional corpus can be thought of as the 'academic' or factual lesson knowledge . . ., it includes as well the cultural logic in use in the display of those facts, and the expected ways of behaving and acting in the classroom" (Austin, Dwyer, and Freebody 2003:27).

Seemingly in contrast to these arguments, educators often emphasize "process" in learning, institutionalizing John Dewey's philosophy that education should focus on the activities of inquiry, rather than collections of knowledge. Curricula and educational standards now explicitly emphasize scientific method, critical thinking, and problem solving. Ironically, charts and tables enumerating discrete "problem-solving techniques" decorate classroom walls and textbook pages, and students are increasingly accountable for labeling the correct procedure for solving a problem in math and science quizzes, in addition to simply identifying the answer—disassembling the process of inquiry into components and treating them as one more set of discrete facts for students to learn. Even in contexts such as laboratory-based science classrooms, in which "the hands-on technique is supposed to be superior to mere lecturing and reading," observers find that "not only is the laboratory procedure an externalization of human capacities for activity . . . , but writing down the results is similarly an externalization of the transformed subjectivity that is supposed to result" (Keane 2008:315). Standard classroom orientations toward componential knowledge are powerful enough that even explicit emphasis by conscientious educators on the process and activity of learning can be quickly objectified and incorporated.

The concept of objectification approaches the idea of "commodification" in Willis's and Foley's accounts. But unlike those authors, for whom commodification is by definition dehumanizing, Massoud and Kuipers emphasize that "objectification is not inherently bad or good: it happens, and it appears to be a fairly active process in . . . classrooms" (2008:218). Similarly Keane writes that, "in contrast to the romantic critique of objectification as, say, inherently alienating or a violation of self-presence . . . , whether objectification is negative or not is a function of who I am for you and what epistemic status I accord that moment of objectification" (2003:239). Still, objectification in the classroom is particularly oriented to assessment by teachers, a process that is alienating in the technical Marxian sense of misrecognizing the products of activity for the social processes of production (Lave and McDermott 2002), and schools' characteristic orientation toward the componentiality of knowledge are building blocks in administrative systems of assessment and ideologies of "achievement" (Varenne, Goldman, and McDermott 1998).

Finally, literacy is a central term in education, and the solitary, formal, and descriptive writing taught in schools is often termed "essayist." In classrooms, talk and writing are often opposed as communicative modalities with very different meanings and consequences:

> Talking is something that causes children to get in trouble more than anything else. Talking provides opportunities for sociability and popularity but also great humiliation; writing can be more solitary, can require more planning, and is often associated with positively sanctioned classroom behavior. Both talking and writing have serious social consequences for students within the classroom, in their relations with other students as well as with the teacher. (Massoud and Kuipers 2008:219)

The ideological separation of talk and writing in schools flattens out the different forms each mode actually takes in various social situations: from correctly answering a question when called on to hollering at a friend during recess, or from writing a sentence in which the form and content carefully conform to instructions to writing a note for a friend on a scrap of paper without regard for spelling or grammar. Distributed access to and valuation of certain forms of textuality and the actual constitution of specific situations in which writing is or is not used have significant implications for the articulation of social power and identity in schools.

Deborah Poole (2008) links these various interactional and ideological orientations together in her close examination of reading group interactions and essayist literacy. The language of essayist literacy is most often characterized as "decontextualized," where broad categories of contextualized and decontextualized language have been seen to differentiate between orality and literacy and between talk on the playground and talk in the classroom:

> The notions of decontextualization or contextualization as applied to written language typically imply a limited scope of meaning, namely, whether or not a text is linked through linguistic or gestural means to its immediate context or to its author, audience or context of production . . . Hence, a so-called "decontextualized" text is said to be devoid of linguistic features such as first or second person pronominal references to author or audience; such a text is also thought to introduce new entities or phenomena in ways that do not assume prior knowledge, often through linguistic features such as relative clauses or the indefinite article. These characteristics of written text are contrasted with contextualizing features of spoken language such as deictic forms that link an utterance explicitly to its immediate physical or visual context. (2008:379–80)

"Contextualized" in this model maps easily onto "indexicality," the term Foley uses to describe the language of working-class and traditional groups. Contextualized and decontextualized language, then, would be broadly characterized by the relative presence of, in Peircian terms, indexical or symbolic signs.[2] The parallel here with the process of objectification is notable. As Keane writes, "objectification commonly involves an upshift from indexicals to symbols, that is, from semantically underspecified marks of causal effects in particular contexts to rules that establish repeatable tokens of established sign types" (2008:314). But just as Massoud and Kuipers point out that objectification often obscures its own "indexical creativity," Poole is careful to point out that "decontexualized" is not a perfectly descriptive label: "these narrow characterizations omit the profound, though less visible, influences of the institutional and sociocultural contexts in which written language is created and encountered. Moreover, . . . the expectations of decontextualized text themselves provide a powerful dimension of context, though again one which is usually invisible and unacknowledged" (2008:380). That is, essayist literacy is always indexically embedded in social contexts—as a significant literature on "situated literacy" demonstrates (e.g., Gee 2008)—even if only insofar as language scrubbed of indexicals necessarily points to an institutional context that militates against such a marked style, and it is important to recognize that decontextualization is "an ideology of academic literacy rather than an inevitable characteristic of written language or its surrounding talk" (Poole 2008:382). Further, Poole argues that decontextualization is "a *stance* characteristic of some texts and often reflected in associated spoken interaction" (2008:382). Decontextualized language and IRE flatten out the social complexity of individuals in classroom or reading situations while producing new relations between participants, and they orient to (and in doing so create) facts that are unique and isolable from one another in a framework of componentiality.

From this perspective on decontextualization and componentiality as a stance or orientation of participants, Poole's analysis of several fifth grade reading groups finds that no single participation framework characterizes any lesson. Rather, each lesson exhibits a shifting range of student- and teacher-initiated orientations toward texts, contexts, and participants. Some of these orientations—characterized by teacher-initiated IRE segments that focus on "facts" abstracted from the text (usually phrases separated out of the context of their sentences) and that do not refer to the other parts of the text, to the text qua writing/print, to illustrations, or to other participants, using little or no indexical language (i.e., a near-complete lack of pronouns)—can be clearly labeled essayist. But "the essayist stance is sometimes interwoven with a more situationally contextualized and personalized form of language use that seems to resist and counterbalance the first" (2008:400). These forms vary from short disruptions of an IRE segment, to longer discussions of illustrations in relation to their surrounding captions and texts, to student-initiated interactions with peers, to occasional jokes or other comments by the teacher. But in general, Poole writes, "the children often shift the interaction to the more contextualized perspective, seeming to prefer and more naturally orient to it. The teacher, on the other hand, primarily guides the group toward a decontextualized orientation, but also seems to play a role of keeping the two in balance; i.e., whenever the interaction seems to veer heavily in one direction, she tends to reorient it to the other" (2008:400). Still, importantly, Poole also points to interactions where students initiate decontextualized orientations and examine the text's facts abstractly.

My claim is that IRE, componentiality, and decontextualization describe formally the interactional and linguistic characteristics of the expressive genres that Willis and Foley discuss in terms of "considered language" or "instrumental speech." As Poole points out the constant slippage in classroom interactional stances from IRE and essayist literacy to other, more contextual modes, we can see the mechanics by which even heavily teacher-regulated classroom interactions are always "messy" with multiple, shifting orientations. While there may be particular elements of language and text that characterize these genres (such as lack of deixis in essayist texts), the generalizable conclusion seems to be shared by Foley and Poole, that the contrast exists primarily in the construction of the interactional frame, stance, or orientation, which is alternately attuned to abstract facts and vertical power relations on the one hand, and context and horizontal peer relationships on the other.

Foley's emphasis on Goffmanian "manipulation," "face-saving," and "impression management" might upset this generalization, characterizing his instrumental communication as especially indexical and attuned to context. This represents a potential disjuncture with IRE and essayist literacy until we remember Poole's position that decontextualization is an "ideology of academic literacy rather than an inevitable characteristic of written language" (2008:382), and Massoud and Kuipers's assertion that "part of the power of objectification comes by its capacity to obscure its own indexical creativity" (2008:218). It is not that classroom texts, componential knowledge, or IRE interactions are in fact disembedded from context but rather that the claim of being context-free is particularly powerful. For example, James Collins (1996) shows how in third-grade classrooms teachers assess students' competence as readers in terms of their out-loud production of texts as objectified and decontextualized: "Interruptions and use of local dialect forms are seen as taking away from the autonomy of a text, and hence its authority as an example of 'good reading.' 'Poor readers' are ones who fail to objectify the text as separate from its social context" (cited in Massoud and Kuipers 2008:217). Naturally these judgments mark against students from minority backgrounds, mapping contextualized and decontextualized language onto community and social groups while normalizing dominant modes of communication.

IRE, componentiality, and decontextualization are one extreme node in a school expressive ecology. As Poole shows, even heavily regulated lessons are sites for mixing of multiple interactional frames—so we can see in these complicated interactional environments how alternative and disputative frames continually emerge and consolidate opposition to authority. What is notable is that the frames that layer with and run up against decontextualization are more or less the same in Poole's relatively tame fifth-grade reading-group scenarios and the much more explicitly oppositional practices described by Foley, Willis, and Eckert, and in countless other studies of kids' resistance to schooling. The contrasting term to decontextualized, instrumental language is, in each case, heightened sociability, a turn away from the solitary, linear, and binary focus of pedagogy toward peers and community.

However necessary essayist literacy is to children's eventual competence and success in bureaucratic adult culture, from the way classrooms organize and regulate students it is clear that "decontextualized" practices are necessarily about power and politics and consent. When kids "resist" such alienated tasks as writing a five-paragraph paper or reading a short text and listing its "facts" in a worksheet, they do not initiate the politicization of the interaction, but are responding *in kind* to teacher-initiated interactions that are already politicized as part of much larger-scale hierarchies of power and status. Moreover teachers, who, of course, competently joke and interact with students, are not simply bureaucratic automatons. Rather, they accomplish to various extents the bureaucratic strategies of school using the same communicative competencies as anyone else.

Dialectics of intimacy and estrangement

These accounts of schooling share a perspective on schools as the agent and symbol of the bureaucratic, instrumental world, and I have proposed that IRE, componentiality, and decontextualization represent the "instrumental" characteristics of school expression to which groups orient themselves in opposition. Less clear from the various accounts is what, exactly, characterizes the oppositional, or counter-school, orientation. Willis proposes that opposition lies in manual labor and masculine jokes or "pisstaking." Foley finds it in historical speech groups or traditions. Eckert sees it as an orientation toward the community outside of school. In Poole's smaller-scale account of classroom settings, students oppose classroom instrumentality by simply reframing their participation to include friends and classmates. A common theme in all of these approaches is a shared focus on non-hierarchical peer relationships, sociability, and community.

Through Poole's account, we can see how expressive styles that mark entire groups of people are also emergent in interactions. That children may initiate decontextualized frames and teachers occasionally interject contextualizations suggests that these contrasting styles are not mutually exclusive; nor do certain groups only have access to one or the other. Contextualization and decontextualization are not separate, bounded, coherent repertoires in themselves, but rather they represent a continuum of available orientations that necessarily refer to each other. The ideological stance of decontextualization does not simply require turning toward instrumental language but also entails turning away from contextual language. And the reverse is true: student orientations to contextualization entail turning away from decontextualization.

This point emerges a bit more clearly if we try to independently examine the different repertoires Foley proposes. If the two orientations are mutually exclusive, they should characterize the expression of entire speech communities. Foley suggests that the indexical, contextual expression of opposition to schooling is located in traditional or historical speech communities. This account sees commonalities in various encounters with modernity by traditional cultures around the world: "various studies of modernity suggest a plausible explanation for why proletarians may be less culturally assimilated in a communicative action sense. In general, low income proletarian communities seem to retain a more traditionalistic organizational character. The practices of an extended family system and fictive kin are more intact in such communities" (1990:183). From this perspective the characteristics of oppositional expression derive from the historical characteristics of bounded, traditional speech communities whose opposition to modern instrumentality is ultimately conservative or preservationist. We can see something similar in Steven Feld's (1988) suggestion that Kaluli expressive culture is characterized by a traditional "master trope" of layering and overlapping of forms ("lift-up-over-sounding") that maps onto the complex (contextual) interactivity of participants in singing, talk, or dance. Feld shows that in situations where Kaluli are asked to perform homophonic missionary music (whose linearity and order seem to index a colonial instrumentality), they resist by pleading inability, or they incorporate aspects of lift-up-over-sounding into their performances.

In contrast, though, examinations of bureaucratic cultures suggest that, despite the institutional forces that militate toward instrumental language, institutional strategies are only ever accomplished through small-scale everyday tactics—the instrumental, "systems" world, as it were, depends on intimate interactions and competencies among the people who produce it. Poole's account demonstrates this clearly: even teachers tasked with producing the extreme instrumentality of IRE, componentiality, and decontextualization in an essayist literacy class manage the lesson by joking with students, addressing off-topic questions, and variously engaging in "contextual" orientations to the students and the lesson. Similarly, Mertz (1996) shows that in law schools (like primary schools, locations for inculcating canonically "instrumental" orientations toward language, facts, and individuals), the measure of student competence in reading case materials is the ability to situate and perform those materials in applicable contexts, rather than to frame them as abstract and decontextualized. "Good ol' boy" networks, connections from elite colleges, or golf outings consolidate power among intimate groups while excluding those with qualifications but without introductions. Lauren Berlant writes, in specific reference to 1990s legal controversies over workplace sexual harassment but with broader application, that "again and again, we see how hard it is to adjudicate the norms of a public world when it is also an intimate one, especially where the mixed-up instrumental and affective relations of collegiality are concerned" (1998:282). Thus it is not clear at all that there are any authentic sites of instrumental communication undiluted through continual counterpoint with intimate expressivity—or that the power of "instrumental" communication does not simply lie in its ideological ability to deflect attention from the intimate relationships it disguises.

Therefore we cannot assume the integrity of these communicative repertoires as they are associated with groups or institutions. Keane (2003) suggests that a dialectic between epistemologies of "intimacy" and "estrangement"—"closeness" and "separation," "immediate" and "mediated," more or less—is ubiquitous in human practice. Keane's "estrangement" involves the objectifications and metalanguages that risk distillation into the bureaucratic "betrayals and reifications" (2003:238) that characterize instrumental communication in modern capitalist contexts. His example involves the oppositionality between scientistic and humanistic orientations to knowledge about social life, where intimacy and estrangement are mobilized as the site of an ideological stance of intellectual distinction. In the case of schools, we can see interactional orientations toward intimacy and estrangement mapping onto orientations to communities and institutions, to modes of communication, to forms of authority, and to larger structural divisions of society into classes and groups.

In a fundamental transformation, schools—and, more broadly, institutions of capitalism—take a mundane, horizontal, immediate, and everyday axis of intimacy (e.g., friendship) and project it onto a massive, vertical, distant, and historical axis of social stratification and hegemony (e.g., class). Capacities for objectification and decontextualization inherent in language are projected onto social difference and institutional power, and so, in Willis's formulation, "resistance to mental work becomes resistance to authority as learnt in school" (1981 [1977]:103). Eckert and McConnell-Ginet write that "[social] categories themselves and the opposition between them can become the object of practice, defining a larger but more loosely connected community of practice focused on conflict over the practices of everyday life in the shared space community members inhabit" (1995:472)—and we might see the social organization of contemporary capitalism as just such a community of practice, "focused on conflict over the practices of everyday life." It may be that some of the specific forms of Hispanic or white Texas working-class or English working-class expression are historically given, as Foley and Willis suggest, but their role within a larger binary expressive ecology is structured by the institutional organization of people in school. Just as there is no authentic site of timeless traditional culture, there is no pure site of authentic bureaucratic culture.

Instrumental and intimate expressivities

In this book I will refer to the binary outlined above in terms of "instrumental" and "intimate." These terms are already keyed to a dialectical opposition of contemporary capitalism (Berlant 1998). The emergence of an "intimate sphere" located in the family was a necessary process in the institutionalization of the public sphere (Calhoun 1992:10; Habermas 1989 [1962]:28, 48), which itself presupposed the "intimacy" of shared and unmarked whiteness and masculinity (Fraser 1992; Warner 1990; also Berlant 2008). Claiming intimacy as the converse term to instrumentality highlights sociability and an emphasis on proximate fellow participants as the consistent converse of instrumental expression. Intimacy, in turning away from "corporate practice," necessarily refers to it. Despite their potential to describe large-scale historical and cultural formations, at the core of each term is an assumption about interactions and relationships between individuals.

Further, neither term is inherently linked to a group of people. Instead instrumentality and intimacy can represent stances toward one situation or another to which any person may or may not have access in any particular situation. Just as both the children and adult in Poole's example each are responsible for initiating essayist or contextualized interactions, each group also clearly has preferences for one style or another. Instead of bounded and determined speech communities, I understand the expressive repertoires of intimacy and instrumentality in terms of the anthropological concept of language ideologies, by which individuals and communities "envision and enact links of language to group and personal identity, to aesthetics, to morality, and to epistemology" (Woolard and Schieffelin 1994:55–56)—emphasizing the acts of articulation between expression and identity, rather than preexisting or natural characteristics. Intimate expressive acts need not be deterministically associated with historically given working-class groups. They take on that characterization because they are framed as oppositional by participants in the communicative ecology of institutions like schools.

Childhood and schooling

When critical studies of schooling continually return to the production and reproduction of class, ethnicity, and gender differences, they frame the school's construction of student subjects as centrally concerned with differences *between students*—differentiating student populations into genders, classes, and ethnicities. But schools do not just produce gendered, classed, and ethnic subjects. From the perspective of bureaucratic institutions explicitly focused on educating neoliberal subjects differentiated only by talent and inclination, gender, class, and ethnicity are messy distractions. Claims of a "level playing field," of course, are themselves fig leaves covering up "the thicket of conflicting people crowding institutions of education with long histories" (Varenne, Goldman, and McDermott 1998:107). Triumphal narratives of social progress through educational equity are packaged with increasingly complex procedures for *measuring* that progress in terms of individual children's "achievement," reinscribing implicitly equal (because abstract) subject positions to children from historically unequal communities: "Social forces are returned to the background as the child is made to occupy the foreground for extended comparison with other children" (Varenne, Goldman, and McDermott 1998:107). But while schools work overtime to paper over historical, class, gender, racial, ethnic, sexual, and religious differences, educators, administrators, and policymakers are explicitly and centrally engaged with another category of person: the "child." To produce the massive educational bureaucracy we now have involved "installing and regulating a standard, administrable model of the clientele, of the Child . . . , attending to the question of who and what were 'the young,' what were their needs, and what did societies need from them?" (Austin, Dwyer, and Freebody 2003:21).[3] It follows that "a crucial plank for these understandings and thus the activities of classrooms is the constitution of Students as a particular category or type of person, and of students as different types of people—primarily as Children, as that is commonly and institutionally understood" (2003:27).

To take an example from the previous discussion: in its abstract, ideal-typical form, the IRE framework does not admit social class difference between students. The abstract procedure of initiation, response, and evaluation positions each child as an individual, autonomous, and equal subject, equivalent to one another in the eyes of the educational bureaucracy. Flattening out social differences in this way, "management strategies used in classrooms [make] students relevant as a class as opposed to as individuals" (Austin, Dwyer, and Freebody 2003:29). Therefore, in their ethnomethodological study of the production of "children" in classrooms, Austin, Dwyer, and Freebody show that students perform different identities in whole-class versus small-group settings: "in interaction with teachers, students ordinarily enacted particular constellations of themselves which made them look like they were somewhat 'incomplete' in relation to those teachers—that, as a cohort, they needed the gaze and guidance of the Teacher—while in interactions between schoolchildren, they were routinely accomplished as competent people" (2003:49). Further, while differentiating between students (through assessment) is a central task of schooling—which, countless studies show, indexes social difference as much as any abstract "achievement"—the categories used to label students are articulated in terms ("normal," "needs improvement," "above/below grade level") of a developmental paradigm that is keyed to age-based assumptions about normative childhoods, and that produce children as "precompetent" (rather than incompetent or competent). That discourses of childhood in such cases provide rhetorical cover for judgments about social difference only increases the need to recognize the ideological power of "childhood" as a category in structuring schooling.

So despite the instrumental orientation of IRE and other classroom frameworks toward interchangeable and abstracted bureaucratic subjects, classrooms necessarily inscribe an original and constitutive distinction between children and adults. Building on the model of opposition and differentiation of Foley and others, we might see the production of children as a basic task of education. As IRE and similar procedures attempt to flatten children's differences, individual children begin to differentiate themselves by how they respond to the ideological weight of that framework, which over the course of schooling contributes to the stratified hierarchies of child and youth social groups in school. In these studies, teachers stand in simply for the bureaucratic, bourgeois orientation with whom conformist students identify. But students from dominant groups "identifying" with teachers is not quite right. When Eckert and McConnell-Ginet point out that burnouts see participation in extracurricular activities as "infantilizing," the criticism is not so much that jocks and other participants are too much *like* bourgeois teachers, but that they subjugate themselves *to* teachers. By taking a solicitous stance toward teachers' power they willingly position themselves as childishly precompetent. The instrumental mode that is being responded to by the oppositionalities of the various stigmatized classes that Willis, Foley, Eckert, and others identify is structured by deep ideological investments in the construction of children and childhood.

I should note that Willis, Foley, and Eckert all deal with high-school students, many of them (in the case of Willis's lads) on the cusp of official "adulthood," whereas the scholars I cite regarding classroom interactions primarily focus on elementary and middle school children. There is a broad (if incomplete) division in the literature, where scholars addressing the large-scale power relations structured through schooling most often consider older students, and those who provide smaller-scale analytical insights into the discursive structure of school language and interaction primarily examine younger students. "Childhood" as a category is incompletely applicable to teenagers, who nonetheless are marked by their status as "youth" in school, law, and politics (Grossberg 2005). That the shedding of carefully calibrated age-based identities in favor of the slipperier age-gradations of full adulthood coincides broadly with completing school and entering the workforce only underscores the importance of age identities for high-school students—though changes in early adulthood may destabilize the link between leaving school and entering adulthood (Arnett 2004; Côté and Allahar 1996). Age and precompetence continue to mark students in high school, though some students may increasingly inhabit legitimate roles as experts in elective music ensembles, vocational programs, clubs, etc.

It is unfortunate that critical studies of schooling often ignore age itself as a parameter of difference, because it seems clear that constructions of youth, even childhood, play a powerful role in the social organization of high schools, and failing to address childhood and youth *as* childhood and youth has a long and problematic history (Hirschfeld 2002). Nonetheless the expressive practices model of social differentiation in school is extremely powerful, and it has clear applications for understanding the production of childhood as a class and an identity in earlier school contexts.

Social construction, development, and pedagogy

Building on the "social constructionist" model of childhood outlined in the introduction, we can see how notions of childhood itself are constructed through binaries of instrumentality and intimacy. Models of childhood as innocent and domestic—sheltered from the harshness of public capitalism—naturalize ideas of "innocence" and "domesticity" that are historically contingent and racially charged (Bernstein 2011; Calvert 1992; Cunningham 1998), which stigmatizes families who do not provide normative home environments and "street children" who transgress into "public" spaces preserved for other sorts of subjects (Boyden 1997; Warner 1992). This model of childhood domesticity ideologically reproduces cultural logics of intimacy and instrumentality. As Nancy Scheper-Hughes writes, "the instrumental value of children has been largely replaced by their expressive value. Children have become relatively worthless (economically) to their parents, but priceless in terms of their psychological worth" (1989:12), though children's historical and contemporary lack of economic value is more ideological than empirical (Zelizer 1985; Folbre 2008).

Notably, the developmental psychology that Prout and James (1997) see as central to modern constructions of a biological, rather than social, childhood (see the introduction), is also the discipline at the center of educational discourse. In education, children are understood to have progressively developing cognitive capacities, and curricula and pedagogy are designed to follow and reinforce children's "progress." In their study of classrooms, Austin, Dwyer, and Freebody found links between developmental models and performances of childhood as "precompetent." Further, they note the historical importance of age to classifications of students in school, pointing out that "as schools assembled children into grades by age, teaching settings, materials and assessment practices became age-tailored, and those theories of Childhood and development that drew on age as a correlate and potential explanation of 'development and learning' became productive instruments of policy for schooling" (2003:22; see also Chudacoff 1989). Age and precompetence are central concepts in developmental models, and it is through the bureaucratic apparatus of schooling that such models are incorporated into students' successful enactment of themselves *as* children in school, creating a feedback loop between ideology and practice:

> [Developmental] propositions about children become organizing principles, systems of interpretation that overwrite other ways of considering people and interpreting their actions. They similarly provide normative specifications that serve as evaluative criteria for the behaviour of people at different points in the life cycle. To meet these norms, in our case to do well at school, students must, among other things, briskly discover what the adults' theories of children are and how they, as teachable students, might enact important features of those theories. (2003:9)

We can see how precompetence and development are incorporated into the expressive repertoires of schooling by noting, for instance, that essayist literacy education proceeds from letter sounds to spelling words to writing sentences, paragraphs, and structured papers. Similarly, music education that focuses on composing music (more common in the United Kingdom and Australia than the United States) builds from "elements" to notes, phrases, melodies, forms, and eventually "compositions." Instrumental training develops elemental musical "skills" progressively toward the goal of competent recital performances. These generative pedagogical ladders are built out of adults' structural decomposition of particular forms of textuality and music into component parts, placed in order of ascending complexity and mapped as natural onto children's imputed cognitive deficiencies at any particular age—all of this despite a vast body of literature that shows that even very young schoolchildren have communicative, writing, and musical competencies that have little or no relation to the componential objects of language, writing, and music they are asked to "learn" in lessons (Dyson 2003; K. Marsh 2008).

Children's expressive traditions

Despite evolutionist attempts to universalize and dehistoricize childhood, children and childhood fit into Foley's (imperfect) account of classes as the "historical speech traditions of status groups." Children have historical expressive traditions, characterized by specific, familiar master tropes. Children's internal relationships with one another are constructed through particular forms of social affinity—"friendship" and "peer culture"—that differentiate their communities from adults. And children's activities are framed in terms of "play" and "fun" as clearly distinct from adult "work." Participating actively in a dialectic of intimacy and instrumentality, children's expressive traditions are a key force in the construction and maintenance of childhood as a distinct social position and cultural identity.

In most places children have their own expressive traditions separate from adults (e.g., Blacking 1967; Gaunt 2006; Opie and Opie 1960; Sutton-Smith 1959). Iona and Peter Opie's study of children's playground games and songs is a classic example:

> The school rhyme circulates from child to child, usually outside the home, and beyond the influence of the family circle . . . The schoolchild's verses are not intended for adult ears. In fact part of their fun is the thought, usually correct, that adults know nothing about them. Grownups have outgrown the schoolchild's lore. If made aware of it they tend to deride it; and they actively seek to suppress its livelier manifestations. Certainly they do nothing to encourage it . . . [Children have] a thriving unselfconscious culture . . . which is as unnoticed by the sophisticated [*sic*] world, and quite as little affected by it . . . [Children] are respecters, even venerators, of custom; and in their self-contained community their basic lore and language seems scarcely to alter from generation to generation. (Opie and Opie 1960:1)

Literacy educators have taken seriously children's expressive cultures outside of the classroom, where, upon investigation, children are found to use writing and language in ways that are systematically, structurally, and persistently opposed to the instrumental and objectifying textual and expressive practices of the classroom (Dyson 2001, 2003; Grugeon 2005; J. Marsh 2004, 2006, 2007). Schoolchildren make constant use of writing to communicate with one another, but their passed notes and scrawlings on desks do not conform to essayist norms (Hubbard 1989; Everhart 1983). The form and content of children's sophisticated and artful language is situated in separate spheres from adults (Bauman 1977, 1982; Sanches and Kirshenblatt-Gimblett 1976). And children have folkloric and ideological traditions such as "cootie lore"—globally distributed but locally articulated practices through which children manage social difference and stigma in ways that "function much like race and caste" (Hirschfeld 2002:619). Just as Eckert (1989) sees high-school students delineating their social affiliations through geographical claims to school spaces, for children school is spatially realized in terms of a binary in which the playground is a central site of intimate expressivity and opposition to school's regulation and instrumentalization of sound, noise, and movement (Beresin 1993, 2004; Blatchford et al. 2002; Campbell 1998; Grugeon 2005; Harwood 1998; K. Marsh 2008; Opie 1994; Willett et al. 2013).

Moreover, children's expressive practices for the most part ignore school's separation of communication into distinct media, as they combine touch and gesture with writing, speech, and music. Their musical practices notably integrate rhythmic syncopations with language play, movement, and especially touch. Despite a constant effort by music educators to teach music in blocks of ascending structure, children's musical cultures are much richer, more varied, and complex. Patricia Shehan Campbell (1998) shows that children talk about music in complex and sophisticated ways. They have interesting and well-developed tastes, they can reflect on the relationship between their musical and social lives, and they incorporate music into a wide range of activities and interactions. Children's musical play in peer groups is formally very complicated (K. Marsh 1995), and their procedures for teaching one another new songs and games are much more integrated and holistic than educators' componential progressions (K. Marsh 2002, 2008). Further, the children's texts that the Opies collected across the United Kingdom were most likely sung, danced, and clapped (Opie 1994; Opie and Opie 1960, 1979, 1985), and such playground songs and games increasingly represent a global repertoire that circulates through migration and media, embedded in locally specific expressive traditions (Lill 2014b; K. Marsh 2008; Bishop 2013).[4] Just as children's musical play integrates dance, movement, song, speech gesture, clapping, and jumping, they also integrate lyrics, melodies, imagery, and themes from a wide range of media, incorporating these into their long-standing traditional practices (Grugeon 2001; K. Marsh 1999, 2001; Burn 2012; Willett 2013, 2014). New media forms of literacy and communication such as mobile texting that are strongly associated with children and young people also incorporate these dense layerings of communicative modes with intimate and interactive connections to friends (boyd 2014), suggesting important continuities with underground literacy practices like passing notes. Despite significant technological, commercial, and political changes, children's playground cultures today clearly reflect significant continuities over long periods of time, especially in their creativity, interactivity, and multimodal layering (J. Marsh 2014; J. Marsh and Bishop 2012).

If children's expressive traditions have a master trope it may be what Brian Sutton-Smith terms "phantasmagoria," the fantastic, violent, sexual, gory, painful, punning, cruel, and gross elements of children's culture: "riddle parodies, bathroom jokes, cruel jokes, gross jokes, elephant jokes, Dolly Parton jokes, Christa McAuliffe jokes, and stories that center on absurdity" (Sutton-Smith 1997:165; also Sutton-Smith and Abrams 1978)[5] and what Roderick McGillis (2003) calls "coprophilia" or the "culture of grossness." Sutton-Smith positions phantasmagoria in specifically literary terms, along an axis of access to rationality and irrationality that structures the politics of children and adults:

> If you add to young children's story disasters their repetitive episodic plots, their preferences for rhyme and alliteration, their nonsense, their obscenity, their crazy titles, morals, and characters, it is not surprising that most adults, even those who believe they are favorable to creative expression, tend to avoid them. Our Western belief in rationality is so important to us that tolerance for such clear bouts of apparent irrationality is limited, even though one could point out that in these cases the irrationality is only of a literary kind, not a behavioral one. (1997:161)

Phantasmagoria may not necessarily be particular to childhood, as we can see its characteristic grossness, absurdity, cruelty, and sexuality in certain adult expressive traditions (often in discourse that is keyed as masculine). Linking fantasy, sex, cruelty, defecation, and silliness as shared elements of a single discourse connects the various absurd or committedly irrational elements of children's culture to broader (adult) forms of transgression: grotesque, contaminated, carnal, and carnivalesque (Stallybrass and White 1986). The inversions, oppositions, and deconstructions of transgression take on a particular character in children's culture, which poses phantasmagoria as a master trope in the relation between childhood and adults:

> It seems that the history of the imagination in childhood is a history of ever greater suppression and rationalization of the irrational. Paradoxically children, who are supposed to be the players among us, are allowed much less freedom for irrational, wild, dark, or deep play in Western culture than are adults, who are thought not to play at all. Studies of child fantasy are largely about the control, domestication, and direction of childhood. So in a sense the rhetoric of the imaginary, with its emphasis on so many varied possible rational and irrational play transformations, is not much used for childhood. (Sutton-Smith 1997:151–52)

Mizuko Ito suggests that Sutton-Smith's analysis of adult repression of phantasmagoria makes better sense in Foucauldian (1978) terms: "we might consider adult efforts to manage children's play not only as a 'repressive' regime that works to silence these dark fantasies, but also as an 'incitement to discourse' that gives voice and form to 'unnatural' and regressive play in opposition to 'natural,' wholesome, and productive play" (Ito 2009:89). Thus children's phantasmagoria is not an inherent or unique characteristic of their expressive traditions. Rather it is partially a product of adults' ideological attempts to order childhood, such that literary tropes of phantasmagoria are projected onto Western epistemologies of irrationality and rationality, which are themselves mapped, as a parameter of intimacy and instrumentality, onto the hierarchical relationship between children and adults.

Childhood also claims particular forms of social relationships. Friendship, in particular, is constitutive of children's social identities in a way that is not true of adulthood. Friendship problematizes neoliberal models of individualization and governmentality by foregrounding the intimacy of relationships, and the production of instrumental subjectivities takes place in the intensity and intimacy of friendship relationships (Hey 2002; Foucault 1997 [1981]). Children construct racial, ethnic, and (especially) gendered identities in terms of the particular social logic of friendships (Allard 2002; Kehily et al. 2002; McLeod 2002; Redman et al. 2002), such that "questions of morality and identity are recast by young people in the register of the etiquette of friendship as questions of taste and trust that situate their core concerns" (Hey 2002:231).

Outside the particular intimacies of friendship, children's relationships with one another are commonly framed as "peer relationships"—a term that expresses horizontal affiliation and joint membership in a particular category (Ladd 1999). Though the term comes naturally when discussing childhood, in other (adult) contexts "peer" is a marked term, used in specific legal or ceremonial contexts to emphasize equality and reciprocity, but rarely in everyday discourse. The ubiquitous application of "peer" to children in relationships with one another reflects a discourse that positions and separates children as a marginal class, where by highlighting equality among children the term itself exposes the ubiquitous and default fact of inequality and hierarchy in relations between children and adults. Despite the term's ideological baggage, an empirical focus on "peer cultures" consistently reveals that children do produce and maintain independent social environments with their own consistent rules and expectations (Adler and Adler 1998; Chen, French, and Schneider 2006; Corsaro 1985; Corsaro and Eder 1990). Further, "peer cultural" environments in which children turn inward, away from adults and toward one another, are prominent locations for the "interpretive reproduction" of practices from dominant adult cultures (Corsaro 1992)—a model that reflects Willis's focus on adolescent peer relationships as the site of reproduction of class cultures. While friendship and peer relationships are often understood by adults as necessary and natural activities in children's development, it may make more sense to see these forms of affinity simply as outcomes of the persistent spatial and social separation of children from adults, and of enforced age gradations among children, in the institutions where children spend their days. That is, "peer culture" depends on the stratification of children and adults, and of different-aged children from each other, that is accomplished in schools. Segmented and bounded, children develop relationships that necessarily reflect and incorporate members' shared status as "peers" in a marginalized group. This marginal status is then taken up by children (in a familiar move of identity politics) as a site of tactical, local empowerment, as children actively intensify their separation from adults to claim increasing spaces of freedom.

Finally, childhood claims "play" and "fun" as characteristic practices (Sutton-Smith 1997), in obvious contrast to adult "work." Play and fun map onto phantasmagoria and irrationality, and play is seen to be a characteristic activity of "peer cultures." Play is what children do together. But play itself is often subdivided. Adults play, but play activities like sports are often so highly structured as to resemble work. Adults and educators often see children's play as simply the disguised work of development: children "play at" adult roles that they will one day inhabit. Educators distinguish between directed and undirected play and between play that results in development versus play that is simply irrational or "fun," and this subdivision of children's play maps further onto class categories, articulating rational play as bourgeois and irrational play as "poor" (Sutton-Smith 1982). Like phantasmagoria, play is not the unique province of children, but the association of play with childhood again maps an ideological binary (play/work) onto a division of society (children/adults).

Childhood intimacy

Children's expressive traditions are an intimate communication style, especially in their attention to context, sociability, and participation, and their grounding in physical and temporal presence. The language of passed notes is full of pronouns and other indexical references to proximate times and places (e.g., "Isn't this stupid?" "What are you doing at recess?" "Want to hold hands on the bus?"), involving a medium whose materiality is carefully attended to in tears and folds of paper, and whose actual transmission involves constant vigilance about the communication's participants (i.e., whether the teacher is looking on), not to mention physical dexterity (accurate but inconspicuous throws across a classroom). Scribbling a message on a desk anticipates a friend's future presence, unlike the essayist literacy that progressively trains writers to address no specific audience at all. Similarly music education focuses on the textual elements of music, emphasizing children's individual production of textual "compositions" or performance of discrete skills, but children's musical play is characteristically participatory—to the extent that their hand-clapping games prominently depend on the complex coordination of gesture and touch with complicated wordplay and syncopated rhythms. Children produce new musical texts and genres not through individual "composition" but through co-construction of new forms in group performances (K. Marsh 2008). Children's active appeal to phantasmagoria rejects the "rational" logics imposed on them by adults in favor of intentionally absurd and irrational expressivity that intimately links them as an interpretive community, further positioning their expressive practices in structural opposition to adult regimes of education and childcare. And friendship and peer culture situate children within a qualitatively particular structure of social relationships, in which "young people's investments in the practice of compulsory sociability is so strong that no amount of neoliberalism is ever likely to overwrite it" (Hey 2002:239).

When Poole points to students initiating orientations toward one another, we can see them as proposing an intimate framework to replace the dominant IRE framework, or layering intimate stances within instrumental classroom interactions. When, as Austin, Dwyer, and Freebody point out that students in a class perform themselves as a cohort, a group of children corporately respond to their teacher, on the one hand they accommodate the IRE participation framework that is oriented toward them as precompetent children, but at the same time they produce the conditions for orienting to one another as peers, friends, and intimates in spaces carved out away from adult oversight. And just as Eckert's burnouts orient not just to one another but to their wider community outside of school, Betsy Rymes (2003) points out that in student-initiated interactions in literacy events like those described by Poole children's indexicality often produces orientations toward much wider contexts in their community, in the media, and even in politicized categories of race and sexuality, all of which are explicitly rejected as inappropriate by teachers' decontextualized stance.

Thus children organize themselves into frequently oppositional sub cultures with their own expressive traditions that are separate from the expressive expectations of adults, against which they are often explicitly contrasted along an axis of intimacy and instrumentality. Childhood, in this sense, fits nicely within a rubric that understands class cultures as "the historical speech traditions of status groups" (Foley 1990:181) or as communities of practice constructed through everyday expressive acts that index and produce group affiliations (Eckert and McConnell-Ginet 1995).

In response to Foley's suggestion that the specifically intimate character of anti-instrumental expressive cultures has its roots in traditional communities, we might note that the domestic spaces of home and family and the semi-public sites of children's peer culture involve more contextual and indexical interactions than truly bureaucratic contexts such as workplaces and classrooms. What's more, while the construction of an intimate sphere in contrast to the public sphere has been examined for producing femininity as domestic and private (Fraser 1985), the concomitant construction of innocent, vulnerable, and economically unproductive children is certainly a necessary implication of that critique.

Childhood, when accounting for its social constitution, the powerful ideologies that make claims on it, its low status within bureaucratic hierarchies, and the historical expressive traditions of children around the world, should be understood as a social category produced in and through the expressive competitions of school. To understand childhood through comparison to the working-class, ethnic, or gendered identities that Willis, Foley, and Eckert study is hopefully not to denigrate those groups as juvenile or childish by implication. For my own purposes, I think we learn more about how bureaucracies, and specifically schools, structure and produce diverse forms of identity than about the similarities among such identities, and that is where the analogy of children to other groups ends for me. Rather than comparing and analogizing groups, we should begin to unpack how age articulates with race, class, gender, sexuality, disability, and various other terms in a constellation of signification about the status of individuals and groups, including as part of hierarchies of social value and worth, and perhaps especially in institutional and bureaucratic contexts. Just as Eckert and McConnell-Ginet point out that certain speech markers correlate simultaneously with class and gender, ultimately positioning working-class girls as especially marked, we can see, for instance, immigrant children multiply stigmatized by their language, ethnicity, *and* age when they are forced to interact with English-speaking bureaucracies on behalf of non-English speaking parents (Reynolds and Orellana 2009).

As James Collins (2009) points out, there are persistent difficulties in analyses that implicate schools as centrally responsible for the reproduction of social inequalities along lines of gender, class, and race. In particular, it is apparent that many other influences in addition to schooling participate in the reproduction of social difference. Collins suggests greater attention to the "interplay of classrooms, schools, and the wider society" (2009:44). This is welcome, but insufficient. The identities that schools are continually producing prominently include those of "child" and "adult." Approaches that seek to identify social stratifications in the adult world through reference to those adults' previous experience as schoolchildren have already subordinated children and childhood to an analytically secondary role, and thus value actual children's experiences only insofar as they produce adult subjectivities—reinscribing, once again, the same view of childhood as transient and children as the "future," rather than a significant segment of the actually existing population (J. Cole and Durham 2008a). Questions about social *re*production and schooling may not be answerable until we understand the initial "production" of children qua children in school, through the constant regulation of distinctions between children and adults and among gradations of age and "development." Thus, fully understanding a question like that posed by Willis of "how working class kids get working class jobs" (1981 [1977]) requires asking how working class kids became working class *kids* in the first place. I think it is clear that the expressive practices approach developed in the work of Willis, Foley, and Eckert has unmistakable analytical force in understanding the institutional organization of schools, but the difficulties of diachronic studies pointed out by Collins will remain so long as synchronic approaches to the social organization of schooling neglect children and childhood.

Coda: entertainment and education

So far I have outlined a largely one dimensional, top-down framework in which power and authority reside in the massive bureaucratic institutions of education and government. Those in social groups (including children) without access to that authority band together in communal defense of their uncommodified communication through repeated performances of intimate expressivity (in a nutshell). But governmental bureaucracies of schooling are not the only powerful, globalized, instrumental institutions in children's lives. The consumer and entertainment industries are certainly as much of a presence in kids' lives as education, and they are equally invested in constructing a suitable vision of childhood among kids and adults. So while Foley provides a near-complete analysis of binary divisions of expressive repertoires that structure the social life of schools at both micro and macro levels, he gives little attention to how entertainment media is incorporated into students' intimate expressive practices, as a resource for claiming intimate solidarity with one another, in opposition to the instrumental frameworks of classroom lessons. In fact, when Foley does address popular culture, he makes almost exactly the opposite point:

> Our everyday national popular culture is generally inculcating people with an instrumental style of speech. Americans "culturally reproduce" their individualistic, competitive,

> and materialistic society through using this alienating, manipulative communicative style. The class segments most deeply integrated into the popular culture practices of leisure and consumption are the most thoroughly socialized and consequently they become the most competent in impression management techniques. As indicated, cultural institutions like schools showcase and valorize these moments of instrumental communication. (1990:193–94)

Foley's use of "American popular culture" focuses on such activities as school sports and dances, and an orientation toward athletics and school-sponsored dances can certainly be seen to reproduce students' institutional orientations. But the idea that the management class is the most "deeply integrated into the popular culture practices of leisure and consumption" seems untenable on its face. That consumer practices are differentiated by class and economic status is a commonplace idea at least since Bourdieu's *Distinction* (1984), and is demonstrable using more recent evidence for the United States (Friedland et al. 2007; D. Holt 1998). It is difficult to know what Foley might mean when he suggests that there is a single set of "popular culture practices" in which only bourgeois individuals participate. But this sense of "popular culture" is certainly too narrow, and may not apply to such popular-cultural fields as music or television. It would be very difficult to argue that entertainment forms like dance music or reality television competitions "showcase and valorize . . . instrumental communication." Here Eckert's (1989) analysis is useful, as she demonstrates that the relevant factor positioning kids' popular cultural participation as a marker of class is the extent to which any cultural form (sports and school clubs as opposed to smoking or certain genres of music) is linked to or officially sponsored by the bureaucratic, instrumental institution of the school.

In fact, what we see in entertainment media is that a rapidly expanding children's media industry increasingly frames child audiences in terms of group solidarity and identity politics (Bickford 2012; Banet-Weiser 2007). While schools construct childhood particularly through authority and separation from adulthood, since the 1980s entertainment media has portrayed children's separation from mainstream adult culture not as marginality but as freedom. This "empowerment" of children as consumers depends on the same dialectics of childhood intimacy and instrumentality, so entertainment media construct childhood in essentially the same terms as schooling—by carefully negotiating concerns over risk and vulnerability, through age-grading of content, and through explicit moves to frame entertainment materials as "childish" (Bickford 2012, 2015, 2016). Ito writes that, "Far from being an unmediated voice of a natural childhood pleasure principle, phantasmagoria and spectacle are distributed, engineered social productions that unite children and media industries" (2005b:100). Phantasmagoria and spectacle unite children and media industries in solidarity with one another and in vague opposition to various adults: to parents and teachers who police purchasing and consumption, and even to adult media figures who criticize, mock, and dismiss kids' media—at least until those kids and their media become too powerful to ignore (Bickford 2012).

The children's media industry grew rapidly during the 1980s and 1990s (Pecora 1995; Montgomery 2007; Mitroff and Herr Stephenson 2007). The prominent success story during this period was Nickelodeon, a cable network introduced in 1979 to cater specifically to children. On cable Nickelodeon was relatively free from homogenizing market demands and government regulations that constrained network television programming for children (Banet-Weiser 2007:17; Pecora 1995). Without the legal compulsion to meet quotas of "educational" programming, Nickelodeon innovatively engaged its young audience with a mantra that said, "let kids be kids" (McDonough 2004). This appeal to the idea that there is something uniquely characteristic of "being a kid" represented the culmination of a history in which marketers of clothing and other consumer products for children only gradually transitioned from targeting parents—specifically mothers—as the audience for advertising, eventually appealing directly to children (Cook 2004). This "discovery" of kids as discerning viewers coincided with the rapid expansion of kids' purchasing power: children directly spend tens of billions of dollars annually, and influence as much as $200 billion in family spending.

Letting "kids be kids" involved adopting the characteristic phantasmagoria of children's expressive culture, such that brightly colored slime, a signature prop from early in the station's history, became iconic of the Nickelodeon brand. Beyond the obvious coprophilia of slime, Banet-Weiser argues that animated shows like *The Ren & Stimpy Show* and *Spongebob Squarepants* framed grossness and absurdity as campy and ironic to "harness a political ideology—gay identity politics, queer theory—and commodify it as an aesthetic practice" (2007:37), thus articulating childhood phantasmagoria as resistant and oppositional through links to parallel identity politics and an economy of irreverent "cool" (2007:180). Constructing children as separate—using specific tropological materials that clearly distinguished and opposed children's entertainment from the mainstream of adult entertainment—went hand in hand with an appeal to children's empowerment, so the accompanying slogan was "kids rule!" Nickelodeon programming also drew on feminist and multicultural discourses to frame children as a particular empowered and oppositional audience (Banet-Weiser 2004; Hains 2007;

Schor 2004:52–53). These elements constructed childhood as separate in part through an appeal to themes (irony, camp, cool, feminism, multiculturalism) from mainstream and adult culture that attracted an adult audience:

> The divisive strategy employed by Nickelodeon that establishes a discrete boundary between adults and children is one that functions brilliantly for the company in terms of profit . . . The exaggerated generational conflict that Nickelodeon cultivates and markets as a kind of fun rebellion actually results in a blurring of the two identity categories [by attracting adult viewers]. Thus Nickelodeon presents a "convergence of generations" where adults are addressed as children on television, and children are encouraged to act like adults. (Banet-Weiser 2004:5)

If Nickelodeon's audience and content at times blurred the lines between actual adults and children, this process did not ultimately destabilize the constitutive binary between adults and children. Cross-over shows, as it were, required a stable boundary to cross over: "according to the Nickelodeon logic, if adults are sometimes not stuffy, just as children are sometimes not innocent and naïve, it proves (or disproves) nothing about the 'essential nature' of adulthood or childhood: it proves only that adults and kids can play at being each other" (Hendershot 2004:184).

Ito points out that this opposition between child and adult has emerged as constitutive of the broader children's entertainment industries: "Media industries have found a new market in both kids and adults who are attracted to a certain depiction of childhood, one that is distinguished from and resistant to certain structures of adult society without being depicted as inferior. Symbolized by . . . triumphs over corrupt adult society, childhood play is represented as mobilizing the power of the margin" (Ito 2007:105). The tropology of this oppositional children's media culture specifically involves phantasmagoria—a historical marker of children's distinct expressive community:

> Entertainment industries participate in the production of institutionalized genres that are packaged and stereotyped into certain formulas that kids recognize and identify with as a liberatory and authentic kids' culture . . . These appear as gross bodily noises, explosions, hyperbole, and increasingly, established licensed characters. This "junk culture" is a particular vernacular that cross-cuts media and commodity types, making its way into snack foods, television, movies, school supplies, and interactive multimedia [as] a site of opposition between adults and kids. (Ito 2005b:101)

To conclude this chapter, I return briefly to the micro-analytic literature in educational linguistics. Linguistic anthropologist Betsy Rymes's writing repeatedly returns to a moment during a phonics lesson in which materials from an entertainment franchise intrude into a classroom lesson (2003, 2004, 2008). In Rymes's example, a six-year-old boy, upon sounding out the word "chancy" on a flashcard, exclaimed "ohp!" and looked quickly to his friend and classmate. Both smiled and said together, "It's a Pokémon!"—playfully mishearing the word on the flashcard as "Chansey," the name of a character from the trading cards and video games that continue to be popular among school-aged boys (see Tobin 2004). The boys shared a smile as they forgot the phonics lesson, but just as they began a new conversation about Pokémon, the teacher quickly reprimanded them, redirecting their attention to the phonics task with "you need to listen." A clear example emerges of the contrast and conflict between the decontextualized, essayist, instrumental stance and the contextual, social, and intimate stance: "As [the two boys] both recognize the word and its meaning through reference to the world of Pokémon, the teacher insists that they make meaning of this word though phonological content alone, and the interaction transforms into a duel over which forms of context should be used to decipher meaning" (2003:132).

Rymes initially analyzes the competing "contexts" as a moment of "contrasting zones of comfortable competence," pointing out that teachers are "comfortable" in an authoritative, directing role, with the pedagogical content fixed and discernible, while kids, she suggests, are more comfortable with the materials of popular culture and entertainment. Rymes suggests that teachers might do well to incorporate popular culture references into literacy lessons, arguing that students "will jump at the chance to use the cultural resources they have available to them creatively—to talk about them, make jokes about them, recombine them, and use them in active, critical, and insightful ways to connect with each other and to understand their connection with the world" (2004:333). But Rymes's initial analysis, by focusing on the popular cultural content as the site of the individual boys' "comfortable competence," neglects the intimacy of the boys' shared grin as they reoriented away from the lesson and toward one another. For teachers to fit Pokémons into the flashcards and writing prompts of literacy education would be simply to claim kids' entertainment not so much as "context," but as one more decontextualized field of componential knowledge.

Pokémon is not simply another neutral "context." Instead, Pokémon is powerful precisely because it is inappropriate, linked to a public world of children's entertainment that in schools is "not merely a different or alternative idiom," but one that is "regarded with hostility or with a sense of indecorousness" (Warner 2002:86). A phonics lesson is normatively instrumental: IRE, essayist, and decontextualized in its focus on the phonological content of letters on the page, which are themselves separated componentially as individual meaning-bearing units (cf. Tedlock 1983). The lesson uses the power and authority of school to flatten out the intimate and contextual relationships between participants—teachers and students who know one another and have familiar ways of interacting. By contrast the boys' shared smile about a Pokémon pun is characteristically intimate: fully contextualized and indexical, as their glance to one another breaks the participation framework of the lesson by reasserting a friendship connection that orients around shared knowledge of material derived from media contexts outside the classroom. So here we see entertainment media fitting neatly within the intimate expressive style, latent with all the potential of intimate expressivity for oppositionality, resistance, and the construction of class or group solidarity—contrasting with Foley's claim that "popular culture . . . inculcat[es] people with an instrumental style of speech" (1990:193). Rather, the opposite is emphatically the case: in sharing this punning, poetic interpretation of the sounds of the word on the flashcard, the boys in Rymes's example interpellate one another as members of a mediated childhood group that is constituted precisely by moves like this—and which is directly opposed to the instrumental objectifications of a "phonics lesson" that they would be placing themselves within were they to be the type of audience that read the word as "chancy."

The boys' turn to one another is the sort of act that is constitutive of their oppositional childhood subjectivities in a bureaucratic school context that seeks to interpellate them differently, and which is (legitimately) threatened by their solidarity. In a later piece Rymes reanalyzes this "Chansey" moment from the perspective of Goffmanian "participation frameworks," suggesting that such popular cultural references "can suddenly create a participation framework that includes relevant classroom peers and excludes the teacher" (Rymes 2008:4). This position resonates more with the political model of childhood in school that I have outlined in this chapter. But still it might understate the breadth and depth of the fields of power—the massive consumer industries devoted to childhood that cultivate precisely this sort of politicized intimacy among children—that are being called upon in these cute and momentary interactions.

My purpose in this book is to understand how the logic of childhood solidarity playing out in the entertainment media is brought to bear in the hierarchical constructions of childhood as a subordinate identity in school. Does the presentation of children as a powerful consumer group in media and commerce provide a resource by which kids can challenge adult authority in schools? How does a mass-mediated logic of subcultural participation inflect kids' everyday peer culture—and how do kids' peer cultural traditions inflect their membership in this mediated subculture? What role do entertainment media—important repositories of "expressive practices"—play in the expressive production of difference and social stratification in schools? I start to answer these questions in the next chapter by examining the ways kids use entertainment media to intimately connect with peers in school, by physically linking friends to friends with the tethering cable of their MP3 players' earbuds.

CHAPTER 2

Earbuds Are Good for Sharing

Headphones, and the portable music players to which they were attached, were intimately embedded in the social interactions of students at Heartsboro Central School. Students' broad ownership and use of portable music devices made them the most prominent media channels at HCS. Listening together to MP3 players, kids activated and delineated relationships and social hierarchies. They solidified certain types of social bonds by sharing headphones with one another, and with the same actions they enforced and regulated the often exclusive and hierarchical organization of children and adults in school. Within the complex logic of genre, celebrity, and consumerism that informed HCS kids' musical tastes and habits, what stood out during my fieldwork was the intimate embedding of earbuds as social anchors among the networks and hierarchies of these elementary- and middle-school children. Upsetting the instrumental and rationalizing logics of privatization and isolation that accrue to headphones and portable music, HCS children creatively reimagined their music devices to fit within the persistent and densely sociable cultures of childhood, as tangible technologies for interaction and intimacy that traced out bonds and tethered friends together in joint activity. I follow kids' earbud cables as they diagram networks of social affinity, finding that sharing earbuds was not simply a diagnostic of close friendships, it was a constitutive practice of sociality through which kids could contest and negotiate their relationships.

These portable music practices were incorporated into the existing ecology of school communication that divided classroom regulation and rationalization of language, talk, and noise from the chaotic, playful, and ideologically unstructured interactions of children's communication among peers during "free" time or surreptitiously during class. In the terms of the preceding chapter, headphones supported decidedly "intimate" communication frames that contrasted directly with instrumental school communication. Shared earbuds served functions similar to such canonical and ongoing practices as whispering, passing notes, or coordinating visits to the bathroom—channels of communication and interaction where kids cultivated intimate connections with one another in spaces intentionally closed to adults. Often listening served less to emphasize particular music than to forge connections in the background of group conversations or other activities. Shared earbuds were an open connection, a link, what Lori Custodero calls "being-with" (2005) or what Alfred Schutz calls "the experience of the 'We'" (1977 [1951]:115)—not unlike the passed notes I regularly witnessed, which as often as not simply represented back-channel cues, confirming connections within the flattened social space of the classroom: "What's up?" "Hey," "How're you?" "Isn't this stupid?" "What are you doing at recess?" "I need to talk to you later," etc. As new media scholar danah boyd notes, practices like passing notes or whispering and young people's mobile communication practices all support the goal of private communication outside adult surveillance—"hiding messages in plain sight" (2014:66). While boyd mostly focuses on mobile phone text messaging, sharing earbuds at HCS activated the same private, intimate, and playful frames as whispered or passed communication. Tucked snugly in clothes and ears, and tangling among complex links of affinity and status, MP3 players and earbuds were an important element of an interactive repertoire that privileged the materiality and intimacy of sociable communication (figure 2.1).

On the first day of school in 2007 I returned to HCS after several years' absence, this time not as the one-day-a-week music teacher but as a full-time researcher. I was new to childhood research, and I did not have very specific ideas about what sorts of practices I would find. I hoped that in the bustling spaces of this little elementary and middle school I would find some insights into how popular music and media found purchase and meaning in face-to-face social environments.

The morning started out uncomfortably. Before school began, kids had been excitedly reconnecting with friends in the gym, and I hovered awkwardly, trying to introduce myself to kids who seemed indifferent. Sitting in on classes that morning I felt like an intruder, making teachers' already difficult first hours even more difficult with my explained but not entirely understood presence. HCS had two morning recesses, an early recess for the elementary students (kindergarten to fourth grade), and a later one for middle school (fifth to eighth grades). During the middle-school recess boys would split into groups to explore the edge of the woods or play football or soccer. A few girls would join the sports, some would wander in

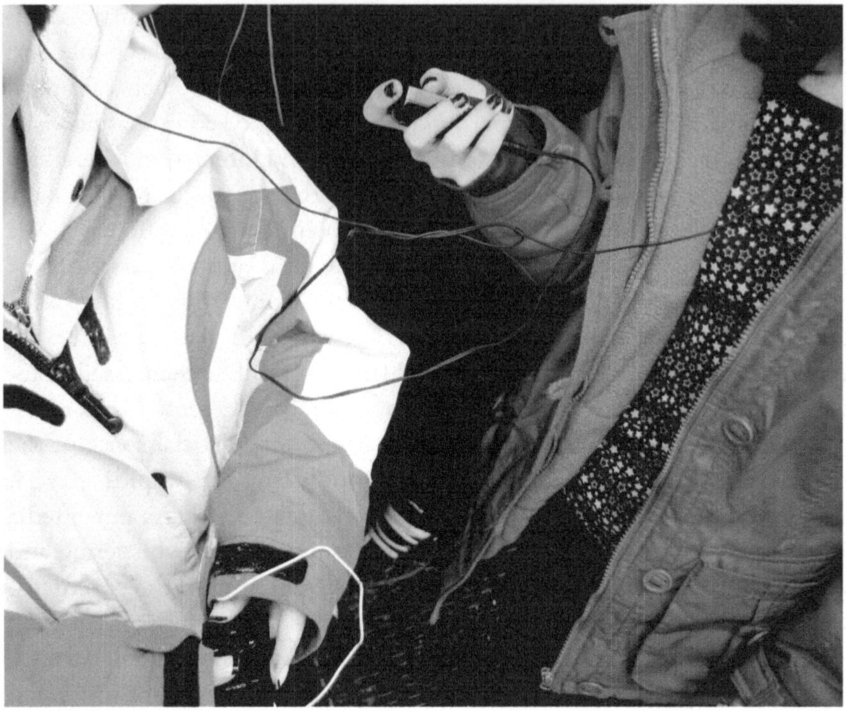

Figure 2.1: Sharing earbuds.

small groups, and many would sit and stand at the swing set behind the classrooms—repurposing the swings as a stationary gathering spot, in clear contrast to their active use for swinging during the elementary recess.

On this first day of school, eighth graders Amber and Daisy sat side by side on adjacent swings, and their classmates Alice and seventh grader Kathy stood in front of them, talking in a circle. Kathy and I remembered each other from years earlier when I taught her as a second grader, but the other girls were new since my time at HCS. From a distance I saw Amber handling an iPod in her lap, so I headed toward the swings to start my research in earnest and see how they were using the music device. I said "hi" to Kathy as I approached the group to introduce myself. She remembered me and blushed a bit as she recalled the drawing she had given me in second grade, a rough rendering of me labeled "the best music teacher ever." That drawing had meant a lot to me then, and Kathy blushed again when I told her I still had it. As Kathy welcomed me and introduced me to her friends, I noticed that Amber had one of her iPod's earbuds in her left ear, and the other earbud was resting in Daisy's ear, its cable stretched across the eighteen inches between the swings. They told me they were listening to a song by Evanescence called "Lithium."

I was impressed that they so easily shared the earbuds even as they swayed back and forth, and I asked if they would ever listen together and swing at the same time. (I did not realize yet that actually swinging on the swings was usually limited to the younger children.) They took my question as a challenge, and Daisy turned to Amber with a mischievous look as they started pumping their legs, almost hitting Kathy and Alice, who scrambled out of the way. As they swung higher and higher they laughed and cheered each other on, coordinating their leg pumps to stay connected by the precariously balanced iPod earbuds in their ears. They swung together like that until they couldn't go any higher, and the earbud only finally dropped out of Daisy's ear when they tried to slow down from the peak of their swing. When they came to a stop Daisy looked at me, pleased and defiant: "See?"

Histories of sonic fragmentation

Scholarship about portable music devices, from the Sony Walkman to Apple's iPod, but also boomboxes, transistor radios, and car stereos, often focuses on the relationships between "public" and "private" that are blurred or destabilized by the mobility and boundary-crossing afforded by these devices. In *Doing Cultural Studies*, Paul du Gay and his coauthors remark, "while there has been a steady move away from mainly public to predominantly private modes of viewing and listening, the Walkman marks an important inversion of this process by taking private listening into the public domain" (1997:114). Alexander Weheliye, in a discussion of the boundaries of public and private that are crossed by noise and music, writes that "the Walkman encountered massive hostility because it supposedly enabled users to 'cut themselves off' from their immediate environment . . . While earlier itinerant technologies, boomboxes for instance, were scrutinized because they subjected 'innocent bystanders' to high decibels of 'noise,' the 'silent' Walkman was ironically taken to task for its 'antisociality'" (2005:135). In a popular audience discussion of the appropriateness of electronics as gifts for young children in 2008, during the rapid rise of widely available MP3 players, psychologist Kathy Hirsh Pasek reflected the same anxiety about MP3 players as greeted the Walkman a generation earlier, telling the *Philadelphia Inquirer*, "Music is great, and it builds listening skills . . . But if a five-year-old is walking around with [earphones] all the time, you're tuning out. You're missing out" (Quinn 2008). Michael Bull (2008) offers a wealth of interview and survey data that support Hirsch-Pasek's anxious identification of an intense antisociality that characterizes iPod users. He writes that "iPods are by their very nature primarily a privatizing technology," which "giv[e] greater prominence to media generated forms of privacy whilst distancing users from the 'proximity' of others" (2008:7). In Bull's framework, the iPod is the "first cultural icon of the twenty-first century" (2008:1), which builds on the cultural movement of private listening practices into public spaces identified by du Gay et al. and represents an extreme "individualization" of culture, an increasing experience of "mediated isolation."[1]

Ironically, du Gay et al. point out that the Sony Walkman was originally designed with two headphone jacks, because "it would be considered rude or discourteous for one person to listen to music alone" (1997:58)—which, as Weheliye notes, it certainly was. After consumer research showed that Walkman users were not using the second jack and instead were listening in more personal, private ways, the follow-up version was introduced with just one jack, which became the standard.

Rather than desiring even more personal, private modes of listening, as Sony identified among early Walkman users, HCS students' preference for sharing earbuds suggested a rejection of the central logic represented by what Jonathan Sterne (2003) calls "headset culture." Sterne identifies headsets, which preceded loudspeakers as the listening devices packaged with early phonographs and radios, as central in the development and diffusion of "audile technique," a process of idealizing hearing and privatizing space that led to the "commodification and collectivization of individuated listening" (2003:155). While such collective listening refers most obviously to the mass audiences of broadcast radio, Sterne identifies several early practices where individuals in immediate proximity to one another would listen "alone together" such as sharing the ear tubes of early parlor phonographs, families' collective listening to one radio on several headsets, and classes for telegraph operators in which students would each wear headphones as they worked on the same lesson.[2] Sterne notes that even once families transitioned from headsets to loudspeakers, the techniques of individual, private, immersive, and detail-oriented listening would remain: "their shared auditory experience is based on a prior segmentation of sound space into auditory private property" (2003:165). Bull's account of iPod culture, then, suggests a linear continuation of the history of audile technique outlined by Sterne. Bull identifies the intensely individual, immersive, and private mobile music practices of iPod culture as "hyper post-Fordism" (2008:29)—an extreme manifestation of postmodern fragmentation and mobility, which extends the "inversion" of privatized listening mentioned by du Gay et al., which itself brought Sterne's privatized sonic spaces into public.

Kids' listening practices at HCS call into question the universality of a progressive narrative of fragmentation and privatization that sees loudspeakers reduced to headsets and multiple headphone jacks pared down to one per device in parallel with the erosion of face-to-face intimacy. HCS students' headset practices made use of the portability and intimacy afforded by headphones, but they cracked open headphones' "hermetically sealed soundscape" (Bull 2008:29) to include one another in their listening. Their technosocial configuration involved listening to music with one ear, while being open to talk or interaction with the co-listener and others with the other ear. Listening was *layered* within talk, touch, gesture, and other interaction. Rather than collective listening being a way to rationalize and control noise, as Sterne describes, shared portable listening represented *one more channel* of sound in an already densely noisy and chaotic social order. Kids at HCS rarely listened with both ears and were therefore constantly attuned to the potential for interaction with those around them. It would not make sense to say that they could be "interrupted," as Bull documents in London adults' "interpersonal strategies" with iPods (2008:54). Instead, they continually passed earbuds among their friends and freely talked over the music they listened to—a "while-doing-something-else" ethos of media use (Fujimoto 2005). While some MP3 players in 2007 came with two jacks, like the original Walkman (and students at HCS even owned a couple of these multijack devices), I never witnessed any HCS students using two headsets at once. Because it would cover up both ears, listening this way would have precluded talk and interaction among the pair of listeners and their proximate friends. With one ear free, kids' soundscapes were certainly not sealed, and being plugged in together was necessarily a different experience from listening in isolation.

Still, in some respects the privacy of headphones outlined by Bull and others was important to HCS students' listening. It was not that kids exploded the privatized sound spaces of headphones to broadcast their music to everyone. Rather, they cracked open the intimate listening environment of their earbuds to share with just one other person. Such inclusion, therefore, depended on some of the same logics of exclusion and isolation described by these theorists of portable music. At HCS earbud cables traced out intimate, close connections between pairs of individuals in groups as a constitutive ingredient of the "friend" relationship, linking them in intersubjective, but exclusive, experience (Porcello 1998; Schutz 1977 [1951]).

Sharing earbuds appears to be a common practice among child and youth listeners in the United States. It is rarely addressed explicitly, but when it does come up it tends to be framed negatively or anxiously. Most often it elicits hygienic concerns that sharing earbuds may also entail sharing fluids, dirt, or germs. At HCS I never witnessed any discourses of cleanliness or attention to hygiene by kids engaged in sharing or by concerned adults, but issues of hygiene seem to represent the great preponderance of online mentions of earbud sharing. The apparent irrelevance of these matters to my informants leaves me with little to say about them, but I note as a suggestion that concerns about dirt, filth, hygiene, disease, invasion, penetration, etc.—especially when directed toward children and youth—are prominent tropes in discourses of transgression, abjection, and "matter out of place" (Stallybrass and White 1986; Kristeva 1982; Douglas 2005 [1966]) through which moral panics are classically produced (Cohen 1987 [1972]). In other contexts, such as food, kids' cultures have been shown to be strongly invested in inverting such adult investments in hygiene, cleanliness, and bodily integrity (James 1982). Here the appeal to hygiene seems to deploy such tropes as part of a generalized stance of disapproval and concern toward kids' peer practices.

Very occasionally sharing earbuds is mentioned in passing in scholarly literature on portable media (e.g., O'Hara, Slayden, and Vorbau 2007:862; Tanaka, Valadon, and Berger 2007:35), but its social implications have been largely ignored, and sharing seems to be understood as a haphazard, ad hoc, or deficient listening practice. A rare exception comes from the late Apple CEO Steve Jobs, who suggested in a 2006 *Newsweek* interview that sharing iPod earbuds was a much more practical, immediate, and *easy* method for sharing music that than the wireless file-transfer function of the Zune, Microsoft's competitor device. Jobs tells his interviewer, "I've seen the demonstrations on the Internet about how you can find another person using a Zune and give them a song they can play three times. It takes forever. By the time you've gone through all that, the girl's got up and left! You're much better off to take one of your earbuds out and put it in her ear. Then you're connected with about two feet of headphone cable" (Levy 2006). By contrast, Hewlett-Packard researchers O'Hara, Slayden, and Vorbau characterize sharing earbuds as a challenge: "Sharing the audio on some devices was also difficult. For example, with the iPod there is no internal loudspeaker available, so people would use one headphone earbud each or cup the earbuds in their hands to try and amplify it or simply not bother with the sound at all" (2007:862). Jobs's view that passing over an earbud is much simpler than establishing a wireless connection between devices certainly corresponds closely with the actual listening practices I observed among kids at HCS. The scenario he describes, of a male teenager trying to impress a girl, emphasizes the familiarity and physical closeness of adolescent courtship, a youthful and intimate social field (and thus not unlike the friendships of younger children) in which anxieties about hygiene or degraded listening would not be especially relevant to participants.

"Digital natives" and Internet sociality

By contrast to discourses of headset isolation, MP3 players in their capacity as "new media" are embedded in a technological and cultural field that scholars increasingly understand in terms of public sociality and participation. Digital music devices are regularly positioned as symbols of a generational gulf separating adults from youthful "digital natives" (Thornham and McFarlane 2010). John Palfrey and Urs Gasser claim the iPod and its iconic earbuds as markers of an entire generation when they characterize the subjects of their book *Born Digital* as "those who wear the earbuds of an iPod on the subway to their first job, not those of us who still remember how to operate a Sony Walkman" (2008:4). Kathryn Montgomery similarly lists "a host of wireless devices and digital products—from video games to cell phones to iPods" before stating that "never before has a generation been so defined in the public mind by its relationship to technology" (2007:2). Unfortunately, despite their early invocations of the iconic iPod, these studies and others—such as the large collaborative study of "digital youth" led by Mizuko Ito (Ito et al. 2010)—do not follow up their introductory remarks with any direct analysis of young people's uses of portable music devices specifically (though Montgomery at least gives some space to the politics of music downloading and RIAA lawsuits), preferring instead to examine how young people use the connective affordances (Hutchby 2001) of the Internet and wireless communications devices.[3]

Instead, discourses about children and new media generally focus on wireless communication and the Internet and frequently look at mobile phones in particular, identifying text messaging and newer social media platforms as prominent features of digital youth cultures. As I point out in the introduction, HCS students were interested in and desired cell phones but were limited by their age, the expense of the devices, and the geographical isolation of their community. Instead, MP3 players were far and away the most widely used media devices at school. While new media studies of youth largely ignore them, kids used MP3 players in ways that reflected consistent findings about social interactions in other digital media, though not necessarily in ways we might expect.

Discussions of MP3 players as new media foreground connections to the Internet and users' practices of sorting, selecting, and sharing songs in playlists, emphasizing the intertextual, rather than interpersonal, affordances of portable music devices (B. Brown and Sellen 2006). Users of portable music devices can share playlists online, download cheap and pirated music easily, and transport large amounts of music with them. Bull sees iPods linking listeners to commercial networks of musical circulation and distribution as a "'tethering' technology" (2008:50)—cables tether listeners to devices and through them to the culture industries. While their connection to the Internet suggests a strong orientation toward "networked publics" (Ito 2008b; boyd 2014), as noted above their actual uses for music listening away from the computer are seen by many to be powerfully antisocial. Notably du Guy et al. and Bull alike also focus on the ability of users to customize song lists through cassette tape mixes or iPod playlists, so it might not be appropriate to view file- and playlist-sharing practices as particularly "new," or uniquely characteristic of digital music devices.

HCS students only occasionally downloaded songs from services such as iTunes or from questionably legal peer-to-peer networks using software like Limewire. In most cases their music was purchased on CDs at discount stores like Walmart. They did share music with one another, but this usually meant an older sibling creating a CD compilation or transferring songs to a younger sibling's MP3 player, simply swapping music devices with one another when a friend would like to hear a certain song, or recording music by setting an earbud from one device against the microphone of another.[4] Though a few students owned expensive (and prestigious) iPods or Zunes, most had much cheaper devices by Samsung, Sony, Ilo (a Walmart brand), and Craig (sold in convenience stores and pharmacies), among others. Ironically some of these cheaper devices were more likely to have extras like the built-in microphones that kids found useful. While their music devices could hold many songs (even relatively inexpensive devices had 512 megabytes of storage, which would store a hundred or more songs), with only a few exceptions kids' devices had songs numbering in the dozens rather than the hundreds. With so few songs, these children did not construct playlists for themselves or for friends; they scrolled through their players' song lists to find one song after another in lists full of misspelled and incomplete metadata.

The scale of these portable music practices was far from the vast "Web 2.0" repositories of instantly accessible tagged and linked songs that commentators emphasize as characterizing music in a digital era. Rather, with the small number of songs, the relative portability, the importance of physical stores, and face-to-face sharing, HCS kids used MP3 players on a much smaller scale, more like they might use portable CD or cassette players. MP3 players were preferable to older technologies for immediate and practical reasons: they were smaller than CD players and, for the most part, hardier. They fit in pockets and would not skip when jarred—necessary traits for objects constantly handled, squeezed, tugged, and tangled in children's active and sociable school lives. Kids largely ignored the particular social and connective affordances of MP3 players' links to stationary computer terminals and the Internet in favor of the social and connective affordances of earbuds' links between physically proximate friends.

So while the Internet played a role in how students at HCS consumed music, the more important market development, in terms of the social practices of music listening at HCS, would be the increased prevalence of earbuds rather than headsets that began to be widely packaged with personal music devices in the 1990s. Without a headband holding the two speakers together, earbuds moved freely from one person's ear to another's. Just as white earbuds visually marked the iPod in advertising, by 2007 earbuds (white, black, many colors of neon) had become iconic of youth in southern Vermont—a hooded sweatshirt and an earbud in one ear marked an adolescent stance in a way that a letterman jacket and cigarette might have in an earlier generation.

It is ironic that for the most part the social uses of MP3 players are acknowledged in contexts where physically separate individuals link to one another over the Internet at stationary computer terminals, but the interactive uses of MP3 players among physically proximate people are largely neglected, or even denied.[5] Despite the general separation from the Internet of HCS kids' uses of MP3 players, their uses did resemble important forms of mediated connectivity between real-world intimates. Thus Ito's description of the mobile Internet as "a snug and intimate technosocial tethering, a personal device supporting communications that are a constant, lightweight, and mundane presence in everyday life" (2005a:1) would apply nicely to the social embeddedness of MP3 players in HCS students' peer culture—with the caveat that the connections drawn by MP3 players were not wireless and distant, but wired and face-to-face. Studies of youth, new media, and wireless communication contemporary with my research consistently found that young people used digital technologies to connect with family and friends that they knew from face-to-face settings (Ito et al. 2010; boyd 2014; Hijazi-Omari and Ribak 2008; Lenhart et al. 2007; Palfrey et al. 2008). At HCS it was not kids' Internet practices, but the embeddedness of their listening practices within a broader ecology of expression and communication, that made their use of portable media devices notably sociable and interactive. Rather than text messaging on cell phones, the most prominent form of mediated connection involved the cables of headphones. Earbud cables traced out bonds between friends while excluding others, and they tethered individuals together in joint activity. At HCS the short cables between earbuds encouraged and even enforced physical proximity and engagement.

Finally, to say that kids put music devices to sociable use is not necessarily to celebrate that they have somehow escaped from problematic configurations of contemporary life. Kids' social organization and media consumption are certainly engaged in regimes of power, which I outline below. But it is necessary to recognize the diversity of practices that characterize the contemporary media landscape and to note that the powerful forces structuring media and the senses are not monolithic or universal. Even within the North American consumer environment the portable music player market is diversifying to account for children's unique approaches to consumption. Off-brand devices have become increasingly affordable and available, and marketers increasingly target kids with celebrity-branded MP3 players, devices like Hasbro's iDog series of portable toy speakers, and MP3 players with multiple headphones jacks (which may have missed the point, as I point out above, but which at least tried to target the shared sociality of kids' social listening practices). In general, children are seen by product marketers as an increasingly profitable and growing demographic of music consumers, and the market may have shifted to accommodate and cultivate modes of music consumption valued by schoolkids, perhaps also disrupting some of the master narratives of privatization and isolation that are bound up with urban adult iPod culture and audile technique.

Social connection

At HCS, earbud-sharing practices varied along parameters of age and gender. Kids began to have their own devices around third grade, as their interest in popular music developed and families allocated more resources to maturing children. All students were willing to share earbuds in certain contexts, and while sharing was most prominent among girls it was also common among boys, many of whom were avid music listeners. On balance boys' attention was occupied a bit more by portable video game devices, which girls also owned and used, so in some settings where girls would invariably be found listening together, boys might instead huddle around a Nintendo DS.[6] Only the older boys in seventh and eighth grade seemed to ever be reluctant to share earbuds. The emotional and affective charge of physical intimacy articulated by shared listening could be uncomfortably construed as feminine or childish, and did not comport with the adolescent, heteronormative masculinities they cultivated (Pascoe 2007; Redman et al. 2002). But even thirteen-year-old boys were not above the occasional intimacies, and I sometimes found them listening with an especially close friend or with a girl classmate—using earbuds to cut across charged gender boundaries in search of a comfortable way of sharing space with a girl.

In some instances, joint listening meant providing access to MP3 players to those who otherwise lacked them, as in the example of Amber and Daisy on the swings at the beginning of this chapter, in which Amber shared music with her friend Daisy who did not have her own device. But the motivation of social connection seemed even more powerful, when such sharing practices continued, and even increased, after the Christmas of 2007 when a majority of kids in third grade and up owned a portable music device of some sort. I was surprised to find that the headphone-sharing practices I observed in the fall continued despite this new saturation of MP3 players. Kids would listen together to a single device, leaving players dormant in pockets, rather than each listening on their own, to their own music on their own device.

This impulse for interaction and connection seemed to trump even mutual interest in music as the motivation for shared listening. Many of the kids' musical tastes overlapped with their friends, but preferences for marked genres like country or metal correlated more with family affiliations than peer groups, and friends frankly acknowledged their musical differences. I noted a couple of instances where a discussion about common taste in music led girls who did not consider each other friends to share a pair of earbuds, but even more often I observed friends with different tastes listening together even though one of them didn't care for the music being played. For the most part, however, kids knew enough about their friends' tastes to silently switch the song to a consensus track when handing over the second earbud. The music playing was generally in the background of kids' attention, which they focused on one another. Further, I never saw listeners coordinating their movements musically, by dancing or timing their steps to the beat of the music, and they rarely sang along to the music while sharing earbuds. That is not to say that children never listen carefully to music. They certainly do, as Jennifer Woodruff (2009) demonstrates with a range of compelling examples of girls attending closely to the details of recorded music in order to coordinate their movements and dance synchronously. Rather, my point is that the particular practice of sharing earbuds with a friend foregrounded social contingencies more than musical ones.

Listening together was so important that at times it eroded individual boundaries of ownership and property, as kids without earbuds tinkered with or even dismantled their headsets to share with one another. Fourth grader Dave's hand-me-down MP3 player had battered old adjustable headphones that had lost the foam cushions over the speakers, which made them particularly uncomfortable to listen to with frozen ears outside at recess in the winter—no matter to these Vermont kids. His best friend Brian did not have a portable music device, but he talked constantly about his interest in "rap" music. Normally these two would pass Dave's MP3 player from one to the other. When Dave was not listening, he would let Brian listen if he wanted. Sometimes on their way out to recess, if Brian noticed Dave was not bringing his player, he would ask if he could listen to it, and Dave would usually agree. But passing the device back and forth was limiting, so one morning as they sat down together with their breakfast trays, Brian took Dave's headphones without asking, pulled the headband to its maximum size, and wiggled one of the speakers until it snapped permanently off. Dave nodded approvingly. Brian passed the headband with its remaining speaker to Dave, who put it over his head. Brian held the newly detached speaker to his own ear, and the two boys listened to Snoop Dogg as they ate their English muffins.

In a social environment in which Brian could feel impunity to destructively dismantle his close friend's device without asking permission, it is important to reconsider what we mean by "sharing." Ownership itself was an unstable, contested, and often disregarded notion at school, and sharing often exceeded the simple act of allowing another to use one's "own" property. So deeply ingrained in the construction of friendship bonds, kids' ethos of listening together problematized the very logics of property and privacy that words like "sharing" presume.

Among friends

Dyadic sharing between best friends was not exclusive. Eighth graders Amber and Alice's extremely close friendship was built upon shared media use: watching Disney Channel shows, social networking on Bebo and YouTube, emailing and instant messaging family, friends, and (they said) celebrities, and listening together to music. Even very close friends like Amber and Alice had other friends, and earbud cables traced out these weaker bonds as well. At the beginning of the year Amber and Alice were the core of a group that also included Kathy and Daisy. These four hung out together during lunch and free time—for instance, sitting on the swings at recess, as I first encountered them. This group fractured over time, but Amber and Alice remained a stable pair.

Amber and Alice spent as much time as possible after school and on weekends at each other's houses. Kathy was a bit of a third wheel to their pair. She joined them for sleepovers and was a full member of the group, but it was clear that Amber and Alice were committed to each other in a way that did not fully include her. Daisy was a bit of a misfit. She got in trouble with her teachers constantly, and she did not spend much of her time outside of school with her school friends, preferring to meet friends from neighboring towns. This group was constituted partly out of necessity; the other group of seventh- and eighth-grade girls were exclusive and "cool," unwelcoming to outsiders other than two boys they would let sit with them at lunch. The only obvious delimiter of the high-status girls (who Amber and Alice termed the "girl posse") was that they had all spent their entire school careers at HCS, while Amber, Alice, and Daisy had enrolled in the last couple of years. Kathy was the exception to this rule, but she had spent the previous year in conflict with seventh grader Betty, one of the "girl posse," and clearly felt unwelcome in Betty's company.

Amber and Alice's friendship centered on the Disney Channel. It would not be an exaggeration to say that they talked about very little besides Hannah Montana, the Jonas Brothers, and especially Dylan and Cole Sprouse, the stars of the hit Disney Channel show, *The Suite Life of Zack and Cody* (see Blue 2013; Bickford 2012, 2015). Kathy joined wholeheartedly in this Disney obsession, but Daisy had no interest in it, and she was self-confident enough not to feel a need to feign interest in Disney Channel brands to be accepted by Amber and Alice. The high-status girls, on the other hand, professed to hate the Disney Channel products, and would have nothing to do with them.

In the spring Kathy and Betty had a rapprochement of sorts, and Kathy began to float between groups. At the same time, she began to publicly forswear the Jonas Brothers, who had become a marker of affinity with Amber and Alice. Daisy also detached somewhat from Amber and Alice as the year progressed, and she spent more time one-on-one with some of the high-status girls. But rather than floating from one group to another, she became an entity unto herself. She lived down the road from Melissa, a sixth grader with similar taste in music and fashion—they both liked dark clothes and shared a style approaching goth—and over the year she and Melissa developed a mutual respect and friendship.

Until Christmas Amber's iPod was this group's only MP3 player, and she shared it freely. But the connections traced out by the headphone cables did not always represent equivalent social bonds. Alice was so close with Amber that sharing was simply assumed, and they had enough trust that Alice never minded if Amber shared with someone else. Kathy would often reach out and grab the earbuds when Amber took out her iPod. One day in March, for instance, Amber took out her iPod at lunch when she could not remember the name of a band—she wanted to complain that her cousin did not like them. She unwound the cable to expose the screen, and Kathy, sitting next to her, immediately reached out and took an earbud, even though Amber had not put on any music and did not seem to intend to play any. Amber left her iPod on the table as she bused her lunch tray, and Kathy picked it up and started a song. When Amber returned, she took the other earbud and listened along with Kathy, while Alice took out her own MP3 player (Amber's back-up Samsung), and listened with one ear. Kathy had her own MP3 player—she had also received one for Christmas—so reaching for Amber's iPod rather than taking out her own suggested a desire to listen jointly and to confirm a less strongly grounded friendship. It may have also suggested the value that accrued to the iPod in particular as a consumer icon. Alice was not at all put out that her best friend would listen with Kathy.

Unlike Kathy, who would reach for the iPod, Daisy, for the most part, would wait for Amber to offer. Daisy never owned an MP3 player, and never expressed a desire for one. She lived alone with her dad, and they had no such luxuries. But sharing with Daisy was not charity. Daisy was tough, independent, and often touchy, and the other girls' lives were comfortable compared to hers. When Amber and Daisy listened together on the swings in September, they listened to Evanescence, one of Daisy's favorites, and not, say, Hannah Montana or Ashley Tisdale (another Disney act), which Amber might have listened to with Alice or Kathy in those months. Listening together with Daisy was a way of reinforcing a somewhat tenuous bond, such that Amber and Daisy were authenticating one another in their sometimes awkward friendship. Conversely, Kathy's listening almost always suggested her effort to strengthen a bond with Amber, and even to crowd in on Alice's best friend status, rather than an expression of mutual respect or encouragement.

Amber and Alice's group could be seen as part of an even larger group that included the sixth-grade girls, who also had very little contact with the high-status girls. At lunch the high-status kids sat at the end of one table, sometimes with two boys they tolerated, and often with an adult that they tolerated. Amber, Alice, Kathy, and Daisy would sit with the sixth-grade girls at another table. They would talk and participate in gross-food contests or other group activities with the sixth graders, but they would share earbuds mostly with one another. At breakfast in October, Alice, Daisy, and Kathy sat with Melissa and Megan, sixth graders and friends (Megan is Alice's sister), catching up on homework for the coming day of classes. None of these girls had MP3 players, so they talked as they worked. Ten minutes before class Amber and Becky, another sixth grader, arrived carrying their MP3 players. Becky handed an earbud to Megan, sitting on the bench. Amber sat down next to Daisy, both straddling the bench at the lunch table and facing each other. She passed Daisy an earbud, and they listened together and talked.

From across the table Melissa quietly asked, "What kind of MP3 player is that?" But Amber and Daisy didn't hear her question—their earbuds were in the ears facing the table, and they couldn't hear her. Melissa leaned over the table, closer, and said again, "Amber?" But Amber still didn't hear her. Melissa gave up, and leaned back and sat quietly. She was good friends with these two, and would have been welcomed into their conversation, but she was also two grades younger and did not seem comfortable raising her voice to get their attention, interrupting them. It was not intentional, but the earbuds had the effect of excluding Melissa from conversation.

Across gender boundaries

As mentioned earlier, older boys were frequently unwilling to share earbuds, though sometimes they found it appropriate to share with girls. Instances of cross-gender sharing that I witnessed tended to occur in groups, and rarely between "couples." Various forms of courtship were common among the fifth through eighth graders, but they tended not to be highly visible at school, which favored more homosocial groupings of friends and made cross-gender pairings awkward. Kids who were "dating" would often pass notes to one another, sit together on the bus home, and meet (or at least ostentatiously schedule meetings) outside of school. Insofar as earbuds outlined most other affinity relationships, it would be unsurprising if sharing earbuds coincided with holding hands or similar practices. Due to the details of my research protocol and agreements with adults in the community, I avoided active investigation of kids' dating, courtship, or sexuality, so I lack significant data on this topic.

Comfort with girls or boys was a marker of status, or "maturity" perhaps, so sharing earbuds across genders was most likely to occur among the high-status kids. Eighth graders Michelle, Sarah, and Erica and seventh graders Jenn and Betty were the "high-status" girls—the "cool" or "popular" kids, except that the school was too small and those words too disputed for them to be widely acknowledged in those terms. They had known each other all their lives, and they shared earbuds in ways similar to Amber and Alice's group. But they did not have a core dyad, best friends around whom the others orbited. Though the strength of their individual bonds shifted throughout the year (and despite a few moments of dramatic conflict), they were a strong and cohesive group. These girls were competitive and challenging with each other and with outsiders, so like almost everyone else at HCS I steered clear of this group, who would often erupt with "*Ewwww!*" and "Go away!" if I approached. Unlike the group around Amber and Alice, these girls had much more interaction with their male classmates. Two boys, eighth grader Jack and seventh grader Sam, would often join them at lunch or hang out with them after school. One episode suggests how earbuds circulated among this group—grabbed and passed and negotiated—and were layered among talk and occasionally even shared with boys, across a gender boundary that was otherwise rather stable. At lunch in October the high-status seventh and eighth graders sat with Jack and me. Jack and the girls had all known one another their whole lives, but his regular presence as a boy in their group created tension that was not necessarily undesirable. In this episode, negotiation over Erica's iPod became an opportunity for a verbal interaction between Sarah and Jack, who was otherwise silent and awkward, which then shifted into listening together to Michelle's device. This encounter was charged with flirtatious tension and competition that was partly mediated by shared listening and the circulation of earbuds.

Michelle and Sarah sat across from each other, listening to Michelle's MP3 player as they ate. Betty sat at the head of the table, listening to Erica's green iPod nano with matching green earbuds. Jack was quiet. Erica demanded her iPod back from Betty, who handed it over. Jack reached for the iPod, and Erica tried to stop him, but Sarah told her, "He's not going to do anything to it."

Jack took the device but he could not turn it on. Erica snatched it back from him, turned off the "hold" button, and handed it back with a sneer.

Sarah said, "I don't know how to turn it on either, but I will when I get one for Christmas!"

Jack browsed the songs, "I don't know any of the songs you guys have here."

Noting the exceptional size of Erica's music collection, Sarah said, "She's got like five hundred or something. Are you going to look at them all?"

"I'm just looking for 'Hell's Bells.'"

I asked, "What's that?"

"It's just a sweet song."

"Who's it by?"

"AC/DC."

Michelle jumped in, "Oh, I have AC/DC. Maybe I have it."

Sarah was holding Michelle's player and tried to browse for the song. She couldn't figure it out and made another comment about not knowing how to work them, "but I'm getting one for Christmas!"

Michelle took the device and fiddled a bit. She handed one earbud to Jack and the other to Sarah. "Is that it?"

"No."

Michelle tried another song. "That?"

"No."

Michelle played a couple more songs for Jack and Sarah, none of which Jack recognized as "Hell's Bells."

The MP3 player's role in this dynamic was to facilitate interactions between Jack and the girls when Jack was otherwise a quiet non-participant in the lunchtime conversation. Its presence gave Jack an opening to join the group action, which shifted to the sort of challenging, competitive dynamic that characterized the boy-girl talk among this group: Erica sneered at Jack's lack of knowledge about the "hold" button, Sarah tried to argue for his inclusion by pointing out her own ignorance, and Michelle's attempt to find the song Jack wanted shifted Erica's competitive frame to one of cooperation and accommodation. Cutting across the gender boundary here, the earbud cable created a context for connection, interaction, and competition.

Earbuds as portable speakers

Even when not directly sharing the earpieces, kids used their headphones in ways that drew out connections among them. Sometimes kids would turn the volume of their earbuds all the way up, until their music could be heard, fuzzy and distorted, from a few feet away. They would use them this way as miniature speakers, resting on a table or dangling over a shoulder. This setup selected a small number of people out of larger social contexts and grouped them as listeners, a variation on the way sharing earbuds connected two people within larger groups. In art class the teacher would often put on music for the class as a strategy for controlling the sound environment and encouraging students to work quietly and not make their own noise. The small class of nine students in eighth grade allowed for more flexibility, but the different friendship groups—one composed of the three boys and two with three girls each—could rarely agree on music to listen to as a class. In the face of such standoffs, sometimes one of the girls would take out her MP3 player and set it on her group's table with its earbuds, turning the volume up so that the earbuds acted as miniature speakers—just loud enough that her group could listen to the music they wanted, but without being such a distraction for the others that the teacher might find reason to object.[7] This practice was so common that kids would complain about earbuds that were not loud enough to be used this way.

Stratification and exclusion

As MP3 players and earbuds were charged with the intimacy and intensity of kids' friendships, they worked accordingly to exclude non-listeners, acting almost as physical barriers visibly showcasing social affiliations and highlighting separation. One fall day while the middle-school boys played soccer during recess (the oldest of them complaining that there were too many players crowding the field), Amber and Kathy walked right into the middle of the game, listening together to Amber's iPod. Intently oblivious to the action around them, they stopped, talking, listening, and completely ignoring the boys who loudly complained at the obstruction—the girls' private interaction dramatically intruding on the public activities of the schoolyard. Penelope Eckert notes that such "walking around"—a canonical practice of middle-school girls—"draws attention to those who do it, by contrasting with the fast movements of their peers, with play, with the larger groups engaged in games, and with the louder tone of children's talk" (1996:184). Conventionally such "walking around" conversations between girls involve gossip about boys. Eckert points out how the prominent display of such "private" conversations stands out as a central practice in the production of a pre-adolescent public sphere that is canonically located on the schoolyard and in semi-public spaces like shopping malls (1996:185). The visibility and physical intimacy of shared earbuds reinforced these established practices, linking private (but not solitary) listening to youthful gossip and heterosexual disaggregation as a constitutive activity of differentiation in the broader social life of school. Amber and Kathy's "accidental" wandering right into the middle of a soccer game—their shared earbuds and turned-in stances broadcasting their insensibility to the action around them—prominently performed the status and privilege claimed by older girls.

Using earbuds as speakers could serve an isolating function too. On a hike after school one day in the fall I tried to walk beside Michelle, an eighth-grade girl who did not seem to want to be there. Her mom and younger sister were on the hike, so she had to be too. Up and down the trail, a pair of seventh-grade boys chattered about spies and ninjas as they investigated pools of water, a group of younger girls struggled to make it up the steep hill, and a handful of parents chatted about work and their kids. Michelle walked by herself, and the earbuds to her MP3 player hung like grapes over her shoulder, blasting fuzzy Top 40 songs. At this point in the year I had not yet been able to get Michelle or any of her friends to share more than a sentence with me. Often they just shouted at me to go away, because early on I told them I would if they ever asked. I caught up to Michelle and tried to make small talk, figuring that without her circle of girlfriends she might be more open. She muttered one-syllable responses to my questions. I heard a song by Lilly Allen playing through her earbud-speakers and expressed excitement because I knew it. But Michelle claimed not to know who Lilly Allen was, and her gruff responses made it very clear that she did not wish to continue the conversation. After a minute I left Michelle alone. The whisper of her music traveled through the quiet Vermont woods, and the rest of us knew to leave her be.

Another afternoon in the fall, classmates Holly (in third grade) and Mary (in fourth grade) waited for their parents to come pick them up after school, sitting side by side on a table in the gym, their backs leaning against the wall. They talked a bit, until Mary took out her MP3 player, put the headset on over both ears, and fiddled with the player to find a song. After a minute Holly asked her what she was listening to. Mary replied, too loudly because her ears were covered, "That 'to the left' song," and sang, "*To the left, to the left*" (referring to Beyoncé's "Irreplaceable"). Holly responded by singing the line back, "*To the left.*" Mary handed the headphones over to Holly, but took them back after a quick moment. Holly told Mary, as she put her headphones back on, "You should get earbuds, you know the ones you put in your ear instead of over your head." With this headset, only one person could listen at a time. Nodding dismissively, Mary explained, too loudly again, that she once had that kind, but they broke, and she got these from her CD player. Holly replied that the earbuds are usually cheaper. Mary said that her older brother was getting a new MP3 player for Christmas and when he did she'd get his earbuds. And with that she quieted, and listened alone; the two girls sat in silence. Mary never acknowledged that earbuds are good for sharing. And while she initially passed her headset over to Holly—she certainly did not snub her—her explanation authoritatively shut down Holly's attempt at interaction. Mary seemed happy to settle in to listening alone, rather than to share with a younger girl with whom she had at best an awkward relationship—especially because Mary was actively concerned with cultivating friendships with the fifth- and sixth-grade girls, so she did not have much time for her younger classmates.

The conspicuous visibility of earbuds as a marker of social connection made shared listening a potential site for negotiating status or lobbying for access to a friendship group. A particularly visible interaction among the four fifth-grade boys revealed the negotiations that sometimes occurred over who would share earbuds with whom. Johnny was not well adapted to the social rigors of middle school, though he tried really hard to fit in with the three other boys in his grade. They were fast friends with one another, and they tolerated Johnny. They were never mean to him but never really welcoming, either. Johnny had picked up on their interest in rap music early in the year, noticing that sometimes they would listen in pairs to the flashy red MP3 player of their most affluent member. Johnny had a portable CD player that he brought to school, usually with Eagles or Fleetwood Mac CDs borrowed from his dad. One morning as these boys were shooting baskets, Johnny took his CD player out of his bag and announced that he had a new Eminem CD. The other boys ignored him, like they usually did. But Johnny was persistent and, holding one of his earbuds out to Ted, walked into the crowded basketball key, saying, "Listen to this, Ted." Ted tolerated Johnny, but he was not about to be stuck sharing a set of earbuds with him, so he retreated. Johnny advanced, and Ted retreated, and then turned on his heels and ran to his other classmates. Johnny ran after, arm held out, saying, "Listen to my new CD!" Unable to catch Ted, he turned his attention to Freddy, who also demurred, but Johnny pressed on and this time chased Freddy across the gym. Johnny continued to chase his classmates across the crowded basketball court, cornering them against the wall until they would sneak under his outstretched arm and run away again, for several minutes, until it was time to go to class. The other boys gasped, half laughing, "Stop, Johnny, leave us alone!" But he pressed on. It became a game, but it was a game based on an underlying asymmetry: sharing earbuds is an intimate act, and however much they liked Eminem or tolerated Johnny, he definitely was not someone with whom they were willing to share such a connection, at least not in so public a place. And for Johnny, who spent a lot of time and effort trying to be more than just tolerated by his classmates, this was a plea for exactly the sort of intimate social linkage that they were committed to refusing him.

Examples like this were uncommon, and the potential for exclusivity of sharing earbuds rarely came to the surface. Moments of dispute were rare, because the conventions were tacit. Johnny understood how consumer media products worked within his classmates' social hierarchies, which is why he pushed so hard to convince them to share earbuds with him. But he may not have understood his own otherwise unstated status in the hierarchy, which was exposed by this "breach" of social rules (Garfinkel 1967). In general, kids knew their social status implicitly, so when they brought media to bear in efforts to change their status they tried to avoid drawing criticism or sanction.

On the other hand, some kids simply knew not to try to share. For instance, Dan was the only boy in the sixth grade. He got along okay with the fifth-grade boys but was not especially close with them. And he wanted to be friends with the seventh- and eighth-grade kids, but they were generally unwelcoming and often mean. Still, he always had someone to sit with at lunch—usually his fifth-grade classmates, though toward the end of the year he started sitting with the seventh and eighth graders who shared his interest in video games. One day in the fall I filled in at the last minute as a substitute teacher for the fifth- and sixth-grade class. As the kids returned from gym for math class, Becky and Kelly were sharing headphones, and they kept them on as they sat down—testing my limits. Seeing them, Dan quickly asked, "If they get to listen to music, can I go get my CD player?"

I suggested we might listen to music as a class while they worked on their assignments. We talked as a class about what we would listen to and eventually, after a lot of haggling, agreed on Miley Cyrus. Kelly said, "That's what we were listening to already."

Dan was the lone holdout, and refused any of the suggestions (whereas Melissa was not happy with the Disney Channel choices, but eventually agreed to the others' choice). So I let him listen to his CD player. He had over-ear headphones and wore them as he slouched over his desk, listening to heavy metal as the rest of us listened to Miley Cyrus. At one point Dan sang to himself, under his breath, and Kelly turned around to tell him to shut up. I encouraged her to focus on her own work.

Otherwise Dan did not often listen to music at school. He brought his CD player to and from school mostly to use in the car during the drive. Dan did not share earbuds in part because he did not have anyone to share with. Demographic chance had determined that Heartsboro would only have one boy his age, and unlike for the older boys, sharing with girls was not an option in sixth grade. So Dan was a special case, but his case also helps set the difference between older and younger boys into relief. Across the chasm of sixth grade, younger boys participated in technology sharing practices just as the girls did, while older boys did not.

So only a few boys listened alone, but none of the older boys listened with one another. Most simply did not listen to music devices at school, avoiding a practice that acquired gendered connotations among the older students. Of the seventh- and eighth-grade boys, several told me that they simply had no interest in listening to music. They would much rather play video games. Jack and Sam had music devices but rarely brought them out during school. Jimmy had a Zune that he would sometimes watch *Family Guy* episodes on in the mornings as he waited for his friends to arrive. On a few occasions Jimmy's friend Zack borrowed the Zune and watched TV shows on it during lunch—using both earbuds and shutting himself out of the other boys' conversation. Jimmy was widely known by a nickname, "Spaz," and was near the bottom of the social order of the seventh- and eight-grade guys. And Zack was perhaps even lower in the hierarchy. Unlike Dan, both boys were full members of the social groups they participated in, but within those groups their role was to bear the brunt of the constant joking, hazing, gay-baiting, insult-filled talk that characterized the boys' group interactions. Neither Jimmy nor Zack told me explicitly that they listened alone because they were tired of being hazed by their friends. But among all the students at HCS only the few boys who were also the subject of frequent hazing listened alone. This suggests that the ways kids used headphone cables usefully diagrammed both the strengths and weaknesses of their relationships with one another.

Inverting audile technique

In all of their shared listening practices, HCS kids subordinated adult values about sound and sociality to their own pragmatic interests in the social configuration of their listening. The MP3 format, for instance, represents an intentional balance between quality and portability, along with particular ideas about acoustical perception (Sterne 2012), but the values implicit in these trade-offs were largely irrelevant to HCS students. Listening with one ear to stereo MP3 recordings—mixed with different left and right channels—meant losing as much as half the signal, but students did not seem to mind or to notice. Using cheap consumer earbuds at volumes loud enough to be heard around a table meant creating a lot of distortion—inverting standard ideals of quality in headphones, where expensive sets cancel out noise and seal out external sounds so that the speakers do not compete with outside noise and cannot be heard by others.

Needless to say, it would not occur to most adults to use earbuds in this way. I was regularly surprised to observe and learn about these practices, which at times shocked my own sensibilities about music, technology, and fidelity. But that might be the point: such practices were simply outside the musical epistemologies normally associated with the Internet, new media, MP3 players, and adult music consumption. Even in cases where HCS kids were ignorant of or uninitiated into mainstream values around fidelity or stereo, it would be wrong to identify deficiencies when their practices so clearly responded to an identifiable system of values and embodied techniques of listening. For kids at HCS to use earbuds as an interpersonal technology for interaction, rather than as a medium for listening to music abstracted by layers of entextualization, recording, and commodification, depended on a particular conception of the intimate social and physical affordances of earbuds, which turned Sterne's (2003) "audile technique" inside out.

This is not to say that they threw out "technique" altogether. If audile technique presents itself as an orientation toward sonic detail, in Sterne's account the careful listening it lays claim to also produces and depends upon particular orderings and stratifications of listeners from one another. Sterne's description of the early stethoscope offers a useful comparison to HCS kids' earbud practices. The stethoscope instrumentalized and rationalized sound as a tool of medicine, isolating and positioning sound precisely in space (and in bodies). Physically and pragmatically homologous to Sterne's stethoscope, earbuds also bounded and located discrete sounds precisely among children's constantly moving social networks. But the task they accomplished pulled the stethoscope's mediations inside out: at HCS earbuds were oriented outward, toward listeners rather than from sites of sonic production—*placing* sounds into social space, like a flashlight or projector, rather than receiving it from some otherwise inaccessible source (inside the body, esoterically written into the grooves of recording media, across time and space to an original acoustic event). The cultural logic of audile technique, which attends carefully to the sources and characteristics of privatized sound as part of a technosocial imaginary that has mediation and the desire for a distant original at its center (Peters 1999), was largely moot here. Instead mediation and circulation were assumed, naturalized, and backgrounded, so rather than the final node in a chain of production, distribution, and (mobile) consumption, MP3 players at HCS were the starting point in a chain of technosocial mediations that embedded music, sound, and listening in the material fabric of children's interpersonal and institutional lives. Kids applied intimate earbud listening techniques in the nooks and crannies of their social lives at school.

Ethnomusicologist Wayne Marshall points to the spread of small speakers on mobile devices as a phenomenon of "treble culture," in which "the everyday inevitability of 'tinny' transmissions appear[s] to affirm a preference for convenience, portability, and publicity, even as a variety of critical listeners express anxiety about what might be lost along with frequencies that go unheard" (2014:43). This suggests that the sonic values I describe here may not be limited to childhood contexts, though Marshall notes that young people—"noisy (and often black) 'kids on buses'" (2014:67)—are the paradigmatic figures of treble culture's critics and proponents. In Marshall's account, like mine, the sonic values of treble culture are not determined by changing technology, but follow from social, cultural, and aesthetic commitments. Children and young people are often seen as "early adopters" of new technologies, but another way to put this might be to call them social and cultural innovators. Just as young people—especially girls and young women—are leaders in linguistic change (Eckert 1988; Labov 2001), children and teenagers can also be seen as originators of media practices and social forms that then spread widely through mainstream adult society, and treble culture may be no different. Here we can see that the *conformity* of new technological and auditory practices with longstanding cultural values linked specifically to childhood, rather than mere "newness" for its own sake, is important to that process.

CHAPTER 3

Tinkering and Tethering

MP3 players were an important part of the material culture of children's lives at HCS. Kids attended to the tangibility of their MP3 players as objects more than as devices for communication or data storage. When friends shared earbuds to listen together, the cables tethered them ear to ear, and they delighted in the bodily challenge of moving in tandem with earbuds balanced delicately between. Kids tinkered constantly with their MP3 players, decorating them with decals, markers, tape, and nail polish, trading unsalvageable ones to save for spare parts, and seeking out charged batteries, in a never ending process of "enlivening" (Skuse 2005; Appadurai 1986) their fragile devices. When they broke, as they often did, kids repaired them or lived with malfunctions. Stories about failed devices were told enthusiastically, and the reasons for their failure were often shrouded in mystery. In these ways, children's MP3 players have been thoroughly domesticated within an intimate and childish material culture already characterized by playful physical interaction and portable objects such as toys, trading cards, and dolls that can be shared, manipulated, and held close. Children's emphasis and interest in the materiality of the devices as objects also informed their conceptions of sound, music, and circulation. They treated circulating songs as resonating sound rather than digital files. They also swapped songs with one another using the earbuds of one person's device to record through the microphone of another's.

Childish things

Media and communication technologies can seem radically disconnected from the material world of bodies, places, and objects. Hence, common narratives about portable music devices see private listening practices intruding upon and fragmenting public spaces, increasingly partitioning individuals within personalized musical soundscapes that detach listeners from their surroundings (Bull 2008; du Gay et al. 1997). Michael Bull argues that users of MP3 players "construct fantasies and maintain feelings of security precisely by not interacting with others of the environment" (2005:350). This non-interaction snowballs into a transcendent experience of separation and isolation from space and surroundings: "as users become immersed in their mobile media sound bubbles, so those spaces they habitually pass through in their daily lives may increasingly lose significance for them and progressively turn into the 'non-spaces' of daily lives which they try, through those self same technologies, to transcend" (2005:353). This way of thinking about mobile music builds on an understanding of sound as a uniquely *im*material medium, and which therefore understands listening as unlinked from its physical environment. To the extent that such narratives understand portable music listening to involve communication or interaction, it is separated from the immediate act of listening and instead occurs across vast distances online, by sharing files or playlists, or by tagging and rating songs. Anxious or nostalgic narratives of the spread of digital music emphasize the disappearance of physical recordings—LPs or CDs and their cover art—and lament the intangibility of digital files (Rothenbuhler and Peters 1997).

Scholars challenging this view argue for understanding new media specifically in terms of "materiality"—acknowledging the unmistakable fact of embodied users interfacing with devices (Munster 2006) and the importance of face-to-face social networks in their use and significance (D. Miller 2010). Phillip Vannini points out that in a fundamental sense technology and material culture are inseparably tied up with one another: "technology is about doing, knowing, and using objects and . . . materiality is about the character of those objects or things" (2009:1). In regard to children, this perspective seems especially salient, as children's own understanding of the meaning and role of new media music devices in their lives seemed to focus especially on the material characteristics and physical utility of such technology. We might even see children's material practices as a more relevant context for understanding their adoption of particular music technologies than their musical taste, though my position here is that children's musical culture is itself inextricably tied up in existing forms of children's material culture.

This approach requires that there is such a thing as "children's material culture." The category of "childish" things has real salience in the lives of children and adults, even if it is not always precisely characterized by fixed traits and has changed dramatically over time (Calvert 1992). Children's movements today are restricted to "islands" set off for them by adults (Gillis 2008), whether playgrounds (Kozlovsky 2008), stores or departments of stores (Cook 2003), media genres (Banet-Weiser 2007; Bickford 2012; Seiter 1993), restricted Internet sites (Grimes 2014; J. Marsh 2010; Montgomery 2007), or designated spaces in homes (Buchli and Lucas 2000). Within such islands, kids have relative freedom; for instance, the movements of kids' bodies in the playground—vertical and horizontal, swinging and climbing, running and crawling—contrast markedly from the restriction and regulation of movement in classrooms. This freedom of movement and activity within confined spaces is often understood in terms of "play"—an activity ideologically associated with children and childhood (Sutton-Smith 1997). And play is associated with a particular class of things: toys. The link between play as an activity and toys as objects helps to define the broad outlines of children's spaces and children's things, as, for instance, in drawing boundaries around children's role as consumers (Cross 1997; Fleming 1996; Kline 1993). Adults, importantly, are often more invested than children in strictly defining toys as distinct from other objects (Sutton-Smith 1986).

Children and adults articulate sophisticated taxonomies of "childish" things. Children, for example, designate certain foods as their own, marking them off through a complex intersection of healthfulness, color, packaging, processing, size, and ability to be handled and played with (Melton 2010), as well as sophisticated awareness of and confrontation with the "adult order" of food rituals based around ideologies of naturalness, cleanliness, bodily integrity, and disgust (James 1982). Robin Bernstein (2011) points out that objects for children are often "scripted" to encourage physically destructive and even violent play, as with (racialized) early twentieth-century rag dolls whose softness and durability, along with their minstrel-show stylization, supported throwing, beating, and other violent acts. Children's objects are often fashioned out of convenient materials, as Sharon Brookshaw calls attention to "makeshift" toys that are "designed, made, named, remodeled, used, and reused solely by children; they represent the creativity and imagination of children and the way in which almost anything can be adapted for their amusement or entertainment" (2009:369). Gunther Kress, similarly, highlights children's use of "what is to hand" to create objects that "are temporary only, and are subject to constant transformation" (1997:29). At HCS, school supplies like masking tape, pencils, and paper clips became the substance for inventive and never-ending creation, especially of medieval weapons like grappling hooks and ball-and-chains.

Brookshaw points out that it can be difficult to separate the material culture of children from materials made for children, in part because children's creations are so often temporary or makeshift assemblages of adult-made materials in their environments. For similar reasons archaeologists interested in children's material culture have not always been able to easily distinguish child-specific objects from objects relevant to childhood but shared by a wider range of people (Baxter 2005), while sometimes miniature objects that are assumed to be for children may have more complicated associations (Derevenski 2000; Mitchell 2014). So rather than distinguishing categorically between objects for and objects made by children, the potential of an object for manipulation and activity, and its capacity to be repurposed for children's use, may be the key diagnostics of potential childishness. Stephanie Melton (2010), for instance, describes an eleven-year-old girl "boxing" a pear as though it were a speed bag, and possibilities for such playful uses suggest why fresh, but not cooked, fruits and vegetables were classified as "kids' food" by the children in her study.

Studies of musical toys produced for children suggest that music, too, needs to be materialized in bright colors, physical manipulability, and interactive potential to be suitably childish. Patricia Shehan Campbell (1998) describes the complex overlapping of visual and sonic stimuli in a large urban toy store, in which electronic sounds are integral (and intentionally designed) elements of the colorful and interactive commercial world of toys. Multicolored and rocking horse–themed instruments, singing dolls and dinosaurs, and even nonmusical toys that inspire or elicit musicking and movement from children all point toward deep connections between music, movement, and objects in children's culture. Similarly, in a study of the everyday home lives of young children in seven countries by Susan Young and Julia Gillen (2007), electronic toys that make music appear to be very common, and children's everyday activities include dancing to child-themed CDs and vocalizing along with music-making pinball toys. Young writes, "in contemporary media, music is interwoven with images, animations, texts, spoken words and sound effects, and these extend into the material items of musical toys and other equipment" (2008:43). Music, here, appears to take its place in a broader phenomenon of "convergence" of categories in children's culture, such as that pointed out by Goldstein, Buckingham, and Brougère (2004) among toys, games, and media.

On the surface, MP3 players seem *not* to share in this "childish" potential of objects. They are small, yes, and sometimes brightly colored, and increasingly they are marketed to children using recognizable visual cues: I have seen Hannah Montana–themed devices and Lego devices with removable pieces, and the toy company Hasbro has had success selling its iDog series of animal-shaped plastic speakers. At HCS there were only two iDog toys and none of the thematically decorated devices. Most of the MP3 players children had were monochrome, many black or gray, a few red, purple, or blue. The cheaper versions most students owned were lightweight, plastic, and uninteresting to look at; as objects they seem designed to disappear, to subsume themselves into the sort of transcendent, "non-space" listening Bull describes. But nonetheless children constantly saw in their MP3 players the childish potential for exactly the sort of manipulability, interactivity, and movement that characterizes the rest of their material culture, reimagining them not in terms of transcendent freedom *from* bodies, spaces, and sociality, but as intimate and tangible anchors *to* their material, embodied, and spatial surroundings, and especially to one another.[1] In this they amply demonstrate Daniel Miller's point that "possessions often remain profound and usually the closer our relationships are with objects, the closer our relationships are with people" (2008:1).

New media devices as childish things

How portable media like MP3 players have been understood in terms of spatial practices and materiality points to some important contradictions, which help reveal the importance of "childishness" in consumer and technology practices. Discussing mobile Internet devices in Japan—or *keitai,* a term translated roughly as "something you carry with you" (Ito 2005a:1)—Ito emphasizes "attention to and immersion in the physical environment and social order" (2005a:13) as a central characteristic of portable media practices. This framing contrasts noticeably with Michael Bull's characterization of iPod practices as "non-interactive in the sense that users construct fantasies and maintain feelings of security precisely by not interacting with others of the environment" (2005:350). By contrast, for *keitai* users, Ito argues that such a "domain of 'cyberian apartness' from everyday physical reality . . . has always been a site of tension and integration between the demands of face-to-face encounters and footwork and the demands of the remotely present encounter and visual attention to the handheld screen" (2005a:13).

By this point it should be clear that through sharing earbuds, HCS children's relationship to their surroundings was much more engaged than what Bull describes. But *why* this is the case requires a deeper understanding. Ito positions mobile Internet practices as part of a broader trend in consumer culture toward "media mixes," the "increasingly pervasive mass-media ecologies that integrate in-home media such as television and game consoles, location-based media such as cinema and special events, and portable media such as trading cards and handheld games" (2007:100). She writes that, "While the Internet has taken center stage in our theorizing of new forms of communication and relationality, media mixes in children's content, below the radar of mainstream adult society, have been quietly radicalizing a new generation's relationship to culture and social life" (2007:100). Ito critiques the idea that "PC-based broadband is the current apex of Internet access models," pointing instead to the Japanese emphasis on the mobile Internet accessed through handheld devices, especially mobile phones: "ubiquity, portability, and lightweight engagement form an alternative constellation of 'advanced' Internet access characteristics that stand in marked contrast to complex functionality and stationary immersive engagement" (2005a:6). While talking on mobile phones, as with listening to portable music devices, is often seen as a private intrusion of public spaces, mobile Internet practices are, as Ito says, "a snug and intimate technosocial tethering" (2005a:1) that creates connections, rather than excluding them.

Key, here, is Ito's framing of media mixes and the intimate connections of *keitai* not in terms of some unique affordance of mobile technologies but as characteristic of a particular consumer culture linked to *childhood,* which is made up of "Tamagotchi, Game Boys, Pokémon cards, and *keitai* [that] are intimate, personal, and often cute media technologies" (2005a:2).[2] Tamagotchi and Game Boys, like *keitai,* are portable digital media devices, and the Pokémon brand appears in Game Boy games and various other digital media, and this varied and pervasive media ecology "enable[s] lightweight imaginative sharing between people going about their everyday business (2007:93). Ito points to the characteristic "cuteness" of this consumer culture and the strong connections of all of these forms to children and youth media: Pokémon and *Yu-Gi-Oh!* trading cards and Tamagotchi are marketed specifically to children, and Game Boys and mobile Internet phones are strongly associated with youth culture, even as they are widely used by adults (see also Allison 2004). On the whole in Japan the ecology of portable media links "childhood, remix, and revaluation cultures . . . with specific phantasmagoric cultural arenas rather than with digital technology per se. Also, importantly, these cultures are more strongly associated with . . . children and working-class youth (Ito 2007:105–6). So at least in the Japanese context we can see how mobile media practices that are embedded in the materiality and sociality of intimate face-to-face interactions build on existing childish cultures of consumption and play. Products like Pokémon and Game Boys marketed by the Japanese media giant Nintendo have long-term appeal to children in the United States, and mobile communication practices—especially text messaging—are increasingly associated with children, as the pervasive discourse of "digital natives" makes very clear (Thornham and McFarlane 2010).

Mobile Internet devices like smart phones are different from MP3 players, and since Ito does not locate portable listening in the cultural fields she outlines, we can ask where music fits in children's media and material culture. The apparently hermetic seal of a pair of earbuds suggests starkly different affordances from the small screen and keypad of a mobile phone. It might not be unreasonable to posit sound as a uniquely privatizing medium, such that mobile listening is necessarily more isolating than other mobile media practices like *keitai*. The historical connections between rationalized sound and privatized space drawn by Sterne and confirmed by Bull and others cannot be easily dismissed. In fact, Bull's conclusions about music devices are confirmed across a much broader sample by a comparative study (also by Ito) of portable technology in London, Los Angeles, and Tokyo. Ito, Okabe, and Anderson (2008) found that adult commuters in each city use music listening as a means of "cocooning" in crowded public transit or traffic. But HCS kids' practices suggest that sound is not a medium uniquely susceptible to privatization, and the material practices of kids' uses of MP3 players suggest that the key difference is childhood: whatever the normative adult association of portable sound to private space, children's listening fits much more naturally among other childish consumer practices. And we can see this point born out precisely in children's *sound* practices, to which I turn at the end of this chapter.

Tethering

MP3 players were objects constantly present on HCS kids' bodies, underscoring Alan Prout's argument that children's bodies are "are inseparable from, produced in, represented by, and performed through their connections with other material objects" (2000:2). A prominent example was sixth grader Melissa, who got a purple iPod Shuffle for Easter along with a matching pair of squishy purple earbuds. Melissa wore jeans and a baggy sweatshirt to school almost every day, and after she got the iPod it remained clipped to her sweatshirt all the time, except when teachers made her put it away during class. (Even then it would remain close, in a pocket.) She kept it on even after school during the hockey program she attended, clipped to her sweatshirt with one earbud in her ear, the other dangling. The cables tossed around and kept getting tangled in hockey sticks, but even though the coach and I repeatedly asked if she might want to put the device away while she was playing, she always declined. She kept it on even when the batteries died and she couldn't listen to music. Eighth grader Amber, too, often kept an earbud in her ear even when not listening to music, and kids would keep their MP3 players on their bodies during school, rather than storing them in their bags or lockers. When they entered the classroom the devices would disappear into pockets and sleeves, snug and close, ready to reappear immediately upon leaving class.

Sharing earbuds between friends also foregrounded material links among kids' bodies, to the extent that it was often difficult to get kids to find anything specific to say about sharing earbuds, as grounded as they were in the tacit intimacy of their embodied sociability. When I asked them about their preferred types of headphones, they nearly always told me they preferred earbuds, but the reasons they gave tended to be along lines of, "The other ones are too bulky," "They're ugly," or "I wear earrings, so they kind of rub—it hurts." When I asked specifically about sharing earbuds, for the most part kids answered that they would listen together because one person did not have theirs with them, or in order not to waste expensive batteries. These answers were ad hoc, developed on the spot in response to my questions. Otherwise sharing earbuds for the most part went undiscussed among kids. They did not seem to have any ready repertoire of talk about sharing earbuds, and they would rarely ask for or verbally offer an earbud to share, preferring to hand them over quietly, or while talking about something else.

Amber and Alice also gave me these same pat answers about earrings, batteries, and ugly big headphones, but when I encouraged them to explain sharing earbuds, Amber's response suggested how sharing earbuds activated kids' bodies *as* bodies, linking them through a physical cable that needed to be carefully balanced in their ears and accounted for as they moved together. When I asked Amber and Alice about sharing earbuds, Amber said, "We just started sharing, and then we'd listen to it and walk around." Remembering, her face lit up in a smile, and she said, "We got really good at, like, opening doors with us both wearing them, and going through them." Alice nodded in enthusiastic agreement, and Amber continued, "That should be a new sport!" Alice nodded again, "Yeah, yeah!" and it was clear that this idea had come up before. Both girls were proud of their skill at working together to accomplish what they recognized as a delicate and athletic task, and they happily remembered their early experiences working through the shared challenge of walking and listening together—not unlike the spectacular feat of physicality and coordination that Amber and Daisy accomplished sharing earbuds on the swings on the first day of school. In each of these cases earbuds were activated to facilitate a task whose challenge was not musical at all but lay rather in the careful coordination of bodies in integrated motion.

A couple weeks later I saw a pair of younger girls gamely working out the problem Amber and Alice had pointed to, trying to walk through doors connected by earbuds. The morning back from Easter break, third grader

Dahlia and her second-grade friend Katie came into the school entryway after dropping their bags off at their lockers, on their way to the gym to wait for school to start. They slowly opened the heavy double doors and carefully stepped through one at a time, a bit off balance, leaning in toward each other while connected ear-to-ear by the earbuds of the purple iPod Shuffle Dahlia carried in her hand.

Seeing me Dahlia exclaimed, "Bicky, I got an iPod for Easter!" Lifting her head to call over to me she almost lost her earbud, so she lowered her head in to Katie's and said, with more restraint, "This is a . . . 'Shuffle.'" The pair shuffled past into the gym, Katie off balance in her loose platform flip-flops but still steadying her head as she leaned in toward Dahlia.

These moments where girls swung together athletically or struggled to walk through doors sharing earbuds reveal earbud sharing as a skill that was actively negotiated, practiced, and honed. Despite the familiarity and facility with which kids passed earbuds around their friendship groups, these practices were learned and perfected, though whether they were passed down or repeatedly invented is difficult to determine. On the one hand, we might see Dahlia and Katie's shuffle as "interpretive reproduction"—William Corsaro's (1992) term for children acting out scripts with each other that they observe among adults (or in this case older students)—as though they were trying out earbud practices commonly witnessed among older kids like Amber and Alice. But Amber and Alice themselves had to figure out how to walk together while sharing earbuds, without apparently learning from even older acquaintances. Whatever the provenance of these activities, it is clear that kids at a range of ages understood earbuds as essentially participatory technologies presenting particular physical and social challenges as they worked out how to incorporate mobile listening into their singularly important friendships. The goal of sharing immediately entails a challenge of embodied coordination and an opportunity to move together, strengthening the affective and unspoken bonds of kids' friendships.

Approaching kids' listening as a physical challenge brings to mind Sterne's treatment of mediated listening in terms of Maussian "techniques" (2003:91–92; Mauss 1979), as a sensory and technological practice that implicates the body and physical learning. Comparing the skillful techniques involved in HCS children's sharing earbuds with Sterne's audile technique reveals how distinct HCS kids' embodied listening practices were from the normative regimes of listening and technology outlined by Sterne, Bull, and du Gay et al. In both cases listening ordered and organized bodies, but whereas audile technique specifically involved separating people from one another—whether headsets partitioning individual space in middle-class dwellings or stethoscopes separating doctors from unclean, lower-class, or female patients (Sterne 2003:114)—sharing earbuds at

HCS intimately linked individuals with a demand of physical proximity and careful coordination with another body in motion.

Tinkering

Like a lot of objects sold to children, the generic MP3 players that most of the HCS kids had were cheap, even disposable. Devices regularly broke or were lost, and kids' use of them demonstrated that "material practice revolves around loss more often than preservation—luster fades, things fall apart" (Colloredo-Mansfield 2003:246). The $40 or $50 that even the least expensive devices cost was significant enough that kids lived with partially broken devices, scrounged around for replacement parts, and tried to repair cracked cases or wires when they could. And though they were aware of the possibility that the devices would break, they were not careful at all with them, keeping them around during active play or sports, and carelessly setting them down where they might forget them. Cranking the volume up to use their earbuds as miniature speakers, they often blew out headsets.

Though they worried about breakage, they also related stories about broken devices with bravado, revealing how "people stake prestige . . . on the techniques and materials of consumption and destruction" (Colloredo-Mansfield 2003:252). Sixth grader Dan, for instance, told me, "I have [an MP3 player], but it's broken. I can't download songs onto it. I don't have the cable, and I think it has a CD that you need. I got it from my cousin [eighth grader Erica], and she's stupid. I think she lost the CD." Dan never did get a working MP3 player during the year, and instead he used his portable CD player. But he also never got rid of his cousin's hand-me-down device, even carrying it to and from school in his backpack, and its presence provided a relished opportunity to complain about his older cousin's ineptness in losing the data cable and software disk.

On another occasion, I sat with seventh and eighth graders Kathy, Alice, and Amber at breakfast, listening to Jordin Sparks and Taylor Swift on Kathy's iDog. The dog bobbed its head in time to the music, and disco lights flashed on its face. The girls' conversation revealed the delight taken in stories about the failure of devices and also the detailed knowledge these friends had about one another's devices. I asked Kathy if she was happy with the MP3 player she got for Christmas. She nodded, but my question prompted Alice to complain, "My MP3 player's being retarded."

Kathy elaborated for her, "It doesn't turn on."

I asked, "Still? Did you try resetting it or whatever?"

Amber jumped in, incredulous: "It doesn't have a reset button!"

Alice said, "My dad, literally, went and picked it up, like this, and went—" she mimed dropping the device, "like that, on the floor [to try to get it to work]. And I did it too! And it won't turn on. I've had it for two weeks, and it's already broken."

Alice and her sister Megan, in sixth grade, had matching MP3 players. I asked Alice, "Your sister's works fine?"

Amber replied for her, "Yeah, except she blew her earphones," and then she bragged, "I've blown two pairs of earphones!"

"How do you do that?"

"It goes too loud and it overblows."

"When you turn up the volume to use them as speakers?"

"No, just as earphones."

"Do you put them real loud in your ear?"

Amber nodded. Alice joined in, "I told Megan not to have hers up cause she's gonna blow them. And she's using my headphones." Since Megan's earbuds were broken, and Alice's device would not turn on, the sisters had consolidated their equipment.

Amber bragged, "I've blown my earphones, my iPod earphones, and my MP3 player earphones. And I traded my mom my dad's earphones—he gave them to me—for my mom's iPod earphones. So I had those, and hers are about to blow, so now I got these, so I have a second pair, my mom's. I blow up earphones very easily," she said with evident pride.

The discussion evidently made Kathy nervous. She pointed to her new iDog and asked, "These could never blow up, right? Could these ever blow up?" Amber and I tried to assure her that the lightweight plastic device should be fine.

Several weeks later the story of the broken device had developed into a comic routine between Alice and Amber, with a mysterious malfunction providing the narrative lead-up to a ready punchline.

During an interview with both girls, Alice remembered, "I got a sucky MP3 player but—"

Amber whispered, "It broke!"

"—it wound up breaking! It broke the first week I got it! Cause, what it was, I had the earphone in my ear, and I had the MP3 in my pocket. What was so weird was that the headphone fell out of my ear and I tried turning it back on and it didn't work after that. After the earphone fell. I didn't even drop it."

Amber asked, apparently for my benefit, "Where'd you get it?"

"A pharmacy," Alice laughed. "CVS."

Amber grinned and delivered the punchline she had set up: "Yeah, don't buy electric things at a pharmacy."

As these stories reveal, breaking and loss did not end the social lives of these objects but were rather the impetus for particular "enlivening" practices in which kids continually worked to maintain and enhance their devices' social utility. Enlivenment "is normatively equated both with the appropriation of commodities, but also with a more mundane practice of maintenance, in the sense that certain commodities such as portable radios require a continual economic investment in the purchase of batteries if they are to remain enlivened in the socio-semantic sense" (Skuse 2005:124–25; also Appadurai 1986). Enlivenment, therefore, continually resists entropy or dispossession, the failure, disposal, or transience of objects (Lucas 2002). When Alice's and Megan's two devices had different failures, the sisters consolidated them and shared. Amber found a seemingly inexhaustible supply of headphones in possession of her family members, and she saw her task as cajoling them into sharing or trading. Dan would later ask me for the USB cable his hand-me-down MP3 player needed to work, and we tried connecting it to one of the school computers, even though he still lacked the necessary software CD. Sometimes students would even break their devices on purpose, as when fourth graders Dave and Brian snapped one earpiece off of an old pair of headband-style earphones so they could share them. Just as the failure of Alice's device was transformed into an occasion for shared storytelling with Amber, in Dave and Brian's case, enlivenment, and increased sociality, is the direct result of destruction, manifesting Colloredo-Mansfield's suggestion that "exhausting commodities frequently opens up channels of connectivity, yet it also reduces individual control of them" (2003:251).

Batteries were central to HCS kids' enlivenment of music devices. Economizing battery power was often mentioned as a reason to share the earbuds to one device between friends. Amber and Alice knew every detail of one another's battery usage, because batteries affected how and when they could listen together. They talked about how they navigated different rules at home and the differences between their devices to listen together as much as possible. Amber told me that one of the reasons she and Alice listened together was because "I charge [my iPod] every day, and she likes to save her battery. I listen to mine a lot, so I have to charge it every day."

Alice agreed, "'Cause I'm limited to so many batteries. My mom bought me a four-pack of batteries. And then I find batteries around the house."

"My battery," Amber continued, "as much as I listen to it, could last me about an hour or two. A full battery."

"My battery can last me two, three weeks."

"'Cause she barely listens to hers, and I listen to mine a lot, like every day."

Alice's Samsung took a single AA battery, while Amber's iPod had an internal battery that was easily charged at an outlet at home, without the need for any cash or purchase from her parents. While her dependence on batteries severely limited Alice's ability to use her device, she and Amber collaborated to avoid Alice's device ever going completely dead. That the girls had such minute knowledge testifies to their closeness and to the important role of these devices as mediators of the girls' friendship. In fact, the MP3 player that Alice had to scrounge batteries for was actually Amber's old Samsung, a device she had before she got her iPod. Alice received this device on indefinite loan from Amber after the player she got at Christmas had broken. So while Amber phrased her explanation in terms of her own frequent listening habits, her ability to listen more than Alice was also structured by her parents' willingness to buy her an iPod and the particular affordances of that device's rechargeable battery. But at school Alice probably listened to music as much as Amber, because Amber would always automatically pass her the second earbud when she took out her iPod.

In addition to such attentive social mediations of battery power, the transience of these devices was tied up in practices of tinkering, repair, and decoration—activities that seemed in many cases to go together—as though the material instability of MP3 players opened up possibilities for kids to interact with them in new ways. Their "cheapness," in this sense, could be seen as a source of constant renewal and interest.

Like Alice, who emphasized the mysterious circumstances of her MP3 player's failure, seventh grader Randy told me that his old earbuds "just melted! I felt some heat on my arm," he said, "and I looked down, and they were melting up!"

I asked, "Really? Just for no reason?"

"Yeah, really! So I tore them apart to see what's inside." Randy pulled them out of his bag to show me (figure 3.1)—he carried even such irreparably damaged items around in his bag, reconstituting them as objects for investigation rather than as deconstituted "trash" (Lucas 2002).

Randy told me he got his current pair from the airplane on his family's recent trip to Disneyland. But unlike his old ones, these weren't marked "L" and "R" for left and right. So he showed me how he would listen to Trace Adkins's "Honky Tonk Badonkadonk" to figure out which ear was which—the song starts, "*left / left / left right left,*" with the words "left" and "right" panned to the respective channels. Then he went into the school office to get a Band-Aid that he could rip up to mark the earbuds so he wouldn't have to keep checking them with the recording. But he couldn't rip the Band-Aid by hand, "because it's thicker than the ones I use at home." Instead he pulled a sheet of decals out of his Game Boy case and wrapped a Confederate flag

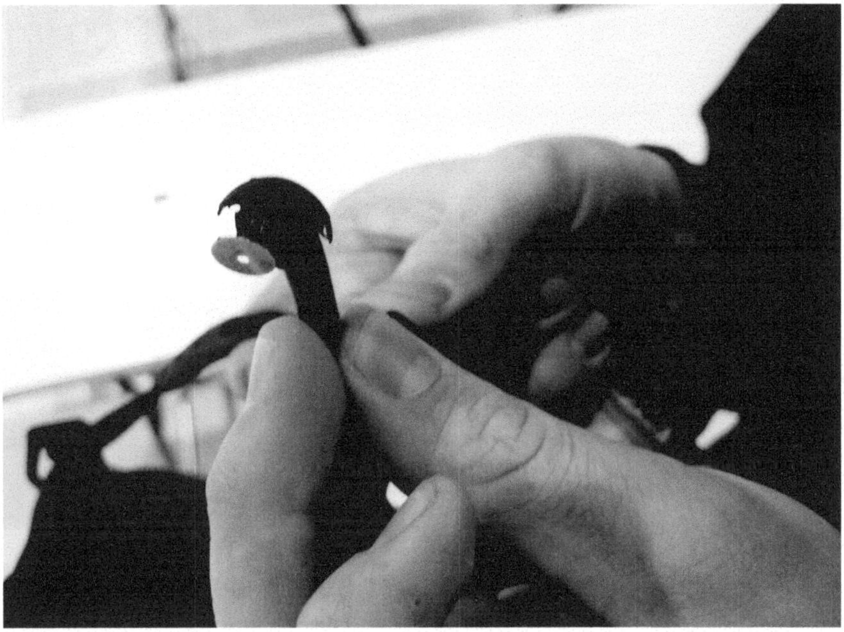

Figure 3.1: Randy tore apart his "melted" earbuds to see what's inside.

sticker around the left earbud. He marked the decal with an "L," using a Sharpie he also pulled out of his Game Boy case, and said with satisfaction, "That's a good redneck way to do it" (figure 3.2).[3]

Other students put stickers on their devices, or accessorized them with headphones with brightly colored cables or with shiny plastic beads hanging from them. Kathy got an MP3 player for Christmas, but by June the screen was held together with tape and she had painted the back case completely with sparkly nail polish (figure 3.3). Such extreme forms of decoration were less common, and in Kathy's case it seemed to reflect the fact that her device was already damaged, suggesting again that breaking is often the inspiration for new efforts at enlivening devices. And portable gaming devices were also sometimes subject to such decoration, as with eighth grader Nate, who cut strips of electrical tape to add tiger stripes to his Game Boy Micro.

Randy was the only kid who even once mentioned the left and right channels of a recording. But, like the rest of the kids at Heartsboro, he never seemed concerned about listening to the full stereo soundscape—which, of course, the widespread practice of listening with just one ear completely devalued. For Randy a new pair of earbuds missing labels presented an opportunity for tinkering and design, more than a problem for faithful listening, and even the sonic organization of the audio track was

Figure 3.2: Randy marked the left earbud with a Confederate flag sticker.

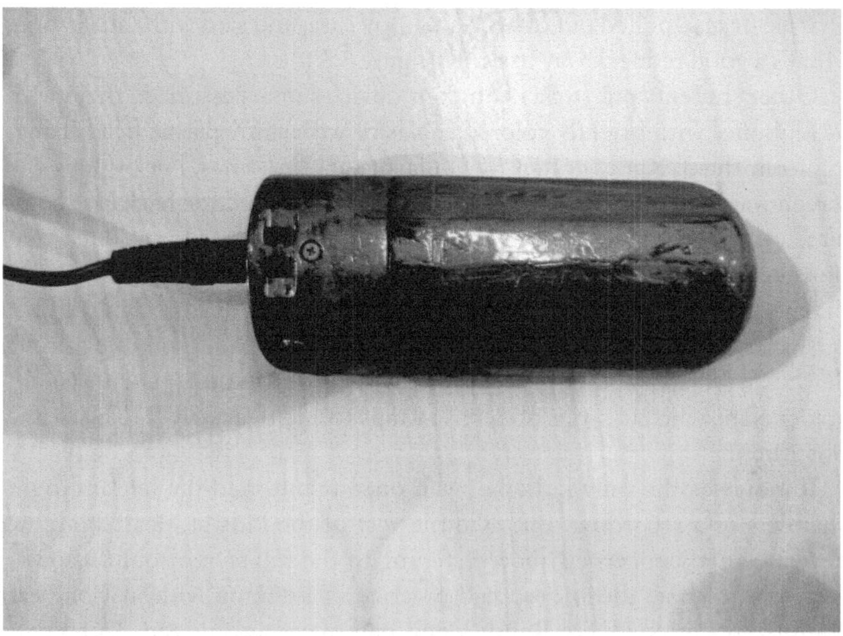

Figure 3.3: Kathy's Christmas MP3 player in June, taped up and covered in nail polish.

put in service of the object and its decoration, rather than appreciated on its own.

Tinkering and tethering in circulation

Noting Randy's use of the stereo sound of a recording to organize his earbuds on his body, rather than to structure his listening as such, children's material orientations toward MP3 players can provide clues about their conceptions of music and sound. Common understandings of sound and music as uniquely ephemeral, even disembodied, suggest that hearing is especially susceptible to technological or schizophonic mediations (Feld 1994). Further, infinite reproducibility—that media files can be transferred and copied without any loss of information, unlike analog recordings or film photographs—is seen as a central feature linking postmodern technological and cultural configurations, the characteristic affordance of digital media. But kids at HCS often ignored or rejected such characteristically "digital" capacities of their devices, instead approaching the circulation of sound recordings in ways that located them within the material world, rather than as placeless and immaterial digital "files." In particular, many used the built-in (and very low quality) microphones in their MP3 players to record and circulate music. They put the microphone up to their television or to computer speakers to record music from a music video, rather than searching for a song on the Internet, downloading it (possibly paying for it with a parent's credit card), and transferring it to their MP3 player. Or they placed an earbud to the microphone, to transfer music from one device to another.

At eighth-grade gym class, held outdoors in June, several girls sat out because it was "too hot." Amber listened to her iPod, while Sarah fiddled with her friend's MP3 player and her very new cell phone—a Motorola RAZR. Flipping open the phone, she looked at the screen for a bit and then played a song using the phone's speakers. I asked her where she got the music—off of the Internet? I imagined she was using one of the new music-downloading services the cell-phone companies had been aggressively advertising. She shook her head and held up the MP3 player. "Off of this."

I was puzzled. MP3 players, I thought, did not connect from device to device—you had to use a computer to transfer files.

So Sarah demonstrated for me, holding one earbud up to the microphone on her phone. As she showed me, the music was interrupted by a loud girlish screech, and Sarah said, "Erica was being loud during that part.

She ruined it." But Sarah let the song play on despite being "ruined," and she and her friends would continue to listen to this track on the phone over the rest of the school year.

During interviews kids would often place their earbuds up to my recorder to "show" me songs.[4] Notably, they only used the microphones on their MP3 players to record or share music; they never used them to record one another. My audio recorder would elicit performative talk from kids of all ages. Younger kids would do funny voices or sing when I took it out, and older kids would say swear words or insults, or call one another names. But the kids never seemed interested in listening to themselves later, even when I offered. And their own devices were just for songs.

Kids would also record music off of the Internet or television, including advertising jingles and TV theme songs. When I asked Randy in an interview, "Would you say you like music?" his immediate response was, "Well, my custom radio says so, yeah!" He went on to tell me about the seven speakers he had attached to an old boombox and wired around his room with strobe lights. When I asked Randy about what types of music he likes, he said, "Rock, heavy metal stuff, country. And the occasional anime shows. You know like—the show's so awesome I can't even remember the name of it. *Blood Plus*. There. That's a good show."

"Yeah?"

"Yeah, they always have cool theme songs. Actually I got like ten of 'em on here," he said, pulling out his MP3 player.

I noticed the white earbuds and asked, "What are these, iPod headphones?"

"No, I stole them from my brother." Randy laughed.

"What's this, like your fifth pair this year or something?"

"I used the ones from the airplane. They sucked." Randy found his song. "This is one of those Japanese anime ones. It's from *Final Fantasy Dirge of Cerberus*. It's a cool song." He held one of the earbuds up to the microphone on my recorder. He whispered to me, to avoid disrupting the recording he was making for me, "That's how I got it on here—I recorded this off the Internet [i.e., from one of the speakers attached to a computer]. Off *Dirge of Cerberus*." We both listened closely to the quiet recording being played on tiny headphones resting on the table. As he transferred music that he had originally recorded from computer speakers onto his MP3 player and then on to my recorder, Randy was executing a fully analogue chain of transfers between digital devices, as though this were a completely normal way to move songs around.

Randy listed several other shows whose songs he liked. He described the theme to *Death Note* for me, and then remembered, "I still need to record that. I gotta write that down." He told me that he would stay up to watch the shows when they came on late on Saturday night. He would set his TV's timer to remind him and then hold the MP3 player up to the TV speakers and record the song. He picked up his MP3 player to show me how. "See that, that's the mike. What you do is when you turn it on, it takes forever. Here we go. You go like this. And it says 'recorder.' Then it'll be like that," he pointed to a menu on the screen, "and you just go like this and it's recording. See? And if you don't want to save it you'll see an X. You just swap over to that and go *tsiu*." Randy finished with a laser-gun sound effect for X'ing out the songs.

Earlier in the year Randy and a couple other boys rode with me on a field trip to hear the author Lois Lowry talk, and I let them pick songs on my iPod to play in the car. When "Stronger," the new Kanye West single, came on, Randy pulled his MP3 player out of his bag and stuck it down at the speaker in the door by his feet. I did not realize he was recording, but several months later I was making a CD of songs for him and asked if he wanted that song. He said no, because he already had it. "Don't you remember, I got it when we were on that trip before?"

At our interview Randy continued through the songs on his MP3 player. He found "Party Like a Rockstar," and said, "That's one of the ones I got from music class." He had recorded it during the music show-and-tell that was a regular part of my music class. He said, "You'll hear it stop, you'll hear Kathy's voice on there eventually."

I asked, "Does the fuzziness bother you at all?"

"No, not really. I know how far to keep them away from the speakers, and sometimes the fuzziness doesn't affect 'em at all. Like this one, this is from *King of Hearts*. This one I need to redo. I mean, it's good, but it's kind of weird."

I suggested, "You might be able to find the actual songs on the Internet."

But Randy dismissed this out of hand: "I don't even know the names of them."

Sarah and Randy were from opposite ends of the social hierarchy. Sarah had a large and close group of friends that was widely acknowledged as having high social status. Randy, on the other hand, had no close friends and few people even to hang out with. He was widely acknowledged to be a social maladroit. Sarah and Randy had very different taste in music. Randy represented an extreme version of this do-it-yourself, tinkering ethos of music listening, and he loved to repair and retrofit his old and broken stereo and his old and broken MP3 player. Sarah and her friends were early adopters of shiny new technology, like Sarah's RAZR phone and Michelle's portable Sirius Radio receiver. Nonetheless, they both moved music around in this remarkable way, from earbud to microphone. My own first reaction to Sarah recording music directly from an earbud was disbelief, and I suggested to Randy that these recorded copies Randy passed from device to device were somehow less real than digital sound files, the "actual songs." It would never occur to me to move songs around like this. The layers of *in*fidelity to high-quality digital reproduction represented by such a practice were stacked upon one another: MP3 encoding already represents concessions of quality to portability; cheap earbuds hardly produce decent playback, and with only one earbud transferring music to the microphone, half the original track is lost; the microphones on MP3 players and cell phones are barely suitable even for casual voice recording; and the audio from the microphone is then subjected to further degradation from another round of low bitrate MP3 encoding.

It would be easy to see these practices as simply kids' accommodation to necessity—they lacked ready income, credit cards, and computer skills to move songs through the "normal" digital channels from the Internet and from one device to another—or even as a deficiency in their understanding of their devices' affordances. But these practices certainly were faithful to an alternate conception of music, in which sound, songs, and recordings were integrated into the physical, spatial, and embodied world that children and their music devices occupy. Sarah and Randy both transferred music by connecting one physically present device to another with the umbilicus of their earbud cables. As they held the earbuds up to the microphones, they transferred sound from one vibrating membrane to another, in real time. If anything, the recordings they made were composed more of "actual" sounds and music than digitally encoded representations. On the Internet songs would be found by searching for meta-data representations—titles, artist names, dates, etc.—but as Randy points out, he did not know the names of many songs on his device. He did, on the other hand, know very clearly how the songs sounded. So, just as MP3 players themselves existed as objects as much as media, it seems as though songs and music existed for HCS kids as sounds more than as files, and so to move music from device to device required the song to actually resound in physical space.

Sound as material culture

Stephen Connor writes that sound "strikes us as at once intensely corporeal—sound literally moves, shakes, and touches us—and mysteriously immaterial" (2004:157). The "immateriality" of sound contributes directly to the transcendence of space and place that Bull documents among adult iPod users, which Ito terms "cocooning." In the face of such powerful and pervasive discourses of immateriality that surround new media and weigh in forcefully on the latter conception of sound, it takes a certain ingenuity for children to orient toward the corporeality of sound, and to see in MP3 players—these iconic objects of new media—material affordances for circulation, movement, embodiment, and sharing. But these practices fit perfectly within the clear and present demands of kids' social and material environment, in which objects and bodies constantly circulate and interact in immediate, face-to-face settings. To seek out some digital file on the Internet would require turning attention away from this rich and solid social world. Sound "constitutes a form of material action" (Witmore 2006:276), and it is this potential for material action—for play, manipulation, tinkering, investigation—that is central to the identification of some thing as "childish." The devices stuck in their clothes and tangled among their bodies, and the sounds those devices produced were thus available to be toyed with, using the sort of immediate agency kids cultivate as they climb in and around their environment and put objects in physical contact. Connor writes about "a restoration of . . . equilibrium in the face of the extreme disembodiment of hearing, a reclaiming of the proximal tactility of the here-and-now body" (2004:171). But it appears that children need not "reclaim" anything at all. Their cultures of hearing have retained the "proximal tactility" of their cultures of materiality, grounded among practices that include boxing a pear, climbing on a jungle gym, collecting and trading cards, or building medieval weapons out of pencils, masking tape, and chains of paper clips.

But if kids would use their MP3 players to record and circulate songs, why wouldn't they use them to record one another's voices? When voices did appear on their recordings, they were always accidental interruptions of a song. When kids performed for my recording device, they were never interested in listening back to themselves, even though they often created rather sophisticated voices and characters for the benefit of the recorder sitting on the lunch table. The above discussion demonstrates that, for these kids, pop songs were understood as material sound that circulated *as* sound. But that does not mean that sound performances are undifferentiated. That songs could be recorded and then passed around as recordings, while kids' voices were, at most, simply recorded and then forgotten, suggests that the distinction lies in textuality and circulation. Songs, though rarely understood by kids as digital computer "files," were, nonetheless, defined texts that had the capacity to circulate (Silverstein and Urban 1996). But kids' singing into the recorder also involves mediations: the entextualization of sounds into music and words into lyrics is a mediation not unlike inscribing recorded sounds into binary code and thus into files with metadata. The distinction, then, is not between objectified sound files and undifferentiated materiality, but rather between various degrees of textual abstraction: rather more abstract digital files, and rather more *im*mediate sounding songs. Relative, rather than absolute, values are important in a school context, where things that are *less* mediated or abstracted take on ideological valences of intimacy. Kids' voices, then, are *even less* available for mediation and abstraction than pop songs, which are already entextualized as songs and commodified as recordings. While kids enjoy the recorder as an audience that elicits their performative vocalizations, to turn around and listen to their performances would activate their language and voices as mediated, entexualized, and objectified, and therefore it is avoided.

The immediate interactivity of bodies and things that characterizes the childish material culture I have been describing in this chapter is a part of a broader logic of intimacy that contrasts decontextualized and instrumental orientations toward communication, other people, and the environment from contextually grounded ones. Associations with children's material culture provide the historically grounded tradition through which kids can distinguish certain modes of expression as natural and childish while other modes are unnatural and unnecessary—pointing to precisely the sort of dynamic of expressive contrast between instrumental and intimate modes discussed in chapter 1. Chapter 5 discusses kids' expressive "inarticulateness"—moments when they refuse to vocalize or discourse about some teacher-prompted topic, preferring instead to communicate with one another through more immediate and intimate means. This chapter, by exploring the materiality of recorded pop songs in kids' practice, provides a context for understanding how the materiality of language, poetics, and communication takes on an increased significance in the expressive ecology of school.

CHAPTER 4

Intimate Media In and Out of the Classroom

Kids used their music devices throughout the school day, including in the classroom and during lessons—which of course was strictly forbidden by teachers. When MP3 players and similar devices like handheld video games were used in school, and specifically in the classroom, kids' consumer media practices were situated not merely in opposition to school but also as an integral part of children's school experience. The social and institutional context of school was a key structuring environment for kids' listening practices, which varied greatly throughout their days.

Before moving to the classroom, it is worth underscoring how kids' listening and interactional practices take on particular meaning and importance in school by pointing to ways in which the same activities appear *not* to have taken place outside of school. Practices like sharing earbuds were ubiquitous in the peculiarly intimate public spaces of school, but they appeared to be much less common in non-school spaces, where the friendships in which they flourished were less pervasive. Though kids might listen together on the bus or when visiting one another's homes, they did not often share earbuds with siblings or parents. Students explained to me repeatedly in interviews that when at home or with family they would listen individually, either in their room with the door closed or wearing both earbuds. These modes of listening point exactly toward the rationalization and compartmentalization described by Sterne, suggesting that the intimate and sociable listening practices I have been describing so far are built into the institutional and social contexts of school itself. This is, on the one hand, a trivial statement of the fact that there are more kids at school, and therefore more friends, and therefore more opportunities for doing things friends do. But that kids spend more time with other kids their own age ("peers") at school than out of school is not trivial at all. Rather, this is the key fact for understanding the social structure of schools. "Peer culture"—the enduring analytical category of childhood and education scholars—is in many ways a product of schooling, which implicitly and explicitly structures the ways children and adults relate and interact with one another, and peer culture certainly could not exist in its modern forms without schools collecting and sorting their communities' children by age for several hours every day. Children's media consumption is structured by schooling mainly because childhood itself is significantly a product of schooling (as argued in chapter 1). Demonstrating that media, entertainment, and consumerism are then articulated to childhood within the institutional co-construction of childhood and schooling is the analytical task at hand.

Throughout my interviews with the kids at HCS, when I asked about music their first response was often to describe the way they used music to negotiate space at home. They mentioned disputes about their music being too loud, limitations on where they could listen to music, or negotiations of what the whole family would listen to on the car stereo (where those who did not get what they wanted would put on their own music with headphones, if they owned a music device).

After Christmas third grader Robbie, Amber's younger brother, drew a revealing picture of his family's complex musical and social environment (figure 4.1). He depicted himself and his sister both listening to earbuds and singing songs from *High School Musical 2*—"Bet On It" and "What Time Is It (Summertime)." In the picture a stereo plugged into the wall plays Hannah Montana's first single, "The Best of Both Worlds." The kids' mom yells, "Stop singing, you [two]." Amber yells, "I hate that song!" and Robbie responds, "I love it." All in all, a lot of noise (music?) is seen coming from voices and speakers (though all the music is from the Disney Channel).

Later Amber elaborated on her family's household noise/music dynamic during an interview. She told me, "I have to keep [my music] down low cause Robbie is usually listening to his music—"

Alice jumped in, "On the computer, blaring it—"

And Amber finished, whispering conspiratorially, "That's why Santa got him headphones," and laughed.

I described the scene in Robbie's picture, and Alice commented, "What he likes to do is he likes to have his headphones, and *sings*."

"It's horrible! You could die in that house."

Robbie's drawing dramatized a partitioning of sound and space, in which each space has its own music playback device: Robbie's earbuds, Amber's

Figure 4.1: Drawing by third grader "Robbie" of Christmas at his family's house, showing his sister Amber (left) and himself singing songs from the movie *High School Musical 2*, as their mother (center) calls for them to "stop singing" and a radio plays a Hannah Montana song in the bottom right corner, January 7, 2008. Used by permission of the artist.

earbuds, and the boombox plugged into the wall. This is the sort of rationalization of sound, space, and social relations that Sterne describes, where parents buy an eight year old headphones so that he can listen to music independently and without disturbing the rest of the family. But here that partitioning fails completely, and Robbie's drawing delights in the chaos and cacophony when music from headphones and loudspeakers are layered with singing and yelling. Even here, where the kids in the house are seen to be wearing earbuds the "right" way, each sealed into their private units, the listening is so noisy that Robbie's mom must intervene. Even her calls for quiet seem only to serve the overall sense of noisily overlapping speakers and voices.

Robbie's drawing exposes the limits of rationalized sound in a household context, but still the primary social consequence of music listening in his drawing is *intrusion*—certainly not interaction or intimate connection. Something like the dynamic expressed in this scene seemed to occur in most households; almost every kid explained to me that when at home they would listen privately, either in their room with the door closed or wearing earbuds. Otherwise, as Amber and Alice pointed out, listening at home in shared spaces could be an unwanted intrusion to others. The separateness of the listening environments in Robbie's drawing suggests that different environments necessitated different listening practices. Just as earbuds did not cross all social boundaries of status, gender, age, and friendship, they also did not link brother and sister, or parent and child. Therefore, the "intimate" practices I've been pointing out can be seen as importantly linked to school. Music listening and educational practices come into direct contact and conflict in the classroom.

Music listening in the classroom

Like Robbie's mom, teachers also called for quiet. I sometimes got the sense that an ideally manageable classroom would involve just the sort of partitioning of each student from every other student that rationalized listening points to. But unlike Robbie's mom yelling "stop singing" to two kids individually singing different favorite songs, teachers' imperatives to "stop talking" or "quiet down" are almost always directed at students who are interacting with each other.

In chapter 2 I mentioned that sometimes in art class kids used earbuds as quiet speakers, which had the felicitous effect of not disrupting groups at other tables who did not want to listen to particular music. This allowed for finer-grained organization of music listening than the art teacher's normal practice of putting music on for the whole class to encourage quiet, independent work. But in classroom settings other than art, teachers almost never played music. In most classes music listening was strictly forbidden. Even if a teacher were to allow music, listening together using earbuds as speakers or sharing them would have been precluded by seating arrangements that often intentionally separated friends to prevent socialization. Students often campaigned to be allowed to listen privately while doing their work, but they were always denied. Still, kids worked together to find ways to bring their small and easily concealed devices into class, despite teachers' restrictions.

At the beginning of the year they tried threading the earbuds through the body of a hooded sweatshirt and up through the neck, hiding the earbuds under its hood. But hats and hoods were also regulated by teachers, and students quickly learned that they couldn't get away with this, because wearing a hood in class would attract the attention of a teacher. Over time a group of older girls worked out that the most effective tactic was to thread the cable not through the neck of their sweatshirts but through the sleeve to the wrist, palming the earbud and listening with their head resting in their hand. With the earbud in their hand, they could quickly hide it in their sleeve if necessary. As other scholars have found with regard to in-class note passing, HCS kids' in-class listening practices worked at the boundary of "overt" and "covert" action (Powell, Danby, and Farrell 2006). Efforts to find the best way to listen in class were collaborative. Despite the fact that in these situations kids listened individually, and despite the care they took to conceal their listening from teachers, they would publicize their surreptitious listening by gesturing to friends and quietly laughing when they could see that the teacher was not looking. They would copy one another and share ideas out of class about how best to avoid detection. These social efforts at finding best practices for concealing music devices in class resembled other activities, like passing notes, where students would collaborate and share results to develop new and creative ways to conceal their behavior from teachers.

In the fall the kids were still figuring out how to sneak their devices into class, and their conversation suggested how they understood music listening to be a practice similar to playing video games and passing notes (Hubbard 1988, 1989). One day in October seventh and eighth graders Jenn, Amber, and Kathy stood around the swings after having taken the NECAP standardized tests that the whole school was taking that week. Jenn explained to her friends that the reason she was always the last one done with the NECAPs was because she would pass notes and talk. "And Mr. B. never notices," she said, referring to their teacher. "Did you see the notes flying around?"

I asked, "Do you guys get in trouble for passing notes?"

Amber and Kathy, not as joyfully rebellious as Jenn, said, "Sort of, not really."

"You're not supposed to."

"But you guys aren't really very careful about it. You just pass them back and forth. Like this—" I swung my arms widely.

Jenn laughed. "Yeah, and he doesn't see. Sometimes he's looking right at me and he doesn't see."

"And yesterday Willy was playing his Game Boy while you were supposed to be reading."

Jenn laughed again and volunteered, "Sometimes we take the headphones," she demonstrated with her MP3 player and neon earbuds, "and slide this part [the headphone cable] up our sweaters and it comes out at the neck. And we listen and he doesn't even know."

Amber: "Yeah, and you can put your hair down to hide the earbuds."

By the end of the year, Jenn and another friend, Michelle, explained to me their more established system for listening to music in class. After talking a bit about when and where they listened to music at home and their negotiations with parents and siblings over noise and taste, I asked them to talk about listening to music in school. Jenn said, "Sometimes we listen in class if we like shove it up our sleeve." I realized that in the time that passed between these two conversations, I hadn't actually witnessed the middle-school kids listening to music in class, though I documented plenty of note passing, spitball throwing, and even video games tucked into open textbooks (as one would do with comics or a magazine).

"I've seen you guys do a lot of stuff, but I don't think I've ever seen you do that."

Michelle said, "That's because we're good at hiding it. 'Cause it's in the sleeve."

Jenn said, "Yeah, you gotta put it in this pocket—" She gestured to the pocket at the belly of her sweatshirt. "And you gotta have it go up—" Her hand followed her sleeve from the shoulder to the wrist. "But you need to do it on your left hand."

"So you can write with your right hand," Michelle finished.

"Ohhhh. So you're not running it up through your hood."

"No."

"You're running it up through your sleeve. And then you can take it right out."

Michelle: "So then you just like hold it in your hand and go like that—" She pressed her ear to her hand, as if she were resting her head. "My brother does it in high school, and he says he walks around all day like this—," she put her hand back to her ear, "and nobody says anything."

"On Monday Erica got like a half an hour to listen to her music until Mr. B. noticed," Jenn reported.

"Oh, he did notice?"

"Yeah, she didn't—she just, like, had it in her ear," Michelle said, noting Erica's failure to use the established best practice.

"Would your teachers ever let you listen to music?"

"No. But you can't tell the difference if we have [the earbud] in or not, so I don't see why it matters," Michelle complained.

Jenn agreed, "As long as you can hear [i.e., the teacher or the lesson], why do they care?"

I mentioned again that sometimes the boys played their Game Boys under their desks. Michelle and Jenn laughed. Michelle said, "But a Game Boy's more noticeable. Because they're like actually sitting there looking down, not concentrating."

"Kind of like when you read your own books," Jenn added, and both girls laughed.

I described one of the seventh grade boys, Zack, who "always has something in his lap. Sometimes it's a book and sometimes it's a Game Boy, but he's just always got something going on."

The girls laughed, and Jenn commented, "I don't understand how he still gets As."

After describing in detail all the ways they sneak MP3 players into class, Jenn's comment that she doesn't understand how Zack can read books or play video games while still being academically successful suggests a complex differentiation of modes of media consumption and orientations to the classroom. When the girls listened to MP3 players in class, they said, they were still doing their schoolwork or following the lesson. At a minimum they had to attend to the teacher to avoid being caught, prepared to palm the earbud and lift their heads in answer to a question. The music from the earbud was in the background of their attention, for the most part, and the girls were careful that with the other ear they participated in the group activities of class. In contrast, sometimes the girls would "read [their] own books" in class, which involved, they suggested, "not concentrating" on lessons or schoolwork. They saw that orientation as more common in the boys' classroom use of video games, which, Jenn and Michelle suggested, were totally immersive and could not accommodate simultaneous attention to the lesson and the game. So while listening in class may not have involved the same physical connections to a co-listener as sharing earbuds during free time, Jenn and Michelle suggest that it did require a similar layering of attention between music and interaction and a similarly intimate integration of the devices with kids' bodily stance and gesture. In their telling, listening to music in class would be inappropriate, and collective efforts to hide their listening were intimacy-building, but, they argued, it did not detract from the pedagogical goals of the lesson. School and media interactions might coexist, Jenn and Michelle seem to think.

Video games in the classroom: layering, interaction, attention

Jenn and Michelle emphasized the necessity of layering their attention, overlapping music listening with classroom "concentration." They seemed to identify visually focused activities like gaming and reading as demanding more attention. Jenn's bewilderment at Zack's ability to read and play games in class is parallel to the responses of many adults to the idea of listening with one ear and talking, reading, or following a lesson with the other. Here I briefly explore the sociality and interactivity of boys' gaming practices, to compare them with portable music practices and to point out that gaming, despite some qualitative differences in the forms of attention, seems to be comparably interactive and socially embedded. As I try to show here, portable gaming devices are caught up in a communicative ecology that includes passing notes, whispering, and sharing earbuds, so examining gaming devices like the Nintendo DS can provide significant context for understanding portable music. One more reason to examine games is because they are, like music players, television, and the Internet, an important repository of music and sound.

Gaming is a topic of a lot of research, though the interactions among people playing games together have received only limited attention. Stevens, Satwicz, and McCarthy (2007) develop a paradigm that distinguishes activities "in-game," "in-room," and "in-world," where the interactions "in-room" by players and people in their proximity are the link between gameplay and players' broader, "in-world" settings. Lenhart et al. (2008) point out that in correlations between gaming and measures of school and social success, the key variable seems to be whether adolescents play games alone or with other people in the same room. Both studies argue that anxious accounts of gaming as antisocial focus excessively on the "immersion" of players into the activities "in-game," when it is apparent that players in fact are able to and do attend to and participate in social situations in their immediate environment.

If sharing earbuds involves a physically intimate linkage between friends, then the general lack of boys' sharing can be understood as part of a broader masculine aversion to certain types of physical intimacy with other boys, which becomes increasingly salient as boys enter adolescence. But playing games together, without the physical tether of an earbud cable mandating proximity, was a similarly sociable activity. In out-of-class peer-group settings it was rare that a kid would play a video game in isolation, focused solely on the game. Usually games were an opportunity to do something together. Even if only one boy was playing, he would have others looking over his shoulder and commenting. So when boys played video games, rather than being sucked into the screen, there would be several kids doing something together—laughing, talking, and bouncing their talk off of what is happening on the screen. There was an intense sociability among the kids around the screen. But by contrast with the sociability of sharing earbuds in a group, in these situations the text of the game itself was usually the focus of the group's talk and attention, whereas music listening was almost always in the background of conversations about other topics.

For example, boys frequently went to websites like addictinggames .com during periods of free time in classrooms. These sites streamed simple games over the Internet, many of which have not changed since they were first developed on much earlier computer systems. One such game, probably the most popular game among the boys during the year, was *Tanks. Tanks* is a simple game where two players have one tank apiece at either end of a two-dimensional landscape. Using a variety of available weapons, they adjust force and trajectory to account for wind, distance, and topography, and they fire projectiles by turn across the small screen to try to blow up the other player's tank. With simple graphical effects, the explosions erode the landscape in bubbly circles and orange flames. At the end of a turn, the player would hand the mouse to his opponent, who would choose a weapon from the list, deliberate over angles and velocities, and eventually fire back. *Tanks* is much simpler than games like *Halo* that many kids had on their gaming consoles at home. But when two boys would play at one terminal, a crowd would often gather standing behind them, laughing at the destruction of the two-dimensional landscape, hollering out suggestions, and joining in with sound effects and comments to narrate the otherwise plodding, turn-by-turn action, despite the incredible simplicity and lack of visual spectacle on the screen. With games like *Tanks* the action and interest seemed to lay primarily in this dense back-and-forth of a group of boys imaginatively narrating the game to one another.

One day early in the year I played *Tanks* with Nate in the computer lab. He had broken his shoulder earlier that week and asked to stay in during recess to play on the computer. As we played he kept up a constant chatter. He beat me handily, and each time his weapon exploded at my tank, he commented in a heightened, chesty voice: "That was BRUtal"; "Oh man, I asSAULted you." Words like "brutal" and "assaulted," pronounced in this emphatic way, took on an expressive resonance that narrated the otherwise two-dimensional and potentially boring game with a sort of kinesthetic physicality and action. Boys had a repertoire of words like this, all marked as outside of normal vocabulary, which they used in expressive moments to narrate their lives to one another. They used words like "heretic," "traitor," "ninja," "assassin," and "midget" to describe one another, always in a heightened register that emphasized both their embodied, sounding voices and the kinetic spectacle that they worked together to add even to games that might otherwise be simple or boring.

Jenn and Michelle's picture of Zack sucked into his game, unable to concentrate on the activities of the classroom around him, reiterates the basic outline of anxious adult narratives of gaming, and it exposes their lack of knowledge about Zack's actual classroom practices (ironically, in light of their own annoyance at teachers' inability to see that they can both listen to music and read at the same time). For instance: in March I observed a science lesson about the seasons, during which the seventh- and eighth-grade teacher, Mr. B., used a flashlight and globe to examine the changing position of the sun at different points in the earth's orbit. Taking advantage of the dimmed lights and his spot toward the rear of the classroom, Zack played his Nintendo DS under his desk. When the teacher asked, "What time of year is it when the sun is pointing to the tropic of cancer?" and demonstrated on the globe, Zack raised his hand, still playing under his desk with the other hand, and answered the question when called on. He continued to participate in the lesson without ending his game. Jenn's comparison to reading was apt: Zack also read books constantly, and he would do the same thing with books in class, reading in his lap while still following and participating in the lesson.

Just like listening to music in class, playing games during a lesson put kids at risk of discipline from teachers. Zack and Mr. B. had an ongoing dispute about his reading books during class, but Mr. B. also encouraged Zack's reading. So when Mr. B. would note Zack's downward gaze and call him on it, if Zack was playing his game he would quickly swap it with a book in his desk, to cop to the lesser infraction of reading outside materials during a lesson. Kids would hide their devices in an open textbook, and slip them quickly away into the desk at a glance from the teacher. Teachers were much less sympathetic to gaming in class than to reading, passing notes, or even listening to music, and by playing games kids risked more serious punishments than the reprimands the other transgressions would elicit.

One winter morning during silent reading, eighth grader Nate looked back at me from his seat in the last row of desks and whispered, "Mr. Bickford." He showed me his DS inside a book below his desk. I smiled in acknowledgement and glanced up to see the teacher noticing our interaction. I looked away but could see from the corner of my eye that Nate was still trying to get my attention, not aware of the teacher's look. Across the room, Ben was also playing his DS, with his head resting on his desk. Nate gave up on getting my attention and the teacher looked away. I noticed that Ben and Nate kept looking over at each other, laughing quietly through their noses. Ben quickly hid his device under his desk as his brother, seventh grader Willy, walked past on his way to the bathroom, apparently hyper-cautious about drawing too much attention rather than concerned that Willy might disapprove and alert the teacher.

Sitting next to Ben, Randy watched him play, without a book or anything to disguise his attention. As Nate and Ben exchanged another look, Nate saw me observing. He smiled and nodded proudly, and smiled at Willy as he returned from the bathroom—showing off, less worried than Ben. Randy took out his own Game Boy Micro and started to play, but the click of his keys seemed much louder than the other devices. The teacher, reading, cleared his throat, and all three game-playing boys started and hid their devices in their desks.

Seeing all was clear, Nate looked back at me and pointed to Ben, mouthing the words, "I'm playing with him."

I mouthed back, "You're playing with Ben?"

He nodded, impressed with himself, and looked back down at his device. The DS can connect wirelessly with other devices.

Ben kept looking over to Nate, wanting to whisper something, but Nate was now making an effort not to look up so much to avoid calling attention to himself—the teacher's cough alerting him to the risk of being caught. Both boys displayed a strong inclination to interact through words and gesture—not just through the gameplay itself but by responding to the gameplay action by communicating directly across the room. Interacting silently, just through gameplay, was not a familiar mode for them.

Nate and Ben continued to play without getting caught until the bell rang for recess. At recess Nate told me they were playing "battle mode" on the game *Mario Kart*, and bragged to me a bit about what they just got away with. He told me about how the DS also allows for wireless chatting, using a stylus to send handwritten notes to other nearby devices—but which would not work for commenting during ongoing gameplay.

That evening was the middle-school dance. I had volunteered as the DJ, and since dancing was not necessarily an appealing activity for the boys in attendance, Nate came and talked to me on the stage for a while. He asked me why I write about their Game Boys in my notebook all the time. I told him that I try to write down as much as possible what happened during the day, and I was interested in media devices like MP3 players and Game Boys, and in how they fit into their lives at school, so getting away with stuff like that in class was especially relevant.

Nate asked me if I wrote about the incident, a couple days earlier, when Willy and Sam had thrown peanuts pilfered from the lunchroom at me while the teacher was briefly out of the room, testing the limits of transgressions I would be willing to forgive and/or not rat them out about to their teacher. Nate laughed when I told him that I did write about that, and he called over to Willy to tell him that I had recorded the incident. It seems that they had gossiped and bragged about it among themselves afterward, savoring having pegged an adult—a quasi-teacher—with projectiles *during class*. The incident framed that day's in-class gaming in terms of rule breaking and transgression, and at my question Nate adopted a formal tone and told my recorder that, "DS's help us kids, mainly kids, communicate to each other in class, during reading. Yes, that's right, during class, the teacher unknowingly knowing [i.e., unaware] that we are doing it. The reason why we do this is [so] the teacher does not see us pass notes, which basically cancels the note passing. Also we don't have to talk over anybody, which also get us in trouble. This is the end of our segment. Good-bye."

A few days earlier I had watched as Daisy and Michelle made Nate the middle man in a marathon of back-and-forth note passing that lasted almost half an hour. Nate was clearly uncomfortable being put in jeopardy with someone else's illicit notes, and he was almost caught holding the note when Mr. B. finally witnessed the exchange and reprimanded the girls. After class he told Daisy, "You guys should get DS's." At the dance I asked about his comment to Daisy, and he told me, "With the DS's . . . you don't even have to move or throw anything. It's so much easier. And they call us geeks. I mean come on—it has it's advantages." This despite the almost urgent need shown by Nate and his friends to add a layer of talk and sound effects to their gameplay, even when playing wirelessly on their portable devices.

Apparently there was a strong mutual misunderstanding between some of the older boys and older girls about each other's communication and media practices. Jenn and Michelle could not understand Zack and the other boys playing games during class because they assumed it would distract from their school work (just as teachers would not understand Jenn and Michelle's music listening for the same reasons). And Nate here could not understand the girls' dismissal of the obvious advantages of devices like his DS for surreptitious communication during class. Nate was probably wrong that old-fashioned notes did not measure up to wireless devices for in-class communication, especially when weighing the severity of getting caught with a note (relatively minor) versus a Game Boy (serious). It is interesting to note Nate's nervousness about being caught with other people's notes in contrast to his enthusiasm for really much riskier uses of portable gaming devices.

Despite their mutual misunderstandings, Jenn, Michelle, and Nate suggest that in kids' minds music listening, gaming, and note passing are relatively interchangeable, or at least comparable, though they come with different affordances that could be measured against different scenarios or using different assumptions. Each practice is understood specifically as a transgression of teachers' expectations for the classroom, while at the same time no one suggests that this would be a reason not to listen to music, pass notes, or play video games. Importantly, though both video games and music listening have the potential for individual immersive isolation, students appear to be as critical of that possibility as adults and defensive when accused that their own media practices might be isolating and detrimental to learning. For the girls, reading a book would be more deleterious to learning than listening to music, even though reading, of course, is a pedagogically sanctioned activity in a way that popular music listening almost never is.

Media, "multitasking," and social differentiation

These kids are weighing in on a broader conversation about "multitasking," and also about "backchannel" communication using digital media in classroom or lecture settings (Yardi 2008; McCarthy and boyd 2005). Of course, the media in question are MP3 players and Game Boys rather than online chat rooms or social networking sites, and Jenn and Michelle don't make a rhetorical appeal to the progressive promise of digital media for transcending interactional limitations of the classroom so much as they find themselves conducting a rearguard action in defense of practices long since staked out by middle-school kids. Backchannel communication in a classroom setting is precisely what "peers" have always attempted and what teachers have always forbidden. Turning one's attention and communication, however briefly, away from the teacher at the head of the class and toward one's classmates is perhaps the canonical move of "peer culture." Certainly such communication restructures IRE frameworks (see chapter 1) away from a teacher-focused orientation or toward a peer-focused one. Sharing earbuds materializes such a move with cables and speakers, but it may be more generally understood as characteristic of children's investments in childhood intimacies and their relative resistance to adult-structured environments.

The examples discussed here suggest rather many different modes of layering attention, all of which might be called "multitasking." Multitasking is frequently associated with children and especially with the exoticizing discourses around technology and "digital natives" (Herring 2008). Hence a 2006 *Time* magazine article titled "The Multitasking Generation," which quotes a fourteen-year-old girl saying, "My parents always tell me I can't do homework while listening to music, but they don't understand that it helps me concentrate" (Wallis 2006). While discourses of multitasking often foreground the question of individuals' abilities to use more than one medium at a time, multitasking may be better understood as a discourse focused on social difference. The salient issue here is not individuals' objective capacities but rather their subjective evaluations of one another's practices of layering attention to media, peers, and classroom lessons. To the extent that "multitasking" is relevant here (since the examples discussed support rather many different modes of layered attention), it is as part of these discourses of criticism and incomprehension that are an important trope in kids' performances of gender difference. The interesting point with multitasking is less whether it is "real" or "effective" or "detrimental" to some specified educational goals than that it seems to stand as an important element in individuals' and groups' misunderstandings of one another, and in their expressions of affiliation and differentiation.

Thinking of multitasking in terms of misunderstanding between individuals from different social groups is the key move here, which is apparent as well in HCS students' discourse. Even when we account for the expressions of incomprehension between girls and boys at HCS, it is clear that the primary distinction they see implicated in multitasking is between children and adults—thus taking on themselves the exoticizing representations placed on them by adult commentators. As multitasking refers to the layering of attention among different, immediate contexts, it makes sense to understand it as part of the broader framework of intimacy and instrumentality outlined in chapter 1—at least insofar as instrumental communication, like essayist literacy and IRE interactions, constructs itself as monologic and decontextualized, and has no brief for "distraction." Therefore, the overall point is that these practices are about setting out the terms of individual and group identifications, and media use can again be seen as central to the construction of children's social roles and affiliations.

Most importantly, "multitasking" in most cases was not simply about individuals doing two different tasks at once, it also highlighted orientations toward intimate peer sociality in contrast with an instrumental classroom order. Kids proudly displayed their in-class music listening or game playing to one another, they kept track and reported on each other's successes, and they shared best practices for getting away with rule breaking. For most students, bringing media into class was not simply about consuming pleasurable materials but also about articulating and strengthening connections with one another. Adult efforts to limit multitasking were framed around cognitive focus, but they also asked kids to orient toward teachers and toward the instrumental IRE structure of classroom lessons, and not to orient toward their peers or friends. In effect, they asked schoolchildren to inhabit the identity of students and to leave behind the identity of kids.

CHAPTER 5
Inappropriate and Inarticulate

MP3 players and earbuds afforded certain modes of intimate interaction, they were embedded within specifically "childish" material traditions, and in school musical media practices were charged with heightened meaning about children's relationship to adult authority. Because elementary school's pedagogical emphasis on literacy and communication already privileged language and expressivity as a field of action, expressive repertoires from entertainment media provided a powerful resource for HCS kids to challenge adult authority and claim childhood as a space of opposition, intimacy, and solidarity. Media practices were organized with expressive repertoires linked to school's bureaucratic social structure, such as "swearing," at one extreme, and instrumental "essayist literacy," at the other. By contrast with literacy education's decontextualized and monologic modes of essayist writing and IRE classroom routines, children's everyday performances revealed distinctive poetic registers—"inappropriateness" and "inarticulateness"—linked to digital technology and entertainment media that emphasized intimacy, interactivity, and embodied indexicality. "Inappropriateness" and "inarticulateness" were the master tropes of the intimately expressive repertoire that opposed school's instrumental communication and claimed childhood as its defining element.

Expressive repertoires

Certain expressive repertoires were codified and named as markers of students' intimate and oppositional identifications as "kids." One of these repertoires was swearing. On the first day of school in September, immediately after eighth graders Amber and Daisy finished their spectacular demonstration of swinging together while sharing earbuds (discussed in the beginning of chapter 2), Daisy looked up at me and asked, by way of introduction, "Do you swear?"

I was already awkward and uncomfortable on my first day at HCS, and I was caught off guard. I indirectly agreed that, okay, like lots of people, sure I swear sometimes. "Why do you ask?"

"Well the only people who don't swear are preps, and you're kind of dressed like a prep. I hate preps." (In slacks and a dress shirt purchased for this occasion, I was a bit overdressed.) Daisy swore gratuitously a couple times, watching me for a reaction. Amber, who I would later learn almost never used strong language (but whom Daisy would not classify as a prep, either), winced. I didn't, and that seemed enough for Daisy.

My training and research interests prepared me to expect language to be a strong marker of kids' affiliation and differentiation, but I was surprised to encounter so early and directly such a challenge to my own identity and language use. I realized later that by catching me off guard and forcing me to make a public declaration that I do, indeed, swear, Daisy had set the terms of my role at HCS for the rest of the year, forcing me to declare an allegiance to the school's kids rather than the adults. Through the rest of the year my unwillingness to censure students' language, a hand forced early on by Daisy's insistent challenge, regularly opened relationships even with kids who themselves may not have been regular swearers: they'd start upon hearing a friend swear in my presence, gesture meaningfully toward me, and relax only when informed that, "It's okay, he doesn't care." Daisy's question, which might have seemed challenging or hostile, was also a way of opening a door to let me in, something that I couldn't really do without this sort of prompting. And it pointed to a very real experience of everyday suspicion, watchfulness, and surveillance as kids monitored their own and their peers' language to avoid adult censure and cultivate relatively closed communities of expressive practice among friends and peers. Swearing, in this context, was as intimate as sharing earbuds—it required a level of trust in one's interlocutors, to whom swearers exposed themselves to potentially serious repercussions.

So a willingness to swear or not was a marker of some sort of oppositional affiliation, but the terms of that oppositionality can be further specified. Daisy's question, "Do you swear?" in part asked, "What kind of adult are you?" Every detail of language and behavior is carefully monitored by adults in school—"literacy," after all, is perhaps the central pedagogical focus of elementary public education—and Daisy legitimately desired to know whether she would have to be on guard in my presence. But when prompted, Daisy framed the available roles for me not as a choice between, say, an authoritative and uptight teacher and a "cool" adult but rather through reference to definitively *youthful* categories: "prep" versus what I'd eventually learn Daisy would term "normal people" (Eckert 1989). These sorts of social categories only really articulate to young people; it is not clear what an adult "prep" would be at all.[1]

Swearing was a marker of a social identity that had clear relevance within an institutional context where expression is strictly and continuously monitored for "appropriateness." But the identity that swearing marked—"normal people"—was limited to young people, and the irony of this is apparent: vulgarity is an expressive repertoire normatively understood to be the province of adults. Children swearing is simply and categorically "inappropriate," but for Daisy, swearing was precisely how one would demonstrate her affiliation with particular groups of children. In the rest of this chapter I explore how this apparent contradiction makes sense from a perspective that sees intimate communicative orientations defined dialectically with instrumental ones. From this view, vulgarity, and associated forms, can be understood as a classically childish genre. Noting that swearing is not an independently constituted expressive genre that in and of itself acquires this articulation to kids' peer society, this chapter explores some of the suggestions that resonate from Daisy's juxtaposition of her defiantly athletic swinging-while-sharing-earbuds and her confrontational performance of vulgarity. There is a fundamental connection between modes of interaction that involve entertainment and media technology, like sharing earbuds, and modes of communication that locate participants as children within an institutional regime governed by adults: the former are a prominent instance of the latter.

As forms of interaction, kids' modes of listening are constitutive elements in their repertoires of expression. As the examples in the remainder of this chapter demonstrate, a distinction between active and passive expression breaks down immediately upon analysis. Instead, music listening turns out to be a mode of communication very much like swearing. All of these elements comprise a larger expressive repertoire that can broadly be characterized as "intimate." Intimacy, in the sense I outline in chapter 1, is only intelligible as part of an even broader ecology of school communication in which it is dialectically opposed to instrumentality. Two key features of intimate communication are important to the co-construction of school and childhood. The first, "inappropriateness," has been suggested in the preceding discussion of swearing. "Appropriate" and "inappropriate" are ubiquitous terms in school, and they are by far the most common frame for evaluating behavior. Like swearing, inappropriateness is constituted negatively, as a rejection of school or adult guidelines for communication, but also affirmatively, as a positive expression of some characteristic childishness. The second element, following Ray McDermott (1988), is "inarticulateness," which is connected to vulgar forms like swearing and is similarly defined in opposition to many of the communicative specifications of the classroom but also involves its own unique and creative expressive modes.

Inappropriate

A key form of "inappropriate" expression at HCS involved MP3 players and sharing earbuds for the simple reason that earbuds allowed kids to listen to music with explicit language that would otherwise be forbidden at school. For example, one morning in January, Kathy explained to me that she decided not to bring her iDog speakers to school because too many of the songs on her MP3 player were "unedited"—that is, full of strong language that had not been edited out into a "clean" version. It would be pointless to bring speakers to school, because listening to such unedited music on them would only invite censure from surrounding adults.

An illustration of the power of portable music devices for underground and "inappropriate" communication among intimates took place one day in March. That morning, as I stood by the stage with a few second-grade boys gathered around a Game Boy playing a Pokémon game, two sixth graders, Kelly and Melissa, broke off from a large group of girls and worked their way across the crowded court, confidently stepping up and saying "hi" to me. They pushed their way in front the second graders to talk to me, and the younger boys' group broke up and went in search of a ball to play with. Kelly remembered that Megan had not heard the "Discovery Channel" song (actually "Bad Touch" by the Bloodhound Gang), so Kelly gestured to Becky to get out her MP3 player. Becky carefully unwound the cord and passed the earbuds to Megan, as she and Kelly bent over the LCD screen to find the song. As it played, Kelly took one of the earbuds from Megan and listened along. Melissa piped in from the edge of this group and asked me if I knew what the song is about, and Kelly responded for me by quoting the chorus, "Do it like they do on the Discovery Channel." Trying to wink and nod, and to avoid directly acknowledging the wordplay and innuendo, I said, "Oh, ha ha, I can guess." But Melissa didn't think I got the reference and confidently told me, "No, you have to hear the song to get it." Kelly quoted a lyric really fast that I did not understand—from the chorus, presumably—and with a significant look Melissa chimed in: "It's about mammals—mammals." In the meantime, Amber and Alice had wandered over to join this emerging group. Alice

Figure 5.1: Sixth graders listening to "Bad Touch" on Becky's MP3 player.

pulled out her own MP3 player and passed an earbud to Melissa. Amber popped up onto the stage to sit quietly, and I turned to chat with her. So there were six girls, two players, four earbuds, eight ears (figure 5.1). Shortly it was time for class.

Later that day at lunch, I sat with Melissa, Becky, Kelly, and Daisy. Kelly (who led her friends more through gregariousness and initiative than popularity or consensus) took this opportunity to educate me about the "Discovery Channel" song, again gesturing to Becky to unwind her MP3 player. Kelly took the earbuds and handed me one, keeping the other for herself—so now I was in the same configuration as Megan was that morning, with Kelly "showing" me a new song on the MP3 player owned and held by Becky. The song has a long instrumental intro, and Becky asked repeatedly, "Have the words started yet?" Kelly, listening, said, "No," and Becky expressed a bit of nervousness in anticipation. When the singing finally did start, Kelly informed Becky, who groaned and blushed. In fact, the lyrics are pretty explicit:

> Sweat, baby, sweat, baby
> Sex is a Texas drought
> Me and you do the kind of stuff
> That only Prince would sing about

So put your hands down my pants
And I'll bet you'll feel nuts
. . .

. . .
I want you smothered, want you covered
Like my Waffle House hashbrowns

Come quicker than FedEx
Never reach an apex just like Coca-Cola stock
You are inclined to make me rise an hour early
Just like Daylight Savings Time

You and me, baby, ain't nothin' but mammals
So let's do it like they do on the Discovery Channel[2]

Daisy, next to me, gestured to Kelly to let her listen, so Kelly handed over her earpiece, and Daisy and I listened through the first verse and chorus. I had trouble following the song and the talk, and I missed some of the more explicit lyrics, while Kelly, Melissa, and Becky laughed as they repeated "Discovery Channel" and the "nothin' but mammals" line. Daisy monitored this talk while she listened, correcting them every time they called it the "Discovery Channel" song: "It's called 'Bad Touch.'" When I asked where they got the song, Becky sheepishly told me she "stole" it from her parents.

As Becky and Kelly looked at me expectantly and with some embarrassment, I realized just how explicit the song was. Despite having not really said anything at all, I seemed to find myself in the midst of a rather graphic discourse about sex. Despite the title, I was caught off guard and embarrassed myself, when this song turned out to be as explicit as it is, so I handed the earpiece back to Kelly. I was relieved to be back in my normal position and part of the (sometimes winking and nodding) talk and action but not necessarily privy to the private channels of the girls' headphones. At the same time I was surprised at how comfortably the girls initially were in including me in their appreciation of this song, though Becky, like me, seemed to quickly get embarrassed. While sometimes kids would hand an earbud over in response to my unending questions about what they were listening to, this was the first time that I was offered one unprompted.

Other songs that seemed to have enough interest for kids to make a point of having me hear them were 2007's "The Gummy Bear Song," by German act Gummibär, and "Barbie Girl," the 1997 European bubblegum pop song by Aqua. Like "Bad Touch," both are novelty songs, jokey and built around the gimmicky use of a "childish" candy or doll as a central image. Another favorite song was from a segment of the irreverent cartoon comedy *The Family Guy* that included the line, "Ding! Fries are done," sung to the ostinato melody of "Carol of the Bells." As the music teacher I had had the students play "Carol of the Bells" on Orff xylophones for the school's holiday concert in December, and the synergy between that school-based lesson and a favorite television show led to the "fries are done" version being sung often throughout the winter. There were also songs with intensely sexual content—Akon's "Smack That" and "I Wanna Love You," for instance—that were listened to widely during the 2007–2008 school year. But unlike the novelty songs these were rarely talked about, and kids did not repeat and relish the lyrics the way Kelly, Melissa, and Becky repeated the lyrics to "Bad Touch" while Daisy and I listened. Similarly, the hit song "Crank Dat" by Soulja Boy—which, along with an accompanying dance, was hugely popular at HCS and around the country in 2007–2008—has as its chorus the line "Superman that ho" (rendered in the "clean" version as "Superman that—oh!"). The dance step at "Superman" involves leaning forward on one foot with arms spread wide, miming a comic hero flying through the air. But the lyrics were rumored to use "Superman" in an extremely vulgar and misogynistic sense to refer to an explicit and humiliating sex act. Through meaningful looks, giggles, blushing, and whispering, a handful of seventh and eighth graders made clear that they knew about this sense of the term. For most of the kids this meaning remained obscure, so the song was only inflected with a nonspecific valence of impropriety, and it was really the reference to a comic book superhero that helped it fit comfortably in this childish milieu. Remix versions of "Crank Dat" circulated on the Internet, substituting other cartoon and comic characters—Spiderman, Batman, Spongebob, Casper the Friendly Ghost, Alvin and the Chipmunks. These led to new, vulgar meanings for those characters being created to fit, but again, HCS students' enjoyment of these new versions seemed to derive specifically from a delight in the ironic inflection of childish images as potential expressions of vulgarity than as a simple interest in vulgarity as such.

The Bloodhound Gang's whole oeuvre is particularly "childish" or "immature." (The name "Bloodhound Gang" itself comes from a kids' TV show on PBS.) Tossing around the catchphrases—"Do it like they do on the Discovery Channel" and "You and me baby ain't nothin' but mammals"—despite Daisy's repeated corrections that the song's name was (the less funny) "Bad Touch," the girls appreciated the cleverness of the lines as much as they reveled in the transgressive meaning, "savoring" (Tannen 1989:64) the complex articulation of sexuality through mention of animals, a canonical topic of school and childhood discourse, and the Discovery Channel, a television network that is particularly "child-friendly" and educational.

(Not to mention common brand names—Coca Cola, Waffle House—that kids would be familiar with, and playground games like "two-hand touch" football.) When Melissa pointed out that morning that "you have to hear the song to get it," she underscored the idea that there was *something to get*, a punchline or pun that rearticulated mundane school topics with a sexually heightened poetics. This punning core is what made the song worth sharing, not simply its explicit content. In fact, with a few exceptions, the song is not properly "explicit": it is full of punning innuendo, ribald and audacious in the length it goes to stretch its metaphors. Connecting this back to Daisy's interest in swearing as a shibboleth for youthful belonging, explicit language is only of interest to kids once it is inflected *as* childish, which takes place through wordplay and ironic inversions. Classic, adult visions of innocent childhoods are turned on their heads as material for a new and independent expression of childishness that uses the power of that expectation of innocence to enjoy its inversion even more. Ironic play with the tropes of childishness may be a key characteristic of kids' understandings of childishness.[3]

It is important to distinguish between this sort of punning and euphemistic sexualized content and more literal or properly explicit songs about sex. Sexual innuendo is squarely part of the fantastic, silly, violent, and "irrational" elements of children's culture that Sutton-Smith (1997) terms phantasmagoria. In chapter 1 I argued that phantasmagoria is a master trope of childish expressive traditions. Sexually suggestive rhymes and verse that use innuendo to thematicize love, marriage, sex, and pregnancy have long histories in the singing and clapping games of children around the world: for example, "I jumped in the lake and swallowed a snake / And came up with a bellyache" and "Boys have got the muscles / Teachers got the brains / Girls have got the sexy legs / And here we go again" (Grugeon 2001:100; see also Ackerley 2007). The snake-bellyache image makes use of tropes similar to those of "Bad Touch," where animals or childish illnesses ("bellyache") clearly but euphemistically suggest phallic and sexual imagery. US popular music has a long history of incorporating characters, themes, and texts from children's literature and folklore into mainstream, commercial songs (Cooper 1989; K. Marsh 2006). That similar ideas, built out of similar repertoires of childish metaphors ("You and me baby ain't nothin' but mammals"), are here mediated through technology and popular music has two contrary effects. On the one hand, whereas playground rhymes might be disseminated entirely through peer-to-peer networks of children, here the mediations of commerce and technology implicate adults—the rock-star members of the Bloodhound Gang and presumably amoral, profit-seeking Hollywood corporations—carrying suggestions of improper "influence" since media and popular culture have long been the subject of moral panics about childhood (not to mention the parents from whom the recording was surreptitiously copied). On the other hand, as the girls passed earbuds among their group, savoring the innuendo of obscure lines about TV and animals that are only elaborated in the private channels of the headphones, they further complicated the layers of secret and public talk, official and unofficial discourse, and the open and underground channels of communication that characterize school (Hubbard 1989).

Here we can begin to see how generic or tropological considerations—"immature" and "inappropriate" songs that make use of specifically phantasmagoric and childish images—are linked to modes of communication and interaction. Identifying the cultural configurations enacted in the girls' interest in "Bad Touch" requires pointing out the layering of communicative channels of talk and listening that accommodated such transgressions, and the girls' ability to use their media devices to selectively cross boundaries by, say, including me and not other adults. Sharing MP3 players, then goes hand in hand with whispering and passing notes, such that children's modes of communication are parallel and necessary to these punning poetics and play with childish tropes of animals and comics.

On the other hand, the privacy afforded by headphones was only necessary in everyday school situations where adults would actively monitor and regulate the sounds kids and their devices made. So Melissa made a point of bringing her portable, battery-powered speakers along with her MP3 player to the eighth-grade graduation ceremony in June (held the evening before the last day of school). After the ceremony, her friends gathered around her and she played Alice Cooper's "School's Out" as loud as she could—an "inappropriate" song that I, in my capacities operating the sound equipment, had refused to play over the loudspeakers, but in its way definitely "appropriate" to the occasion.

Content and form

While adjectives like "childish" or "puerile" or "silly" or "phantasmagorical" help characterize the genre of texts that make up the content that circulates in this intimate sphere of children's friendships, I choose to name this genre "inappropriate," partly because that's the word that kids themselves might use to describe these texts and also to foreground the institutional context that charges this underground circulation with heightened affective and social power. Inappropriate content like "Bad Touch" depends on these private channels of communication for its circulation, and the transgressive character of such content in turn charges those private communicative channels with a powerfully social intimacy.

There is a constitutive association here between form and content, where the embodied and intimate channels of communication afforded by MP3 players and other such devices create a privileged space for the circulation of particular types of media content linked to childhood. Following McDermott (1988), I call the form in which these inappropriate materials circulate "inarticulate." This term emphasizes children's refusal of institutional modes of discourse that place competence and fluency over other values. Inarticulateness in McDermott's sense does not mean inability or incompetence. Rather it highlights the refusal or rejection of norms of intelligibility and coherence and the performance of alternatives. I hesitate to identify those alternatives as simply articulate or fluent according to their own standards, though of course they are largely successful and competent communicative interventions. But in their own structure the performances that I will call "inarticulate" here seem to reject those sorts of evaluative criteria altogether, and perhaps they suggest other ways for utterances to be valuable. Even though kids themselves wouldn't use this term, I would suggest that something like intentional and solidary inarticulateness really does describe their own motivations in pursuing these intimate modes of circulation in the context of school.

Mutterances

In the fall of 2008, after my full-time field work concluded, I returned to Heartsboro and sat in on art class, where the teacher was dedicating time during a couple of early classes to establish the rules and procedures that would govern behavior for the coming year. For the second and third graders she explained the "take-a-break" chair she had set up in a corner. She demonstrated the procedure, tapping herself on the shoulder and calmly, with an air of dejection, walking over to the chair, emphasizing quiet, orderly acquiescence. This sort of teacher-pretending-to-be-a-student routine will usually elicit an enthusiastic response from younger students who thrill at the idea of adults as children. So, as the teacher walked to the chair, two third-grade boys sang "*WAH WAH WAH WAH*," like the "sad trombone"/"You lose!" music from a cartoon or video game (figure 5.2). And before the teacher had a chance to correct them, the whole class perked up in recognition of the appropriateness of the sound effect to the situation being acted out, and everyone raised their voices and pointed their fingers: "*WAH WAH WAH WAAAAAH*." The teacher talked over the kids, trying to point out how such a response from the class would probably hurt the feelings of a person going to the take-a-break chair (in this situation, the teacher herself). But as she talked, the first boy looked at his classmates

Figure 5.2: "Sad Trombone."

and said, "Come on, on 'three'—one, two, three!" And he waved his arms to conduct the whole class together in shouting, "*WAH WAH WAAAAH!*" The teacher continued calmly to settle the class as individuals repeated the melody, laughing. Third grader Jake said, to no one in particular, "I think it sounds like a video game, like when you get a gutterball." The kids all laughed at how appropriately the familiar musical trope from media was applied to this real-world situation, taking pleasure in their "competent" performance (cf. Bauman 1975). They collectively defied and thus undermined the teacher's immediate instructional point thematizing quiet and order in response to discipline. And in ganging up as a class to point fingers and ridicule, they performed a familiar negative aspect of the peer solidarity they cultivated so assiduously.

Joining together in this way they didn't just invert the normal teacher-student power dynamics to put themselves on top, they also replaced one interactional frame with another. Initially framed as a behavior management lesson in support of official learning goals that identify "art" as a unique subject to be broken up into a hierarchy of skills and taught in sequence to individuated students whose competence is presumptively limited (Austin, Dwyer, and Freebody 2003), they reframed the situation as a video game. It became an exuberant performance not of individual development and acquisition of componential skills but rather of group solidarity, a shared experience of repetitive media consumption, and a strong sense of the value and pleasure of silliness. Their collective outburst bears out Halberstam's (2011) argument that the phantasmagorical imagery and spectacular silliness of children's media is deeply linked to a richly imagined politics of collectivity that refuses narratives of individual development to explore instead alternative and non-institutional modes of sociality and solidarity.

The students also positioned themselves at least momentarily against the dominant institutional mode of language use and communication in school, "essayist literacy" (discussed in chapter 1). On another occasion, during a social studies lesson on the Civil War, the seventh- and eighth-grade teacher asked the class, "What did the South do in response to Lincoln resupplying Fort Sumter?" Before anyone could raise their hand and be called on, seventh grader Willy piped in loudly: "They were like, '*Noooooo*!' '*Arrrrrgh*!' '*NINJA*!' and they attacked them!" Like the second and third graders' "sad trombone" outburst, Willy's interjection was not simply an absurd non sequitur, and he was not just bringing a comfortable repertoire to bear on uncomfortable material. Rather, he did something socially and interactively more powerful: he reframed the class material in terms of the spectacle and narrative structure of video games, comic books, and children's TV shows—in which anger and incitement to violence might trigger the transformation of an ordinary person into a superhero with such sound effects (think the Incredible Hulk), or the assumption of a "ninja" identity to address a fighting scenario.[4] Rather than reply to the teacher's third-person *initiation* with an equally third-person *response*, Willy's reply was in the form of direct reported speech (Voloshinov 1986 [1929]), such that Willy himself spoke in the narratively heightened voice of the Southerners. Thus he theatricalized the characteristically decontextualized frames of classroom IRE interactions (discussed in chapter 1), in which everyone talks in the abstract about some third thing, transforming it into a dramatic space of performance that linked his own voice and body to spectacular narrative media and characteristically childish noise and vocal play.

Later during the same class the teacher listed some Civil War vocabulary words on the board—"Union," "Dixie," "Confederate"—and when he got to "blue" and "gray," Nate shouted out, "Blue versus Red!" Nate's friend Sam piped in. "Blue versus Red! Kill the Reds! Kill the Reds!"—quoting lines from a popular Internet cartoon made using footage from the even more popular video game *Halo*.[5] Like Willy moments before, these boys rearticulated the IRE classroom interaction in order to share an enthusiastic wordplay with one another linked to video games. Both outbursts during that class deployed knowledgeable participation in gaming culture as an immediate expression of solidarity and intimacy with a small number of close and physically present friends, while powerfully asserting the ability to order the interactional structure of the classroom according to values they chose.

Thus the classroom was less a space for imparting expressive ideologies to children than it was a site of continual contestation between repertoires of sound and expressivity governing when, where, and how noise, talk, and media use would frustrate or facilitate the goals and procedures of classroom instruction. Such contest was a prominent, audible force in the social organization of school, yielding a dynamic tension between peer sociability, consumption, and instruction to produce the complex, stratified, and mutable orderings of kids and adults, friends and peers, girls and boys, and older and younger. The power relations between kids, schools, and media played out in everyday interactions, where "silly" and sociable vocalizations overlapped with and incorporated entertainment forms from MP3s, the Internet, video games, and broadcast media, challenging communicative repertoires learned and enforced in the classroom.

I want to connect such moments in which media-related sounds intervene in classroom lessons to what Ray McDermott calls "mutterances":

> apparently disruptive, disorganized, or otherwise nonsensical moves on the parts of the children often precisely at the moments when it is their turn to perform some task: moves such as a whine, a curse, a scream, a burp, a gaze away, a silence, something in the eye, a wisecrack, a complaint; tasks such as answering, getting a turn, taking a turn, reading, or simply showing attention. (1988:48)

In contrast with decontextualized essayist literacy, mutterances only take on meaning as deeply contextualized responses to specific social situations. While the childish media-oriented content of these outbursts was clearly inappropriate to the classroom context, in their form they rejected IRE and essayist modes of discourse in favor of one that was broadly illegible to the IRE order of the classroom. And in fact, while Willy's "ninja" response was essentially a correct answer to the question posed—the South did respond aggressively to Lincoln's resupplying Fort Sumter—the teacher neither acknowledged Willy's outburst for its demonstration of content mastery nor sanctioned it as inappropriate. Instead he simply ignored it and closed the IRE routine with an evaluation of another student's more properly phrased response. In doing so the teacher arranged, as McDermott puts it, to hear less of Willy's "request for action" (1988:50), and thereby reinscribed the official non-recognition of such ways of speaking as "inarticulate." Another way to phrase this is to say that Willy prominently displayed what Ben Rampton identifies as a "commitment to school knowledge often combined with a lack of regard for procedural decorum managed by the teacher" (2006:31). Content and knowledge, for both the teacher and the student, seemed to take a back seat here to disputes over procedure, decorum, and appropriateness. Examples like these suggest that the nonsensical moves McDermott points to often have specific *content* beyond the social power of their interruption, and that content, in many cases, is linked to entertainment media. Kids' expressive and communicative culture points to a strong link between between entertainment media and the ideological construction of childhood as an oppositional identity.[6]

Inarticulate

In these examples, spectacular tropes from video games and digital narratives provide the inappropriate content that marks children's performances as inarticulate in their form, in part by emphasizing horizontal solidarities between children as against hierarchical relationships with adults (Hey

2002). As the "Bad Touch" example suggests, kids' talk about the music they listened to was, more often than not, indexical or imitative. They might repeat notable phrases and orient their shared attention toward a song, but rarely would they discuss or describe the music they listened to in non-indexical, third-person terms. In chapter 3, I noted that Randy claimed not to even know the names of the songs he recorded from TV. Similarly, everyone but Daisy persisted in calling "Bad Touch" the "Discovery Channel Song"—repeating the prominent funny phrase immediately audible in the chorus rather than acknowledging an otherwise unheard title. Labeling and describing are central characteristics of "essayist literacy," and in this section I explore how discursive practices around popular music that *avoid* such tropes of decontextualization might be understood as intimate, childish interventions in an educational regime of instrumental communication. So in a final example I want to explore how digital technologies themselves may mediate even embodied, intimate interactions between children.

In January I sat down with sixth graders Kelly and Melissa for an interview. Melissa had brought her Ilo MP3 player—a brand made exclusively for Walmart—and it served as a useful prop. My recording of the interview includes constant low-level music from the earbuds resting on the table, and the conversation changed direction several times in response to the MP3 players' output. I had been trying to think about popular music as cultural capital, but the processes by which songs and artists took on currency among the kids seemed random and unstructured. I spent several minutes asking ill-formed questions about how particular music becomes popular among HCS students, and Melissa and Kelly were clearly getting frustrated. We were very friendly, and they were happy to get out of their silent-reading period to chat with me about music. But they were definitely not interested in using this free time to analyze the social structures that informed their taste. Kelly repeatedly personalized my questions about classic rock bands whose popularity I had been surprised by, telling me that she liked AC/DC and other bands because of her dad, whereas I was looking for answers about why *so many* students, regardless of their parents' tastes, seemed interested in classic rock. By contrast, Melissa gave in to my questions with frustration in her voice, telling me that "people at the school who are interested in music tell each other, and then like they listen to it on like the radio." By the tone of her voice it was clear that Melissa was telling me what I wanted to hear, and she had no interest in thinking further about the circulation of music in her peer relationships. Neither the pat abstraction and generality of this answer nor the specificity of Kelly's references to her dad really seemed to address the particular mechanics of taste in peer culture that I was hoping to get at. I found repeatedly in situations like this that students were much more likely to have clear ideas about how music fit into their families than how it fit into their friendships.

So when a song by the band Evanescence began playing from Melissa's earbuds, I tried a new approach, focusing on a specific situation. Melissa was a close friend of Daisy, an eighth grader, with whom she would spend time outside of school, since they lived near one another. Both girls also shared a strong interest in Evanescence, and I asked if their interest might correlate somehow with their friendship. Melissa flatly denied any connection between her friendship with Daisy and their shared interest in Evanescence—either that their shared musical affinity might reflect personalities compatible to friendship, or that their existing friendship might lead to similar musical tastes. As I asked her repeated iterations of the question, getting frustrated myself that her responses were increasingly reduced to monosyllabic nos and ums, Kelly interrupted to ask, "Who is—what is Evanescence?" (Kelly and Melissa were close friends, too, and Kelly's lack of shared knowledge about music Melissa liked seems to support Melissa's point that friendship did not necessarily correlate with musical interest.)

Unlike her reluctance to answer my questions, Melissa responded immediately to Kelly's question, handing her over an earbud. "This, ready?" She pressed a button to start the song over.

I interrupted, hoping that maybe *this* might be a (culturally appropriate) situation for getting Melissa to talk in detail about her music. "Wait," I said to Melissa, trying to prevent her from pressing play. "Can you describe the group?"

"Errr . . . rock?"

"Well, how would you explain it to Kelly if you couldn't play it for her?"

But Melissa had already turned to Kelly and introduced the song as Kelly tucked the earbud in her ear, "Kelly, this is the best song ever—"

I objected, again, trying to get Melissa to talk about the music. Playing the song for Kelly would not produce the sort of discourse about music I thought I needed to record and analyze. I switched to my teacher voice, sharply: "Wait. Hold on. Stop. Before you press play, I'm curious about this. What if you didn't have your player right here, and she wanted to know what was Evanescence, and you *had* to tell her?"

Melissa gave me a withering look and sneered, "I'd tell her to go to Walmart." To buy the CD. Kelly laughed loudly, recognizing that Melissa had put me in my place.

"You would just wait until you could have a recording of it."

"Exactly," Melissa deadpanned, turning to get back to showing her friend a favorite song.

While the girls mostly humored my pestering and uninteresting questions, when I finally tried to use my authority as an adult to compel Melissa to produce the sort of talk I was looking for, her response was quick and penetrating. We had long before established goodwill, even friendship, and Melissa's barbed comment was not rude, no more than I was used to taking and giving in playful interaction. But I was nonplussed by her response: being unwilling to talk to even a close friend about a band without a recording seemed completely impractical, and I did not believe Melissa. My reply, "You would just wait until you could have a recording," was skeptical, even a bit sarcastic. But Melissa doubled down. "Exactly."

I want to emphasize the very different communicative strategies present in this exchange. On the one hand Melissa responded to Kelly's question about a band with a quick and unselfconscious move to pass an earbud to her. By contrast, I was trying hard to organize the interview around speech, and, in particular, descriptive, denotative, decontextualized, and expository speech—essentially "essayist" discourse. Hypotheticals like "how would you describe Evanescence to your friend?" are characteristically teacherly. My question could easily have taken the form of an essay assignment. I tried to force a context on a situation that was not based in any actually occurring social situation (however plausible the imagined scenario might be), with the sole purpose of eliciting a particular type of decontextualized, expository discourse. In fact, it is hard to imagine a more decontextualizing move than to propose a hypothetical situation as a direct replacement for the current one. That the content of my goal involved popular music and entertainment rather than potentially more sterile topics of classroom teachers does nothing to change the structure and format of the discourse I tried to impose with this intervention. For the purposes of my research, Melissa having Kelly listen to her MP3 player rather than talk about a song was literally inarticulate—completely illegible as research data, just as it would be illegible to an educator trying to assess their literacy skills. So I was getting a bit desperate to get these kids to produce some sort of discourse *about* their peer-cultural musical practices, without realizing that that was precisely the sort of discourse they were committed to withholding.

Kelly and I both posed questions to Melissa about Evanescence, but we sought very different kinds of information, and we brought to the table very different discursive repertoires. By this point I had spent months observing the kids in their interactions and recording and participating in free-time talk with music and around music, and I hoped these more formal interviews would facilitate direct discourse *about* these peer cultural musical practices. But it had not occurred to me that kids might be unable, uninterested, or unwilling to talk about music. I did not consider that *not talking about music* could itself be a convention inscribed within the kids' music consumption. The constant presence and availability of MP3 players made music listening a shared, and frequently *unspoken*, element of kids' peer culture.

This point merits emphasis. Kids *did* talk with one another about celebrity musicians, saying, "I like so-and-so," "He's cool," or "He's hot" (i.e., attractive). But they almost never talked about the content of media. Over the entire school year, with my ethnomusicological focus almost obsessively attuned to "speech about music" (Feld 1984), I witnessed only a single spontaneous instance of speech that referred to a part of music as an object: while Amber and Kathy listened to Akon's "Smack That" while sharing earbuds on the playground, Amber said to Kathy, "*That's* the part [of the song] I like." Otherwise, like the girls listening to "Bad Touch," kids would sometimes repeat lyrics from songs or even sing along to them, but they almost never made any descriptive, analytical, or evaluative statements about songs. One element of this phenomenon is the trouble kids had using the names of songs to find them on the Internet or even on their own devices. To generalize, kids' discourse about music was almost always indexical or mimetic (iconic), rarely symbolic or decontextualized. The connection to classroom situations like Willy's "ninja" sound effects is important: in that moment, though he did provide the decontextualized facts that answered the social studies question, Willy reframed those facts as reported speech and inflected them with emotional content and specificity through the prominent addition of expressive sounds. He turned a request for decontextualized information into an opportunity for mimetic performance. The second and third graders, similarly, used the performance of sound effects to comment indexically on the social situation they were witnessing. Rather than a meta-discourse *about* music, they used *music* as a meta-discourse about the teacher's demonstration of the consequences of rule breaking. Jake's comment that, "it sounds like a video game, like when you get a gutterball," blurs this distinction somewhat. But despite objectifying the music the class was making, his comment nonetheless took its meaning from the indexical connections between situation and sound effect.

Music seemed to be understood by these kids as ontologically immediate: a material presence in actually occurring social situations, not an abstract object of discourse. Melissa's statement that she'd tell Kelly to purchase the CD at Walmart reflected a logic of immediate, materially available sound similar to that which inspired kids like Sarah and Randy to circulate music among devices and friends using speakers and microphones rather than copying digital files (described in chapter 3). The same logic structured the interactions around the "Discovery Channel" song, when Kelly simply "showed" me the song by passing one of Becky's earbuds, and Melissa made it clear that "you have to hear the song to get it" (while making no effort to explain or describe the joke). And as I listened to the recording and the girls repeated lines from the song, only Daisy attempted to clarify that the song's title wasn't the same as its refrain, but the other girls ignored her intervention.

By contrast to her dismissive response to my questions, Melissa responded to Kelly's question about a band with a quick and unselfconscious move to pass an earbud to her, a move made possible by the easy portability of her digital device. As Dell Hymes points out, "The cost, as between expressing things easily and concisely, and expressing them with difficulty and at great length, is a real cost, commonly operative, and a constraint on the theoretical potentiality of language in daily life" (1973:73). Devices like Melissa's MP3 player help skew that cost-benefit calculation even further—not to mention the materiality and physical intimacy of sharing earbuds, or the fact that simply showing someone something is a deeply contextualized and embodied form of communication. (The utterance "This, ready?" is about as dense with indexical references to specific time, space, objects, bodies, and actions as two words can be.) With her mention of Walmart, Melissa even suggested that big-box stores are almost as ready-to-hand as the digital devices and recordings you might buy within them, and certainly (if a bit ironically) more ready-to-hand than the decontextualized language you might use to describe the music to be purchased there—a suggestion made even more pointed by the fact that Heartsboro was at least a forty-minute drive from the nearest Walmart.

My questions to the girls may have been poorly designed, and it is tempting to analyze this interaction as an interviewer's inattentiveness to culturally appropriate modes of discourse (Briggs 1986). But poorly designed interview questions would not account for the fact that Melissa had such a competent, and subtle, repertoire for dismissing my questions and redirecting her attention to a demonstration of the music for Kelly. Rather, my line of questioning was exceedingly familiar as a mode of discourse, because it resembled almost exactly the back-and-forth, IRE interactions and essayist assignments of teachers leading classrooms—not at all unfamiliar or inappropriate to Melissa, but specifically undesired and rejected. Teachers regularly asked kids to produce unmotivated discourse about uninteresting topics, as exercises in literacy education.

McDermott charges us to consider any instance of inarticulateness not as an absence of fluency, but as a moment where particular discursive modes—which are usually naturalized within powerful institutions, like schools—are actively avoided or rejected. Paul Willis similarly notes that for working class kids a refusal of language can be powerful, even in situations of real powerlessness:

> Part of the reaction to the school institution is . . . a rejection of words and considered language as the expression of mental life. The way in which these creative insights are expressed, therefore, is one of expressive antagonism to the dominant bourgeois mode of signification—language. In a real sense for the working-class the cultural is in a battle with language. This is not to reduce the cultural to anti-abstract behavior. It is to posit it, in part, as an antagonistic way of expressing abstract and mental life centered, not on the individual subject, but on the group: not on the provided language but on lived demonstration, direct involvement and practical mastery. (1981 [1977]:124–25)

As my attempts to elicit talk about music eventually lapsed into a clear expression of adult authority (a command: "Do this language task that I've set you"), Melissa responded in kind with a cutting reply, and the liminal frame—of a friendly out-of-class research interview in which kids and adults might briefly interact as equals—collapsed completely. It was replaced with a discursive binary that posed decontextualized, essayist communication against the "lived demonstration, direct involvement, and practical mastery" of sharing earbuds, which centers, notably, on the group: that is, on Melissa's embodied relationship with Kelly that excluded both me and the disembodied individualized space of hypothetical abstraction. Earbuds, in their immediate, ready-to-hand accessibility as a tool for interaction and communication, were like language—even obviating certain functions of language—and as such their use needs to be seen as part of a larger ecology not just of listening but of expressivity.

Continuing to follow Willis, the point here is not to "reduce the cultural to anti-abstract behavior." Rather, it is to see, as McDermott suggests, these moments of non-communication as instances of politically charged interactions between individuals with different access to the institutional resources of power and authority, which in schools are embedded thoroughly in orientations to language and communication. A contrast between "talking-about" and "showing" might map broadly onto "adults" versus "kids," but these discursive modes are not preconstituted repertoires that naturally articulate to certain types of people. Rather, my own shifting position during this interview—as I variously inhabited one and then another discursive position, eventually settling into a recognizable, teacherly, and inescapably politicized mode of IRE questions and essayist hypotheticals—demonstrates how these modes exist as resources through which individuals orient in relation to one another. This sort of shifting orientation to modes of communication reflects almost exactly that laid out by Poole (and discussed in chapter 1) in a fifth-grade reading lesson, where the key distinction between peer-oriented and teacher-directed language use involved whether the communicative action was *framed* as fully contextualized or as abstract and decontextualized. By rejecting "talking-about" in favor of the intimate indexicality of sharing earbuds Melissa positioned herself clearly on one side of this opposition, and she situated me, with disapproval, in a teacherly role—just as Daisy positioned me on the side of "normal people" when she put me off balance and got me to admit to swearing on the first day of school.

More than just orientations to communication, we can see media and portable technologies embedded within this structural contrast between "considered language" and "demonstrations" that Willis points to as characteristic of a "counter-school" culture. Willis identifies this opposition as arising out of school and schooling, not simply a "natural" "working-class" mode, and by situating portable media within that framework, we can see how entertainment, perhaps counterintuitively, takes on an institutionalized role in school. Not simply some foreign consumer entity that is imported into a coherent school culture, media and popular culture might be understood as *native* to schooling, insofar as they play a central role in structuring the expressive ecology of the entire school social system. As McDermott writes, "occasions in which people are left without words are systematic outcomes of a set of relations among a group of persons bound in a social structure" (1988:38), and by refusing words Melissa here positioned herself not outside of, but *within* a social structure in which a particular notion of articulateness is the key organizing trope.

McDermott's idea of "mutterances" carries a suggestion of solidarity. His key example involves a sixth-grade African American student who says "Fuck you" in answer to a request to sit down, and at another time volunteers the nonsensical rhyme, "latitude an attitude," in response to a question about geography made to the whole class. McDermott notes that the rest of the students were "beaming" (1988:52). Certainly the students Betsy Rymes sees punning "Chansey" for "chancy," discussed in chapter 1, are producing something not unlike a "mutterance"—articulate, but illegible from the perspective of an ESL phonics lesson—just as Melissa and Kelly have no trouble in communicating successfully with one another, despite their active rejection of the frameworks I attempted to impose. There is plenty of content in such "inarticulate" utterances, and my focus here is to point out how that content involves, with remarkable frequency, entertainment media and consumerism. At least in school, entertainment is in every case either inappropriate, inarticulate, or intimate. Therefore it is not simply suppressed by the educational apparatus, but rendered largely illegible to and within schooling—all the better for the kids' use in cultivating solidarity (and all the better for the consumer industries, who cultivate kids cultivating solidarity).

In McDermott's account inarticulateness is a barrier to circulation. Mutterances are sudden dams in the normal flow of discourse. In the examples I have considered, such mutterances do forcefully stop certain flows of discourse, but only as they open the sluices for the circulation of other, mediated, childish, consumerist flows. These moments of inarticulateness are nodes in the circulation of media. They do not simply say, "No," they say, "Not that, this!" But also maybe, "Not you, us!" They simultaneously turn inward toward an intimate, protected sphere of childhood; and they turn outward toward an unbounded public sphere of consumption and circulation. In light of my arguments in chapter 1, we ought to understand inarticulateness not simply as opposition, which is the thrust of McDermott's analysis, but also as intimacy. Melissa and Kelly's rejection of my instrumental, decontextualizing questions in favor of immediate, material, and audible listening involved a turn not simply away from the adult across the table but toward another kid—a move that, as Melissa's reference to Walmart suggests, is profoundly mediated by consumer products.

Conclusion

Kids' Rules

Kids proposed their own basis for authority in opposition to adult rule making. In art class the day after the "sad trombone" episode, the teacher asked the sixth- and seventh-grade students to help her compose a list of rules to govern their behavior for the year—a common method for getting kids to take ownership of the classroom order. Going around the circle, each kid "passed," declining to volunteer a rule—asserting a lack of fluency in this discourse, perhaps—to the teacher's frustration. Finally Kelly said, "Our rules don't fit with your rules," fundamentally objecting to the exercise. I jumped in to point out that neither Kelly nor anyone else had actually proposed any rules, so how could we know that they might not "fit"? Kelly shrugged: "Well, we don't really have any rules . . . or our rules are just do whatever you want."

In my time at HCS I heard mention of "kids' rules" on numerous occasions. The only consistent thing about "kids' rules" seemed to be that kids got to tell adults what to do (this was usually invoked to try to get me to do their bidding in some mischief). But, as Kelly's comment made clear, it was not that she and her classmates had in mind some list of rules they claimed as "ours" that would not "fit" those the art teacher would presumably require (after this obvious charade of an exercise). Rather, "kids' rules" was inherently contradictory, because its substance was a committed lack of actual rules—an anti-classroom, anti-adult, anti-structure framework where kids could "authentically" be kids in unstructured peer interactivity: "our rules are just do whatever you want." Of course, kids' peer interactivity was structured by various scripts, routines, expectations, "rules," etc. But like "essayist literacy," which claims decontextualized language for itself despite the constant presence of contextual cues (successfully excluding the "wrong" types of contextualized language), kids posed a vision of "ruleless-ness" in an institutional context explicitly and constantly organized by innumerable rules.

Kids "rule" when they join together as a class to vocalize a soundtrack that reframes their teacher as a hapless cartoon character buffoon. And kids rule when they reframe their social studies lesson as a spectacular narrative with characters whose emotional power is expressed through dramatic vocal sounds. Kids rule when they listen together to music that is inaudible by surrounding adults but whose content is starkly inappropriate for school. Kids rule when they sneak media devices into class and show off to their friends that they got one over on the teacher, again. Kids rule when they reject the very premise of an adult's question and turn to one another, instead, to communicate by means of the ready-to-hand material of their consumer media devices. Kids rule when they tell an adult with a straight face that it's more convenient to go to Walmart and buy a CD than to perform acts of essayist literacy on command. And "Kids Rule!" was of course the slogan of Nickelodeon's triumphant revisioning of child audiences for cable television (Banet-Weiser 2007). Marketing mottos like Nickelodeon's "Let kids be kids," or the Chuck E. Cheese restaurant chain's "Where a kid can be a kid," imply that some quality of being a kid is absent or supressed in homes and schools and needs to be set free. Kelly's "our rules" contains the suggestion of some set of practices or expectations authentically "ours" and authentically childish.

So Kelly's version of kids' rules was not specifically connected to consumer practice, media, or entertainment. But hopefully from the material in this book it is increasingly clear how consumer practices in school fit into such an oppositional framework. By emphasizing relationships with friends, and by articulating those relationships as a form of solidarity, kids at school are doing something similar to what is happening in the media with the children's entertainment industry: they are framing themselves as a group with an identity, an identity with public and political implications.

Music as social capital

In this book I have not attended so much to the content of the specific music kids listen to or produce. That is partly because, as I have described, HCS kids themselves largely avoided talking about the content of their music. Instead I focused on the structure of interactions in which kids listen to or produce music. Such a distinction between content and structure only holds intermittently, and linguists and anthropologists have demonstrated how the structure of discourse embeds and constitutes meaning and social relationships (Silverstein 1976; Urban 1991). The distinction I am making might be better understood as between music listening as cultural capital and music listening as social capital (Bourdieu 1984). In its role as cultural capital, musical knowledge, of artists, genres, and songs, maps on to social status. But as social capital, listening to music involves not so much acquiring expertise as acquiring and strengthening relationships. Social capital is what is ultimately at stake in expressions of solidarity. Cultural capital and social capital are potentially fungible and in the right circumstances (or the right marketplace) can be converted from one to another. The example of Melissa and Kelly in the previous chapter demonstrates this well: Melissa was decidedly unwilling to consider whether the interest in the band Evanescence that she shared with Daisy was a form of cultural capital that they both acknowledged in one another. But presented with the opportunity to reject a particularly structured social interaction dominated by me, and to initiate a new connection with Kelly sitting next to her, she jumped on it. That reestablishment of her friendship with Kelly as a sort of social capital that worked against the authoritative relationship I was putting forward could perhaps then be converted into cultural capital in the form of Kelly learning "what is Evanescence."

Music scholars, like scholars of literature and the arts generally, are likely to understand music in terms of cultural capital and to see its social power in the potential for converting that capital into status (which was clearly my goal in the line of questioning about Evanescence and Daisy). By focusing on such practices as sharing earbuds, in which the actual music playing on those earbuds is deemphasized if not altogether unimportant, I might like to say that I am pursuing the same project from the other direction, that is, identifying how music listening built out of social capital might be translated into cultural capital hierarchies of taste. But the truth is, I simply did not see much evidence among the kids I worked with that hierarchies of musical taste played more than a middling role in establishing hierarchies of social status. Melissa certainly did not devalue Kelly's status when she admitted to not knowing Evanescence, and Kelly never became a "fan" of Evanescence after being introduced, which we might expect were such taste a marker of cultural capital.

It makes more sense to me to understand music at HCS as a relatively undifferentiated medium for conducting social relationships. That is not to say that kids were not aware of or sensitive to issues of genre and taste in general. But for the specific question of how music practices participated in the social organization of school, it mattered much more *whom* one listened with than *what* one listened to. In many cases co-listeners were selected in spite of different tastes in musical genres, which were no more than trivial markers of friendship or group membership. Therefore, the central example in this book, sharing earbuds, is best understood as a practice in which music listening articulates, consolidates, and expresses social capital—or, more simply, in which music listening, which links people together, simply *is* social capital. From a wider perspective, while musical taste largely did not seem to stratify kids from one another, it certainly did serve as capital for differentiating them from adults—in which childish and "inappropriate" content was understood as categorically distinct and opposed to educationally "appropriate" content.

This point is relevant to education scholarship. Many scholars of education who have addressed popular culture and argued for its useful pedagogical application have treated children's popular culture as a sphere of cultural capital—of widely shared knowledge, taste, and interest.[1] While much of the material in such educational literature does address friendships, family relationships, and social interactions as important elements, the theoretical and interpretive emphasis is more on textual material, imagery, tropes, and knowledge of popular culture. Thus Rymes's analysis of the "Chansey" incident (discussed in chapter 1) is initially framed in terms of zones of competence, or fields of cultural knowledge to which students have distributed access. Similarly, when Anne Haas Dyson (2001) asks critically, "where are the childhoods in childhood literacy?" she suggests that a key aspect of "childhood" is popular cultural knowledge as a site of intertextual reference in student writing. Jackie Marsh (2002) explicitly describes children's play with electronic toys as an important site of acquiring cultural capital, recognizing that skillful knowledge of technology and media are markers of social status, and she emphasizes cultural capital as the particular form of capital relevant to literacy education (J. Marsh 2006; J. Marsh and Millard 2001). There is no question that knowledge of popular culture and media can form precisely such a repository of cultural capital, whose textuality makes it especially relevant to music and literacy education. But by noting the same theoretical and interpretive emphasis on cultural capital rather than social capital that we also find in music scholarship, I think we can identify an opening to move toward an even broader and more satisfying understanding of how children relate to learning and to one another in schools, and more broadly, to open new perspectives on how texts of various forms function in everyday social life.[2]

My emphasis here on social capital is intended to move away from a focus on the knowledge and skills that children acquire or don't acquire in school and toward a perspective that sees social relationships in school as fundamental to understanding the practices of schooling. Hence my interest in sharing earbuds as a key practice that points to how media use involves not just taste and knowledge but also specific interactions and configurations of individual people in a social and institutional context. Notably, a focus on musical activities seems to encourage such an interest in interaction over textuality, which is apparent in efforts in music education studies to move toward a critical ethnographic understanding of children's musical practices (Campbell 1998; Harwood 1998; Lill 2014a, 2014b; K. Marsh 2008, 2009; Young 2003, 2008; Young and Gillen 2007), in parallel to critical ethnographic interventions in literacy education scholarship by Dyson and others. This music education research often focuses on children's playground songs and hand-clapping games, which means that discussions of composition, intertextuality, and innovation are always necessarily grounded in embodied social interactions between individuals in social contexts (especially K. Marsh 2008). Music is so often about individuals sharing space and coordinating their movements with friends. And friend relations are potentially more destabilizing to core educational ideologies than are new areas of knowledge. The social relationships, and social capital, of friendships make possible a sort of politicized solidarity that, by its very constitution in face-to-face intimate relationships, cannot legitimately be subjected to or appropriated into the authority of schooling.

Education versus consumerism

I don't think that we can understand children's uses of portable media in school without a larger theoretical intervention regarding the relationship between education and consumerism. In addition to hierarchical distinctions between children and adults as groups of different (and always unequal) status, there is no reason we cannot see horizontal distinctions involving opposition or conflict between institutions or industries that are not so easily plotted in relation to one another on a graph of distinction. Education, according to theorists like Willis, Foley, and Eckert, is a site of capitalist reproduction of social difference from generation to generation. Though framed largely as critique, that view need not be seen as controversial: commonly stated goals of education policy, as well as common sense and everyday discourses, see the role of compulsory universal education as producing a future labor force, and this is even more true in contemporary neoliberal discourses that emphasize "human capital" as the key to future growth. That education is a central element in a capitalist society is a truism, but it is no less true for that.

This view of education is about producing *labor* and not about consumption at all. Consumption, as a central aspect of capitalist expressive practices, seems like it also ought to be tied up in the instrumentality that Willis and Foley identify as so fundamental to bourgeois life, but, instead, consumption is generally coded as intimate. For instance, Sam Binkley writes that, "within the experiential domain of consumption there persists a tendency toward expressive as opposed to instrumental action, to the imaginary associations of desire and fantasy as opposed to the objective, calculating interests that prevail in the professional realms of work and productivity" (2006:352). From this, if we were to take the social class model of instrumentality too seriously, consumption as non-instrumental (and phantasmagorical) would be definitively keyed as minoritized or working class, which, given the central fact of bourgeois consumption and the dominance of consumer industries by global corporations, is not exactly correct. Consumption and popular culture nonetheless are strongly coded as working-class (Levine 1990), feminine (E. Willis 2014 [1970]), and also, importantly, *childish* (Barber 2007).

Education, in particular, is implicitly and explicitly understood as somehow contrary to consumption, in part through its pervasive cultivation of instrumental communication. That view can be seen perhaps most clearly in critiques of advertising and marketing in schools (Manning 1999; Schor 2004), which suggest that bringing advertising into schools contradicts the mission of schools to safely nurture children's development partly by *protecting* children from the potential harms of public commerce (Schor 2006). But an analytical division between education and consumerism may not be sustainable, as the growth of "edutainment" as a commercial and educational phenomenon suggests (Ito 2009). The increasing presence of marketing in schools has occurred in parallel with an increasing adoption by educators of the tropes of entertainment as a potential source for motivating student learning, the growth of industries producing educational materials for use in schools, and the increasing market outside of school for media and entertainment that are presented as fostering specifically educational goals. There's an irony here, in which commerce is widely understood as "dangerous" to kids but is simultaneously represented as somehow authentic or native to childhood. As Langer writes, "What is crucial to the children's culture industry is . . . the designation of childhood as a cultural space constituted by consumption" (2004:260).

Ito argues that an "opposition between entertainment and education is a compelling dichotomy—a pair of material, semiotic, technical genres—that manifests in a wide range of institutionalized relations" (2005b:83), which cannot be simply analyzed as an extension of bureaucratic, instrumental communicative practices. Instead Ito points out how pleasure and fun are joined with entertainment in opposition to education:

> Pleasure and fun—whether for adults, youth, or children—are symbolically set off from the instrumental domains of work, discipline, and achievement, highlighting the cultural opposition between "active" production and "passive" consumption. Media

> industries capitalize on the discursive regime that produces play as a site of authentic childhood agency, specifically by mobilizing phantasmagoria as a site of regressive, illicit, and oppositional power. (2009:91)

Through an examination of "participation genres," Ito's approach fits into the model of interactive and expressive frameworks that I outline in the previous chapter. For Ito, entertainment and education do not simply apply to fields of production or categories of texts. They also outline persistent and conventional practices through which people engage with media products and texts: "We recognize certain patterns of representations (media genres), and in turn engage with them in routinized ways (participation genres)" (2008a:91). Phantasmagoric and spectacular textual characteristics of entertainment software connect to intimate social orientations: "All gaming titles in some way cater to a hankering for spectacle, which is a cornerstone of participation genres associated with entertainment media. Children are quick to recognize these forms of engagement as 'fun' and part of their peer cultural exchange rather than the achievement economy of adults and education" (2008a:110). By contrast, Ito's analysis points to the componentiality and decontextualization characteristic of essayist literacy, reproducing instrumental orientations even in progressive, process-oriented environments: "The focus on external assessment and the linear sequencing of the game encourages an orientation to accomplishing the technical conditions of success rather than deeper exploration of the problem domain. Even . . . where adults try to push kids toward exploratory and imaginative play, the kids quickly recognize the genre expectations of educational achievement" (2008a:107–8). Thus educational media is analyzable as "instrumental" in ways characteristic of other school orientations to textuality, knowledge, and participation, while entertainment appears neatly linked to the characteristic practices and tropes of childhood intimacy.

If we understand the expressive economy of schools to project intimacy and instrumentality onto a vertical axis of social differentiation, reflecting and reproducing binary social hierarchies like child/adult, we might be inclined to add entertainment/education as an important pairing. But entertainment and education do not apparently relate to each other the way child and adult do, as marked and unmarked categories that calibrate a hierarchical spectrum. Rather, an orientation toward entertainment does not encompass only an intimate turn to proximate friends or community. It also entails a turn to powerful global institutions of capitalism that are not entirely unlike schools:

> When one adds media industries and high technology to the relational mix, the equation becomes more complicated . . . What constitutes an authoritative institution is a

> contingent effect of local micropolitics, where pop culture identification confers status in children's status hierarchies and "fun" gets mobilized vis-à-vis adults as an authenticating trope of a "natural" childlike pleasure principle. This is not a simple story of adult repression of authentic childhood impulses but is a distributed social field that produces the opposition between childhood pleasure and adult achievement norms as a contingent cultural effect, subject to local reshapings. (Ito 2005b:100)

The same intimacies that position children in opposition to school produce affiliations with entertainment and technology industries, through the cultural logic of consumption.

Childhood, schooling, and friendship

Insofar as constituting one space involves drawing boundaries with another, it is clear that, in schools, spaces constituted by peer culture and the relative absence of adult oversight are simultaneously spaces whose sociality is notably full of consumption. Intimate spaces constituted by consumption are simultaneously constituting the classroom as instrumental, and vice versa. Skillfully crossing such boundaries from "carnivalesque" sites of consumption to spaces of work, home, and school is a key task of "governmentality"—an ethical task of self-discipline:

> Consumers must be made up as people able to immerse themselves in the phantasmagorical transformations of the carnivalesque, without losing themselves entirely. But what is important is the boundary between these realms, and the way in which it is reproduced as itself an ethical program . . . As an ethic of the self, the boundary between carnivalesque consumption and everyday life is transposed from the spatial and temporal coordinates of real market places, consumption locales and leisure times, into a characterological feature, a relation of self to self, or a technique of governmentality. (Binkley 2006:355)

The energy schools put into forbidding noisy socialization as well as media consumption practices within classrooms, and fencing them off in playgrounds, lunchrooms, and hallways, might be understood as fostering precisely such practices of crossing boundaries, rather than as an attempt to train such practices out of children altogether. From this perspective, entertainment and consumer practices are not something foreign to schools that kids bring in to interfere with the real mission of schooling, but rather they are key elements of schooling—perhaps not as schooling is explicitly understood by adults, but certainly in the underlying structures that actually organize schooling.

In fact, the particular institutions of childhood and school—which necessarily constitute one another, as I argue in chapter 1—problematize the binaries of education and entertainment, work and consumption, and public and private, at their core. "Childhood" is the social imaginary at the center of education, but childhood dissolves public and private: children are at once the definitive private subjects, canonically located in the home (even the bedroom) and with no legitimate public role, and they are simultaneously the population most subject to public—governmental, bureaucratic—intervention (Boyden 1997; Stephens 1995). This is fundamentally a contradiction. Children are canonically private subjects who need to be protected from potential dangers from the public, adult world. But it is precisely that vulnerability that makes "public" institutions claim access to childhood as a basic social good. Thus governments, for example, can intervene into homes to protect children from abuse, and, more basically, governments institute compulsory schooling because successful childhoods are seen as public, not private, outcomes. But schools, still, are not fully public spaces. Schools restrict access to non-authorized adults, and more than that a basic element of school practice involves intimacy and care. This is especially the case for younger children, for whom relationships with teachers are normatively caring and intimate, but it holds true even at older ages, where discourses and ideals of nurturing and caring remain common. Douglas Foley's Habermasian perspective on language and communication would precisely see the sort of rational-critical language that gets produced in literacy education as what happens in the "public sphere." But that sort of "public" communication is happening in a space that is conscientiously "protected" from public.

Ito's framework in which "pop culture identification confers status" points toward a classic reading of media in school as a form of cultural capital, which is a compelling perspective. But I think the social capital involved in childhood *friendships* provides an even more compelling basis for understanding children's investment in media and popular culture. Valerie Hey argues that at its core, children's (especially girls') friendship relationships problematize a "neoliberal" model of "subjects who exist outside of sociality, place, history, and almost time . . . social cyphers [who] have no families, certainly no friends, nobody except themselves and their individual 'freedom'" (2002:229). Instead, childhood friendships are evidence that "subjects cannot simply evade the regulation that flows from interconnectedness, mutuality, and interdependence . . . Taken together, young people's investments in the practice of compulsory sociability is so strong that no amount of neoliberalism is ever likely to overwrite it" (2002:239). In Hey's account, friendship is a relationship that opposes what Foley would call "instrumentality" in its fundamental composition as mutual and interdependent—and friendships reveal the fact of interconnectedness more broadly in an otherwise fragmented and privatized society.

But at the same time, Hey argues, friendship

> draws so heavily upon the discourse of individual freedom. Historically, friendship premises itself on ideas about "choice" and uniqueness and it thus makes a particular claim on young people, since it appears as an ideal or first practice of the "reflexive" self . . . [Friendship] is lived by these young people as an ontology and epistemology of the self through the "other." (2002:239)

This "freedom" of expressive, intimate practice has remarkable parallels to the intimate freedoms of consumerism: "the freedom of the consumer is the freedom to transform the self by stepping back in thought, but the medium of such thinking is not that of instrumental planning but of something quite different—it is one of fantasy, play, distraction and imaginary escape" (Binkley 2006:351). Further, it is not appropriate to say that friendships are simply "private"; rather, intimate friendships create their own publics in spaces like the playground or mall, as Eckert argues:

> The crowd dominates the public sphere, partially inserting the private sphere into it. Heightened activity and style draw attention to those who are engaged in it, and makes their private affairs public events. In this way, they take on status as public people. This "going public" is a crucial component of the process of maturation taking place in this age group. Such things as girls' trips to the mall, and gang-oriented territoriality, are primarily about inserting and viewing the self as an independent agent in the public domain. (1996:185)

Thus friendship, the canonically "childish" relationship at the center of peer culture, is a relationship structured in such a way that its intimacy is naturally opposed to school's instrumentality, while its emphasis on individual expression through sociality helps integrate consumption as an essential practice of friendship.[3]

School rules

Friendship, insofar as it is constructed out of the intensity and intimacy of childhood relationships, configures the peculiarly intimate public spaces of school into a robust site for disrupting the privatization and isolation of individuals. Friendship poses one system of social capital based on political and emotional solidarity among children in opposition to another system, based on individuality and instrumental communication. Add in the affective intensity of consumer media's phantasmagoric desire, and items like MP3 players are legitimately threatening to school's institutional authority. They fundamentally reconfigure how the politics of school are understood, away from hierarchical adult power and toward a more dynamic and essentially agonistic structure.

So teachers and administrators at HCS had good reason to be suspicious of MP3 players, seeing them as distracting and disruptive. At staff meetings MP3 players were often listed with hats, soda, and chewing gum as objectionable objects that negatively influenced student behavior, and some adults proposed banning such items from the building, "so that the kids know they're at school." On the other hand, some teachers disagreed with this view, arguing instead that there is pedagogical value in items like music players or chewing gum for helping students concentrate and defending kids' "free time" against proliferating regulations. But at the beginning of the 2008 school year, after my full-time fieldwork ended, students returned from summer vacation to a total ban on all portable electronics. (In fact, HCS was years late in this development. Most schools in the region had long forbidden such devices or never allowed them in the first place.) So we might say that MP3 players and earbuds were ultimately subject to the unrelenting disciplining power of bureaucratic adult authority.

But schools regularly ban all sorts of things, especially commercial and sociable "fads" like Pokémon cards or Pogs—or MP3 players—through which kids turn their concentration intensely toward one another. Perhaps these cycles of fads and bans do not suggest repression so much as incitement to the private, intimate, interactive, and playful practices that persistently characterizes children's sociable peer culture in school. It is hard to see such instrumental adult interventions into kids' listening as effectually socializing kids toward essayist habits of instrumental literacy (or rationalized habits of isolated listening). Rather, by framing banned items as hidden, close, and intimate, they further articulate them to the marginal and subordinated peer sociability and intimacy—and to the particular affective modes of consumer practices—to which kids are so committed. Of course, adult regulations are only ever partial, as practices like passing notes and whispering persist throughout continual adult attempts to manage kids' illicit peer communications.

When I would return to visit HCS, after the ban on portable media devices, it was hard to identify much difference in kids' sociality without MP3 players, although absent the colorful cables visibly diagramming kids' social networks it would sometimes take a second glance to see friends leaning in to one another, intimately sharing space.

NOTES

INTRODUCTION

1. "Heartsboro" is a pseudonym, as are the names of all the individuals mentioned in this book, to protect the confidentiality and anonymity of the children who participated. In several instances in this section I do not provide complete citations for demographic data in order to protect the participants' confidentiality.
2. The population of Heartsboro as a whole was 99 percent white (United States Census Bureau/American FactFinder 2010). Forty-seven percent of students at HCS were eligible for free or reduced (government-subsidized) school lunch in 2007–2008, compared to 43 percent for the United States and 29.6 percent for the state of Vermont (National Center for Educational Statistics 2010; Hoffman 2009:16). According to the American Community Survey, the median household income in 2009 was approximately $36,000, compared to about $51,000 for both the United States and the state of Vermont (United States Census Bureau/American FactFinder 2009). Heartsboro's median income was below the $46,000 county median as well.
3. According to a 2005 town profile prepared by the county commission, more than 70 percent of residents' jobs were located outside of Heartsboro.
4. Here I am using data from the "Heartsboro" Town Plan of 2005, but I refrain from including the full reference in the interest of maintaining confidentiality.
5. From 1990 to 2000 employment in "education, health, and social services," already the largest category, increased by over 60 percent, and employment in leisure and hospitality ("arts, entertainment, recreation, accommodation, and food") more than tripled. Government employment also increased, while other categories, notably including "agriculture, forestry, fishing, hunting, and mining," declined significantly. In a town with such a small population the percentage changes can be misleading. The increase in leisure and hospitality categories was from seventeen to fifty-four jobs, and the increase in "education, health, and social services" was from fifty-nine to ninety-six. (This data is from a county commission's 2005 profile of Heartsboro.) Town-specific data are not available from the more recent census in 2010, but for the larger county, during a period that included the Great Recession, the labor force as a whole decreased by 6.9 percent, and most new jobs from 2001–2011 were added in education, health services, and state and local government. (These statistics are from a "Regional Profile" of the county prepared by the county commission in 2014.)
6. Internal cultural divisions among Heartsboro residents were not strongly apparent in the 2000s and those that did exist were usually articulated in terms of class and geography. This was not always the case. According to longtime residents I spoke to, as well as oral history interviews conducted with elderly people and published by HCS students in 1979, in the early twentieth century (the interviewees do not give specific dates) there was a

surge of anti-Catholic Ku Klux Klan activity targeted against Italian immigrants. One Italian American interviewee reported, "They were against the black people. There were not black people in this town, but there were a lot of aliens [nonnative immigrants] here. People that came from over across, they didn't want any of them around. They didn't want any Catholics in town, they didn't want any religion, in fact, because the Ku Klux Klan are against any religion—of any type" (quoted in a 1979 self-published book of oral history authored by HCS students). Certainly by the time I was conducting research there was no sense at all of religious or ethnic conflict, and families with Italian surnames were at the core of the life of the town, while racial diversity remained very limited. I note this history to point out that the contemporary racial/ethnic homogeneity of Heartsboro was not always so apparent.

7. The pay was prorated at 20 percent of a full-time teacher's salary ($22/hour), but the length of the commute and teachers' inability to combine several 20-percent positions into one with full-time benefits meant these positions had high turnover and were difficult to staff.
8. Over the course of the year HCS paid me $3,346 for music teaching from November 2007 to June 2008. My primary means of support was a graduate student fellowship at Columbia University that allowed me to work remotely and my spouse's salary as a public school teacher in New York City.
9. Technically, "MP3" is a "format" for encoding and compressing music as a digital file (Sterne 2012), so an "MP3 player" is a playback device for music encoded with the MP3 format, and the term "MP3" more commonly refers to an individual song file, whatever format it is encoded in.
10. This categorical slippage was present among adults, too, some of whom understood iPod and MP3 as competing brands from Apple and Microsoft, on analogy to "Mac" versus "Windows" in the personal computer market.
11. These are not the actual strings of characters reported by my interlocutors as their Internet passwords.
12. Marc Perlman, reviewing *My Music*, makes a similar point: "We badly need a study of musical taste that combines My Music's attention to detail with panoramic views of the social, economic, and historical context" (1993).
13. Queer theorists have paid particular attention to temporality as a structuring social field, and childhood and adulthood are key terms in theorizations of queer temporality. Halberstam, for example, highlights the centrality of "the adult/youth binary" (2005:2) to normative constructions of heterosexual reproductivity, in which adulthood, reproduction, and the patriarchal family all coincide, while people who don't conform to a narrowly defined life course are pathologized as immature and worse: "Queer time for me is the dark nightclub, the perverse turn away from the narrative coherence of adolescence–early adulthood–marriage–reproduction–child rearing–retirement–death, the embrace of late childhood in place of early adulthood or immaturity in place of responsibility" (Halberstam in Dinshaw et al. 2007:182).
14. To a meaningful extent, that the politics of the private sphere might be seen as powerfully structured by childhood presents a fundamental problem for liberal societies interested in individual freedom and autonomy. Childbearing and childrearing are much thornier problems for liberal feminism—and therefore for liberalism—than (relatively) straightforward claims of equal rights and demonstration of equal capacities. Even in a liberal utopia in which every adult is free, autonomous, and equal, the work of bearing and raising dependent children remains. The relationship between feminist studies and childhood studies, and between women and children as historically constructed social classes, is the subject of a long-standing and productive strand of feminist thought (Alanen 1994, 2005; Firestone 1970; Oakley 1993; Thorne 1987).

15. See, for example, Nussbaum's discussions of "issues of fairness in the relations among family members" (2006:106).

CHAPTER 1

1. Foley objects to Willis's mental/manual framework on the grounds that it is too classically structural Marxist, but here Foley's critique misses or ignores Willis's emphasis on a working-class imperative to maintain expressive/mental practices as a privileged site of freedom from bureaucratic alienation.
2. See Richard Parmentier (1994) for a useful introduction to Peircian semiotic terminology.
3. As Sharon Stephens (1995) has asked, why refer to "the child" when we might discuss actual "children"? Austin, Dwyer, and Freebody capitalize "Child" along with "Student" and "Teacher" to refer to conventionalized roles that are performed in schools. Their ethnomethodological approach sees these categories constructed in everyday practice, and their "Child" is not the same essentialized category as can be found in, say, developmental or philosophical discourses.
4. Children's folkloric traditions can and have been used to position them as "primitive" and their expressivity as "authentic" or close to nature, that is, as evidence for evolutionist, developmental views (Minks 2002; K. Marsh 2008). While this remains a common inclination, we should reject those frameworks for children's folklore in the same way and for the same reasons we reject them for any other folklore traditions (Bauman 1982).
5. Christa McAuliffe was the schoolteacher who died when the space shuttle Challenger exploded during takeoff in 1986.

CHAPTER 2

1. Bull's book is about iPods and their iconic cultural status specifically, but he points out that his conclusions about listening are applicable to other portable music devices. Since my concerns are not directly with the iconic status of the iPod, but with listening practices and earbuds, I engage with Bull's discussion with the assumption that "MP3 player" means effectively the same thing as "iPod." That said, I should note that many of the students at HCS refused to categorize iPods as a subset of MP3 players, demanding instead that they were decidedly different categories of device (see the introduction). Nonetheless, their peculiar taxonomy seemed to have no effect on how they used the items. In any event, this chapter is not about taxonomies or brands (interesting as those topics are), it is about earbuds, so I set these issues aside.
2. Sterne attributes "alone together" to William Kenney (1999). More recently Sherry Turkle (2011) has used that phrase to diagnose contemporary cultures of communication technology. Turkle's lament focuses special attention on recent disruptions of intimate bonds among children and families, though Sterne's longer history suggests similarities in earlier instances of the domestication of media technology within the family.
3. In this chapter and throughout I use the term "affordances" in the sense that it is used in science and technology studies, to emphasize the complex relationships between material technologies and their social contexts. The term is part of an intervention that seeks a middle ground between technologically determinist views in which the material properties of technologies, independent of their social contexts, are seen as wholly responsible for the activities those technologies are used for, and a social constructionist rejection of any constraining or enabling potential inherent in the material form of technologies or objects, in favor of unlimited interpretive possibilities depending on social context. The "affordances" view deemphasizes both "essential" characteristics and discursive representations of technologies, in favor of "questions of the use-in-situated-social-interaction of technological devices (Hutchby 2003:582). Insofar as I am interested in children's uses of earbuds and MP3 players for unexpected social purposes that are still deeply attentive

to the actual form of those devices, "affordances" is the appropriate term. For an overview of these issues, see the debate between Ian Hutchby and Brian Rappert in *Sociology* (Hutchby 2001, 2003; Rappert 2003).

4. A surprising and remarkable activity. I discuss this mode of transferring music from one device to another in the next chapter.
5. In a volume titled *Consuming Music Together* (O'Hara and Brown 2006), which includes chapters with titles like "Sharing and Listening to Music" (B. Brown and Sellen 2006) and "Investigating the Culture of Mobile Listening" (Bull 2006), practices like sharing earbuds and listening together to maxed-out headphones as speakers are entirely absent.
6. A 2008 study by the Pew Internet and American Life Project (Lenhart et al. 2008) showed that 94 percent of US girls play video games, compared to 99 percent of boys, problematizing common assumptions about a gender divide in gaming and pointing to the ascendance of gaming as a nearly universal cultural phenomenon among youth in this country, which conforms to my observations. Still, the Pew study points out that boys and girls do tend to play different types of games, in different social environments, and for different amounts of time. It may be that girls' relatively heightened interest in music listening—and the overall gendering of pop music itself (Weisbard 2014)—contributes to the gendered differentiation of video game practices.
7. Managing social space through inclusion or exclusion in the listenership of speakers recalls the similar, if inverted, phenomenon of portable stereos ("boomboxes") in public spaces. With boomboxes, though, sound from portable speakers "spills over" into others' listening environments, aggressively pushing the boundaries of individual space (Schloss and Boyer 2014; Weheliye 2005). With earbuds used as speakers, social inclusion and exclusion can be managed much more precisely.

CHAPTER 3

1. Research by Allen (2004), Bergen (2004), Fabregat et al. (2004), and Plowman (2004) similarly suggest that children use new technologies in "traditional" ways, without too much concern for their digital enhancements.
2. Tamagotchi are "virtual pets"—handheld consumer devices with which users feed and care for a cartoon animal (see Bloch and Lemish 1999; Allison 2006). Pokémon and the Game Boy are both international brands owned by Nintendo. Game Boys are portable video game devices. Pokémon is a collection of cartoon characters and storylines that appear in video games, TV shows, movies, and, centrally, trading cards (see Tobin 2004).
3. Randy's use of the term "redneck" was unique at the school or in the broader community, as far as I know, and stemmed in part from his interest in comedian Larry the Cable Guy. His interest in the Confederate flag was always directly linked to the "General Lee," the hot rod car with the flag on its roof from the television show and movie *Dukes of Hazzard*. Rather than positioning him within the local sensibility of rusticity shared by his peers, Randy's identification as "redneck" and use of Confederate iconography contributed to his relative social isolation.
4. This turned out to be useful documentation of what might have been playing on kids' devices during recordings where otherwise the microphone would only pick up their talk.

CHAPTER 5

1. In fact categories like "prep," "jock," or "geek" were relatively rare at HCS and only used much at all by the eighth graders. The strict social divisions outlined by Eckert (1989) and Milner (2004) among high schoolers are less well established in middle and especially elementary school. Moreover, the small size of HCS would necessarily destabilize any strict categorizations, simply because there were too few kids to define adequate

aggregate taxonomies. For the most part, the eighth graders would only use these terms when prompted. If I specifically asked them to name the social categories, they would come up with "prep," "jock," "normal people," and "video game boys" or "geeks." Daisy's unprompted use of "prep" in this instance, then, seemed to highlight, to the extent of naming, the heightened emphasis on social belonging and identity that characterized this first day of school, when confronted with the newness of an overdressed adult researcher.

2. "Bad Touch," performed by the Bloodhound Gang. Lyrics by James M. Franks. © 2000 Universal Songs of Polygram International Inc, Hey Rudy Music Publishing, and the Jimmy Franks Publishing Company. Reprinted by permission.
3. By contrast with this humorous play with tropes of childishness, when the seventh and eighth graders were asked to read George Orwell's novel *Animal Farm* in class, they uniformly hated it, and pointed to its "talking animals" as especially objectionable. One said, "It's what my brother reads," referring to her nine-year-old younger sibling. In my discussions with students about the book, they were unimpressed by the allegorical aspects of the novel ("Who cares if it's political?" one said), but it was the childishness of talking animals that they latched on to as a ready source of scorn. I would argue that the source of humor in "Bad Touch" is the same as the source of scorn for *Animal Farm*: childishness is fraught with implications about respect, authority, self-worth, and independence. It is a recognizable feature of identity politics that such markers would be a source of power when initiated by kids, but charged with the suggestion of disrespect or worse when coming from adults. That the teacher would give these students a book about talking animals was a real affront.
4. The word "ninja" had taken on a greatly expanded slang meaning, especially in online and gaming-oriented youth culture, where it would appear as a verb, adjective, and exclamation. So "They were like ninja!" was a reasonably grammatical sentence.
5. Making movies with video captured from video games is called "machinima" ("machine" + "cinema") and is an increasingly common form of cultural production (Ito 2011; Lowood 2006). "Kill the Reds" is from "The Best Laid Plans," *Red vs. Blue*, season 3, episode 39, originally released October 12, 2004. The episode can be viewed at http://roosterteeth.com/episode/red-vs-blue-season-3-episode-39 and http://www.youtube.com/watch?v=rFwad7UE5JY.
6. Educators, not least among them music educators, are increasingly interested in fostering rather than censuring the connections students make between formal and informal learning contexts (see, for example, Lill 2014a, 2015; Green 2008; Ito et al. 2010; Ito et al. 2013). Nate's and Willy's outbursts in this civil war history lesson might be seen as expressions of "informal learning" or "connected learning" that can productively contribute to the formal learning goals of the lesson.

CONCLUSION

1. Lefstein and Snell provide a contrasting approach that looks to "discourse genres" (2011). The discussion in this paragraph and the following is meant less as a critique or even to generalize about literacy studies than to use examples from literacy studies to clarify the analytical distinction between cultural and social capital.
2. To be, perhaps, more critical, an educational perspective on popular culture as cultural capital may reproduce a problematic view of learning as knowledge transmission and acquisition that is common in schools but also the frequent object of criticism from educators and scholars; hence proposals that teachers should make an effort to include materials from popular culture in their lessons, so that students can apply the same knowledge-acquisition techniques to those materials as they do to traditional classroom content. I find theories of learning as membership in a community (Lave and Wenger 1991) to be more

persuasive, and such a perspective is more amenable to analysis in terms of social capital. I am also open to the idea that the notion of "learning" itself is the problem (McDermott 2011), which, also, fits with the social capital analysis I am proposing here.

3. Lee Higgins (2012) suggests that friendship is central to how community musicians understand their relationships to participants and each other, in ways that might suggest a similar analysis of music's role as social capital to the one I am putting forward here.

REFERENCES

Abu-Lughod, Lila. 2001. *Dramas of Nationhood: The Politics of Television in Egypt.* Chicago: University of Chicago Press.

Ackerley, Janice. 2007. "The Subversive World of New Zealand Children's Playground Rhymes." *Journal of Folklore Research* 44 (2/3): 205–25.

Adler, Patricia A., and Peter Adler. 1998. *Peer Power: Preadolescent Culture and Identity.* New Brunswick, NJ: Rutgers University Press.

Adorno, Theodor W. 1991 [1938]. "On the Fetish Character of Music and the Regression of Listening." In *The Culture Industry: Selected Essays on Mass Culture,* edited by J. M. Bernstein, pp. 29–60. New York: Routledge Classics.

Alanen, Leena. 1994. "Gender and Generation: Feminism and the 'Child Question.'" In *Childhood Matters: Social Theory, Practice, and Politics,* edited by Jens Qvortrup, et al., pp. 27–42. Aldershot, UK: Avebury.

———. 2005. "Women's Studies/Childhood Studies: Parallels, Links, and Perspectives." In *Children Taken Seriously in Theory, Policy, and Practice,* edited by Jan Mason and Toby Fattore, pp. 31–45. London: Jessica Kingsley Publishers.

Allard, Andrea C. 2002. "'Aussies' and 'Wogs' and the 'Group in-between': Year 10 Students' Constructions of Cross-cultural Friendships." *Discourse: Studies in the Cultural Politics of Education* 23 (2): 193–209.

Allen, Mark. 2004. "Tangible Interfaces in Smart Toys." In *Toys, Games, and Media,* edited by Jeffrey Goldstein, David Buckingham, and Gilles Brougère, pp. 179–94. Mahwah, NJ: Lawrence Erlbaum.

Allison, Anne. 2004. "Cuteness as Japan's Millenial Product." In *Pikachu's Global Adventure: The Rise and Fall of Pokémon,* edited by Joseph J. Tobin, pp. 34–52. Durham, NC: Duke University Press.

———. 2006. *Millenial Monsters: Japanese Toys and the Global Imagination.* Berkeley: University of California Press.

Appadurai, Arjun. 1986. "Introduction: Commodities and the Politics of Value." In *The Social Life of Things: Commodities in Cultural Perspective,* edited by Arjun Appadurai, pp. 3–63. New York: Cambridge University Press.

———. 1996. *Modernity at Large: Cultural Dimensions of Globalization.* Minneapolis: University of Minnesota Press.

Arnett, Jeffrey Jensen. 2004. *Emerging Adulthood: The Winding Road from Late Teens through the Twenties.* New York: Oxford University Press.

Austin, Helena, Bronwyn Dwyer, and Peter Freebody. 2003. *Schooling the Child: The Making of Students in Classrooms.* New York: Routledge.

Banet-Weiser, Sarah. 2004. "Girls Rule! Gender, Feminism, and Nickelodeon." *Critical Studies in Media Communication* 21 (2): 119–39.

———. 2007. *Kids Rule! Nickelodeon and Consumer Citizenship*. Durham, NC: Duke University Press.

Barber, Benjamin R. 2007. *Con$umed: How Markets Corrupt Children, Infantilize Adults, and Swallow Citizens Whole*. New York: Norton.

Bauman, Richard. 1975. "Verbal Art as Performance." *American Anthropologist* 77 (2): 290–311.

———. 1977. "Linguistics, Anthropology, and Verbal Art: Toward a Unified Perspective, with a Special Discussion of Children's Folklore." In *Linguistics and Anthropology*, edited by Muriel Saville-Troike, pp. 13–36. Washington, DC: Georgetown University Press.

———. 1982. "Ethnography of Children's Folklore." In *Children In and Out of School: Ethnography and Education*, edited by Perry Gilmore and Allan A. Glatthorn, pp. 172–86. Washington, DC: Center for Applied Linguistics.

Baxter, Jane Eva. 2005. *The Archaeology of Childhood: Children, Gender, and Material Culture*. Walnut Creek, CA: AltaMira Press.

Baym, Nancy K., and Andrew Ledbetter. 2009. "Tunes that Bind? Predicting Friendship Strength in a Music-based Social Network." *Information, Communication, and Society* 12 (3): 408–27.

Becker, Howard S. 1972. "A School Is a Lousy Place to Learn Anything In." *The American Behavioral Scientist* 16 (1): 85–105.

Beresin, Anna Richman. 1993. "The Play of Peer Culture in a City School Yard: 'Reeling,' 'Writhing,' and a 'Rhythmic Kick.'" PhD diss., University of Pennsylvania.

———. 2004. "School Power, Children's Play, and the Timing of Recess Violence." In *Cultural Shaping of Violence: Victimization, Escalation, Response*, edited by Myrdene Anderson, pp. 18–23. West Lafayette, IN: Purdue University Press.

Bergen, Doris. 2004. "Preschool Children's Play with 'Talking' and 'Nontalking' Rescue Heroes: Effects of Technology-Enhanced Figures on the Types and Themes of Play." In *Toys, Games, and Media*, edited by Jeffrey Goldstein, David Buckingham, and Gilles Brougère, pp. 195–206. Mahwah, NJ: Lawrence Erlbaum.

Berlant, Lauren. 1997. *The Queen of America Goes to Washington City: Essays on Sex and Citizenship*. Durham, NC: Duke University Press.

———. 1998. "Intimacy: A Special Issue." *Critical Inquiry* 24 (2): 281–88.

———. 2008. *The Female Complaint: The Unfinished Business of Sentimentality in American Culture*. Durham, NC: Duke University Press.

Berlant, Lauren, and Michael Warner. 1998. "Sex in Public." *Critical Inquiry* 24 (2): 547–66.

Bernstein, Robin. 2011. *Racial Innocence: Performing American Childhood from Slavery to Civil Rights*. New York: New York University Press.

Bérubé, Michael. 2003. "Citizenship and Disability." *Dissent* 50 (2): 52–57.

Bickford, Tyler. 2008. "The Social Economy of Headphone Use in a New England Primary School." Paper presented to the annual meeting of the Mid-Atlantic Chapter of the Society for Ethnomusicology, New York, March 30.

———. 2012. "The New 'Tween' Music Industry: The Disney Channel, Kidz Bop, and an Emerging Childhood Counterpublic." *Popular Music* 31 (3): 417–36.

———. 2015. "Tween Intimacy and the Problem of Public Life in Children's Media: 'Having It All' on the Disney Channel's *Hannah Montana*." *WSQ: Women's Studies Quarterly* 43 (1/2): 66–82.

———. 2016. "Justin Bieber, YouTube, and New Media Celebrity: The Tween Prodigy at Home and Online." In *Musical Prodigies: Interpretations from Psychology, Education, Musicology, and Ethnomusicology*, edited by Gary E. McPherson, pp. 749–67. New York: Oxford University Press.

Binkley, Sam. 2006. "The Perilous Freedoms of Consumption: Toward a Theory of the Conduct of Consumer Conduct." *Journal for Cultural Research* 10 (4): 343–62.

Bird, S. Elizabeth. 2003. *The Audience in Everyday Life: Living in a Media World*. New York: Routledge.

Bishop, Julia C. 2013. "'That's how the whole hand-clap thing passes on': Online/Offline Transmission and Multimodal Variation in a Children's Clapping Game." In *Children's Games in the New Media Age: Childlore, Media, and the Playground*, edited by Andrew Burn and Chris Richards, pp. 53–84. Burlington, VT: Ashgate.

Black, Rebecca W. 2010. "The Language of Webkinz: Early Childhood Literacy in an Online Virtual World." *Digital Culture and Education* 2 (1): 7–24.

Blacking, John. 1967. *Venda Children's Songs: A Study in Ethnomusicological Analysis*. Johannesburg: Witwatersrand University Press.

Blatchford, Peter, Tony Pellegrini, Ed Baines, and Kato Kentaro. 2002. "Playground Games: Their Social Context in Elementary/Junior School." Spencer Foundation, http://www.breaktime.org.uk/SpencerFinalReport02.pdf.

Blatterer, Harry. 2007. "Contemporary Adulthood: Reconceptualizing an Uncontested Category." *Current Sociology* 55 (6): 771–92.

Bloch, Linda-Renée, and Dafna Lemish. 1999. "Disposable Love: The Rise and Fall of a Virtual Pet." *New Media and Society* 1 (3): 283–303.

Blue, Morgan Genevieve. 2013. "Performing 21st-Century Girlhood: Girls, Postfeminist Discourse, and the Disney Star Machine." PhD diss., University of Texas, Austin.

Boellstorff, Tom. 2008. *Coming of Age in Second Life: An Anthropologist Explores the Virtually Human*. Princeton, NJ: Princeton University Press.

Boris, Eileen, and Rhacel Salazar Parreñas, eds. 2010. *Intimate Labors: Cultures, Technologies, and the Politics of Care*. Stanford, CA: Stanford University Press.

Bourdieu, Pierre. 1984. *Distinction: A Social Critique of the Judgment of Taste*. Cambridge, MA: Harvard University Press.

boyd, danah. 2007. "None of This Is Real: Identity and Participation in Friendster." In *Structures of Participation in Digital Culture*, edited by Joe Karaganis, pp. 132–57. New York: Social Science Research Council.

———. 2014. *It's Complicated: The Social Lives of Networked Teens*. New Haven, CT: Yale University Press.

boyd, danah, Eszter Hargittai, Jason Schultz, and John Palfrey. 2011. "Why Parents Help Their Children Lie to Facebook about Age: Unintended Consequences of the 'Children's Online Privacy Protection Act.'" *First Monday* 16 (11): http://firstmonday.org/htbin/cgiwrap/bin/ojs/index.php/fm/article/viewArticle/3850/075.

Boyden, Jo. 1997. "Childhood and the Policy Makers: A Comparative Perspective on the Globalization of Childhood." In *Constructing and Reconstructing Childhood: Contemporary Issues in the Sociological Study of Childhood*, 2nd ed., edited by Allison James and Alan Prout, pp. 187–225. New York: Falmer Press.

Briggs, Charles L. 1986. *Learning How to Ask: A Sociolinguistic Appraisal of the Role of the Interview in Social Science Research*. New York: Cambridge University Press.

Brookshaw, Sharon. 2009. "The Material Culture of Children and Childhood: Understanding Childhood Objects in the Museum Context." *Journal of Material Culture* 14 (3): 365–83.

Brown, Barry, and Abigail Sellen. 2006. "Sharing and Listening to Music." In *Consuming Music Together: Social and Collaborative Aspects of Music Consumption Technologies*, edited by Kenton O'Hara and Barry Brown, pp. 37–56. Dordrecht: Springer.

Brown, Dona. 1995. *Inventing New England: Regional Tourism in the Nineteenth Century*. Washington, DC: Smithsonian Institution Press.

Buchli, Victor, and Gavin Lucas. 2000. "Children, Gender, and the Material Culture of Domestic Abandonment in the Late Twentieth Century." In *Children and Material Culture*, edited by Joanna Sofaer Derevenski, pp. 131–38. New York: Routledge.

Bull, Michael. 2005. "No Dead Air! The iPod and the Culture of Mobile Listening." *Leisure Studies* 24 (4): 343–55.

———. 2006. "Investigating the Culture of Mobile Listening: From Walkman to iPod." In *Consuming Music Together: Social and Collaborative Aspects of Music Consumption Technologies*, edited by Kenton O'Hara and Barry Brown, pp. 131–49. Dordrecht: Springer.

———. 2008. *Sound Moves: iPod Culture and Urban Experience*. New York: Routledge.

Burn, Andrew. 2012. "The Case of the Wildcat Sailors: The Hybrid Lore and Multimodal Languages of the Playground." In *Children, Childhood, and Cultural Heritage*, edited by Kate Darian-Smith and Carla Pascoe, pp. 55–73. New York: Routledge.

Butler, Judith. 1990. *Gender Trouble: Feminism and the Subversion of Identity*. New York: Routledge.

Calhoun, Craig. 1992. "Introduction: Habermas and the Public Sphere." In *Habermas and the Public Sphere*, edited by Craig Calhoun, pp. 1–48. Cambridge, MA: MIT Press.

Calvert, Karin. 1992. *Children in the House: The Material Culture of Early Childhood, 1600–1900*. Boston: Northeastern University Press.

Campbell, Patricia Shehan. 1998. *Songs in Their Heads: Music and Its Meaning in Children's Lives*. New York: Oxford University Press.

de Certeau, Michel. 1984. *The Practice of Everyday Life*, translated by Steven Rendall. Berkeley: University of California Press.

Chen, Xinyin, Doran C. French, and Barry H. Schneider, eds. 2006. *Peer Relationships in Cultural Context*. New York: Cambridge University Press.

Cheney, Kristin E. 2011. "Children as Ethnographers: Reflections on the Importance of Participatory Research in Assessing Orphans' Needs." *Childhood* 18 (2): 166–79.

Christensen, Pia. 2004. "Children's Participation in Ethnographic Research: Issues of Power and Representation." *Children and Society* 18 (2): 165–76.

Christensen, Pia, and Allison James, eds. 2000. *Research with Children: Perspectives and Practices*. London: Falmer.

Chudacoff, Howard P. 1989. *How Old Are You? Age Consciousness in American Culture*. Princeton, NJ: Princeton University Press.

Clifford, James, and George E. Marcus, eds. 1986. *Writing Culture: The Poetics and Politics of Ethnography*. Berkeley: University of California Press.

Cloke, Paul, and Jo Little, eds. 1997. *Contested Countryside Cultures: Otherness, Marginalisation, and Rurality*. New York: Routledge.

Cohen, Stanley. 1987 [1972]. *Folk Devils and Moral Panics: The Creation of the Mods and Rockers*. New York: Basil Blackwell.

Cole, Jennifer, and Deborah Durham, eds. 2008a. *Figuring the Future: Globalization and the Temporalities of Children and Youth*. Santa Fe, NM: School for Advanced Research Press.

———. 2008b. "Introduction: Globalization and the Temporality of Children and Youth." In *Figuring the Future: Globalization and the Temporalities of Children and Youth*. Santa Fe, NM: School for Advanced Research Press.

Cole, Timothy. 2010. "Up Against the Blackboard: Youth and Children's Liberation in the 1970s." Paper presented to "Exploring Childhood Studies" conference, Department of Childhood Studies, Rutgers University–Camden, Camden, New Jersey, April 9.

Coleman, E. Gabriella. 2010. "Ethnographic Approaches to Digital Media." *Annual Review of Anthropology* 39: 1–19.

Collins, James. 1996. "Socialization to Text: Structure and Contradiction in Schooled Literacy." In *Natural Histories of Discourse*, edited by Michael Silverstein and Greg Urban, pp. 203–28. Chicago: University of Chicago Press.

———. 2009. "Social Reproduction in Classrooms and Schools." *Annual Review of Anthropology* 38: 33–48.

Colloredo-Mansfield, Rudi. 2003. "Matter Unbound." *Journal of Material Culture* 8 (3): 245–54.

Conforti, Joseph A. 2001. *Imagining New England: Explorations of Regional Identity from the Pilgrims to the Mid-Twentieth Century*. Chapel Hill: University of North Carolina Press.

Connor, Steven. 2004. "Edison's Teeth: Touching Hearing." In *Hearing Cultures: Essays on Sound, Listening, and Modernity*, edited by Veit Erlmann, pp. 153–72. New York: Berg.

Cook, Daniel Thomas. 2003. "Spatial Biographies of Children's Consumption: Market Places and Spaces of Childhood in the 1930s and Beyond." *Journal of Consumer Culture* 3 (2): 147–69.

———. 2004. *The Commodification of Childhood: The Children's Clothing Industry and the Rise of the Child Consumer*. Durham, NC: Duke University Press.

———. 2011. "Editorial: A Ghostly Presence." *Childhood* 18 (1): 3–6.

Cook, Daniel Thomas, and Susan B. Kaiser. 2004. "Betwixt and be Tween: Age Ambiguity and the Sexualization of the Female Consuming Subject." *Journal of Consumer Culture* 4 (2): 203–27.

Cooper, B. Lee. 1989. "Rhythm 'n' Rhymes: Character and Theme Images from Children's Literature in Contemporary Recordings, 1950–1985." *Popular Music and Society* 13 (1): 53–71.

Corsaro, William A. 1985. *Friendship and Peer Culture in the Early Years*. Norwood, NJ: Ablex Publishing Corp.

———. 1992. "Interpretive Reproduction in Children's Peer Culture." *Social Psychology Quarterly* 55 (2): 160–77.

Corsaro, William A., and Donna Eder. 1990. "Children's Peer Cultures." *Annual Review of Sociology* 16: 197–220.

Côté, James E., and Anton L. Allahar. 1996. *Generation on Hold: Coming of Age in the Late Twentieth Century*. New York: New York University Press.

Crafts, Susan D., Daniel Cavicchi, Charles Keil, and The Music in Daily Life Project. 1993. *My Music*. Hanover, NH: University Press of New England for Wesleyan University Press.

Cross, Gary. 1997. *Kids' Stuff: Toys and the Changing World of American Childhood*. Cambridge, MA: Harvard University Press.

Cunningham, Hugh. 1998. "Review Essay: Histories of Childhood." *American Historical Review* 103 (4): 1195–208.

Cusick, Suzanne G. 2006. "Music as Torture / Music as Weapon." *Trans: Revista Transcultural de Música* 10: http://www.sibetrans.com/trans/articulo/152/music-as-torture-music-as-weapon.

———. 2008. "'You are in a place that is out of the world . . .': Music in the Detention Camps of the 'Global War on Terror.'" *Journal of the Society for American Music* 2 (1): 1–26.

Custodero, Lori A. 2005. "'Being With': The Resonant Legacy of Childhood's Creative Aesthetic." *Journal of Aesthetic Education* 39 (2): 36–57.

Daughtry, J. Martin. 2015. *Listening to War: Sound, Music, Trauma, and Survival in Wartime Iraq*. New York: Oxford University Press.

Derevenski, Joanna Sofaer. 2000. "Material Culture Shock: Confronting Expectations in the Material Culture of Children." In *Children and Material Culture*, edited by Joanna Sofaer Derevenski, pp. 3–16. New York: Routledge.

Dinshaw, Carolyn, Lee Edelman, Roderick A. Ferguson, Carla Freccero, Elizabeth Freeman, Judith Halberstam, Annamarie Jagose, Christopher Nealon, and Nguyen Tan Hoang. 2007. "Theorizing Queer Temporalities: A Roundtable Discussion." *GLQ: A Journal of Lesbian and Gay Studies* 13 (2/3): 177–95.

Douglas, Mary. 2005 [1966]. *Purity and Danger: An Analysis of the Concept of Pollution and Taboo*. New York: Routledge.

du Gay, Paul, Stuart Hall, Linda Janes, Hugh Mackay, and Keith Negus. 1997. *Doing Cultural Studies: The Story of the Sony Walkman*. Thousand Oaks, CA: SAGE.

Dyson, Anne Haas. 2001. "Where are the Childhoods in Childhood Literacy? An Exploration in Outer (School) Space." *Journal of Early Childhood Literacy* 1 (1): 9–39.

———. 2003. *The Brothers and Sisters Learn to Write: Popular Literacies in Childhood and School Cultures*. New York: Teachers College Press.

Eckert, Penelope. 1988. "Adolescent Social Structure and the Spread of Linguistic Change." *Language in Society* 17 (2): 183–207.

———. 1989. *Jocks and Burnouts: Social Categories and Identity in the High School*. New York: Teacher's College Press.

———. 1996. "Vowels and Nail Polish: The Emergence of Linguistic Style in the Preadolescent Heterosexual Marketplace." In *Gender and Belief Systems: Proceedings of the Fourth Berkeley Women and Language Conference*, edited by Natasha Warner, pp. 183–90. Berkeley, CA: Berkeley Women and Language Group.

Eckert, Penelope, and Sally McConnell-Ginet. 1995. "Constructing Meaning, Constructing Selves: Snapshots of Language, Gender, and Class from Belten High." In *Gender Articulated: Language and the Socially Constructed Self*, edited by Kira Hall and Mary Bucholtz, pp. 469–507. New York: Routledge.

Edelman, Lee. 2004. *No Future: Queer Theory and the Death Drive*. Durham, NC: Duke University Press.

Emberly, Andrea. 2013. "Venda Children's Musical Culture in Limpopo, South Africa." In *The Oxford Handbook of Children's Musical Cultures*, edited by Patricia Shehan Campbell and Trevor Wiggins, pp. 77–95. New York: Oxford University Press.

Everhart, Robert B. 1983. *Reading, Writing, and Resistance: Adolescence and Labor in a Junior High School*. Boston: Routledge and Kegan Paul.

Fabian, Johannes. 1983. *Time and the Other: How Anthropology Makes Its Object*. New York: Columbia University Press.

Fabregat, Malena, Maria Costa, and M. Romero. 2004. "Adaptation of Traditional Toys and Games to New Technologies: New Products Generation." In *Toys, Games, and Media*, edited by Jeffrey Goldstein, David Buckingham, and Gilles Brougère, pp. 225–40. Mahwah, NJ: Lawrence Erlbaum.

Federici, Silvia. 1975. *Wages Against Housework*. Bristol: Power of Women Collective and Falling Wall Press.

Feld, Steven. 1984. "Communication, Music, and Speech about Music." *Yearbook for Traditional Music* 16: 1–18.

———. 1988. "Aesthetics As Iconicity of Style, or 'Lift-up-over Sounding': Getting Into the Kaluli Groove." *Yearbook for Traditional Music* 20: 74–113.

———. 1990. *Sound and Sentiment: Birds, Weeping, Poetics, and Song in Kaluli Expression*, 2nd ed. Philadelphia: University of Pennsylvania Press.

———. 1994. "From Schizophonia to Schismogenesis: On the Discourses and Commodification Practices of 'World Music' and 'World Beat.'" In *Music Grooves: Essays and Dialogues*, edited by Charles Keil and Steven Feld, pp. 257–89. Chicago: University of Chicago Press.

Field, Corinne. 2014. *The Struggle for Equal Adulthood: Gender, Race, Age, and the Fight for Citizenship in Antebellum America*. Charlotte: University of North Carolina Press.

Firestone, Shulamith. 1970. *The Dialectic of Sex: The Case for Feminist Revolution*. New York: Bantam Books.

Fleming, Dan. 1996. *Powerplay: Toys as Popular Culture*. Manchester, UK: Manchester University Press.

Folbre, Nancy. 2008. *Valuing Children: Rethinking the Economics of the Family*. Cambridge, MA: Harvard University Press.

Foley, Douglas A. 1990. *Learning Capitalist Culture: Deep in the Heart of Tejas*. Philadelphia: University of Pennsylvania Press.

Foucault, Michel. 1978. *The History of Sexuality*, vol. 1, translated by Robert Hurley. New York: Vintage.

———. 1997 [1981]. "Friendship as a Way of Life." In *Ethics: Subjectivity and Truth*, translated by Robert Hurley, edited by Paul Rabinow, pp. 135–40. New York: New Press.

Fox, Aaron. 2004. *Real Country: Music and Language in Working-Class Culture*. Durham, NC: Duke University Press.

Fraser, Nancy. 1985. "What's Critical about Critical Theory? The Case of Habermas and Gender." *New German Critique* 35: 97–131.

———. 1992. "Rethinking the Public Sphere: A Contribution to the Critique of Actually Existing Democracy." In *Habermas and the Public Sphere*, edited by Craig Calhoun, pp. 109–42. Cambridge, MA: MIT Press.

Friedland, Lewis, Dhavan V. Shah, Nam-Jin Lee, Mark A. Rademacher, Lucy Atkinson, and Thomas Hove. 2007. "Capital, Consumption, Communication, and Citizenship: The Social Positioning of Taste and Civic Culture in the United States." *Annals of the American Academy of Political and Social Science* 611: 31–50.

Fujimoto, Kenichi. 2005. "The Third-Stage Paradigm: Territory Machines from the Girls' Pager Revolution to Mobile Aesthetics." In *Personal, Portable, Pedestrian: Mobile Phones in Japanese Life*, edited by Mizuko Ito, Daisuke Okabe, and Misa Matsuda, pp. 77–101. Cambridge, MA: MIT Press.

Gallacher, Lesley-Anne, and Michael Gallagher. 2008. "Methodological Immaturity in Childhood Research? Thinking through 'Participatory Methods.'" *Childhood* 15 (4): 499–516.

Garfinkel, Harold. 1967. *Studies in Ethnomethodology*. Englewood Cliffs, NJ: Prentice-Hall.

Gaunt, Kyra D. 2006. *The Games Black Girls Play: Learning the Ropes from Double-Dutch to Hip-Hop*. New York: New York University Press.

Gee, James Paul. 2008. *Social Linguistics and Literacies: Ideology in Discourses*, 3rd ed. New York: Routledge.

Gill-Peterson, Julian. 2015. "The Value of the Future: The Child as Human Capital and the Neoliberal Labor of Race." *WSQ: Women's Studies Quarterly* 43 (1/2): 181–96.

Gillis, John R. 2008. "The Islanding of Children—Reshaping the Mythical Landscapes of Children." In *Designing Modern Childhoods: History, Space, and the Material Culture of Children*, edited by Marta Gutman and Ning de Coninck-Smith, pp. 316–30. New Brunswick, NJ: Rutgers University Press.

Gilmore, Perry, and Allan A. Glatthorn, eds. 1982. *Children In and Out of School: Ethnography and Education*. Washington, DC: Center for Applied Linguistics.

Gittell, Ross, and Charles S. Colgan. 2004. "New England Regionalism: Economic Motivations and Barriers." In *Regionalism in a Global Society: Persistence and Change in Atlantic Canada and New England*, edited by Stephen G. Tomblin and Charles S. Colgan, pp. 127–47. Peterborough, ON: Broadview Press.

Goff, Phillip Atiba, Matthew Christian Jackson, Brooke Allison Lewis Di Leone, Carmen Culotta, and Natalie Ann DiTomasso. 2014. "The Essence of Innocence: Consequences of Dehumanizing Black Children." *Journal of Personality and Social Psychology* 106 (4): 526–45.

Goldstein, Jeffrey, David Buckingham, and Gilles Brougère. 2004. "Introduction: Toys, Games, and Media." In *Toys, Games, and Media*, edited by Jeffrey Goldstein, David Buckingham, and Gilles Brougère, pp. 1–8. Mahwah, NJ: Lawrence Erlbaum.

Goodwin, Marjorie Harness. 2006. *The Hidden Life of Girls: Games of Stance, Status, and Exclusion*. Oxford: Blackwell.

Gordon, Hava Rachel. 2009. *We Fight to Win: Inequality and the Politics of Youth Activism*. New Brunswick, NJ: Rutgers University Press.

Graham, Kara Elizabeth. 2005. "The Massachusetts Museum of Contemporary Art: How an Arts Organization Became a Small Town's Unlikely Economic Savior." MA thesis, American University.

Green, Lucy. 2008. *Music, Informal Learning, and the School: A New Classroom Pedagogy*. London: Ashgate.

Grimes, Sara M. 2014. "Configuring the Child Player." *Science, Technology, and Human Values* 40 (1): 126–48.

Grimes, Sara M., and Andrew Feenberg. 2009. "Rationalizing Play: A Critical Theory of Digital Gaming." *The Information Society* 25 (2): 105–18.

Grossberg, Lawrence. 2005. *Caught in the Crossfire: Kids, Politics, and America's Future*. Boulder: Paradigm Publishers.

Grugeon, Elizabeth. 2001. "'We like singing the Spice Girl songs . . . and we like Tig and Stuck in the Mud': Girls' Traditional Games on Two Playgrounds." In *Play Today in the Primary School Playground*, edited by Julia Bishop and Mavis Curtis, pp. 98–114. Buckingham, UK: Open University Press.

———. 2005. "Listening to Learning Outside the Classroom: Student Teachers Study Playground Literacies." *Literacy* 39 (1): 3–9.

Gubar, Marah. 2013. "Risky Business: Talking about Children in Children's Literature Criticism." *Children's Literature Association Quarterly* 38 (4): 450–57.

———. 2016. "The Hermeneutics of Recuperation: What a Kinship-Model Approach to Children's Agency Could Do for Children's Literature and Childhood Studies." *Jeunesse: Young People, Texts, Cultures* 8 (1): 291–310.

Gupta, Akhil, and James Ferguson. 1997. "Culture, Power, Place: Ethnography at the End of an Era." In *Culture, Power, Place: Explorations in Critical Anthropology*, edited by Akhil Gupta and James Ferguson, pp. 1–29. Durham, NC: Duke University Press.

Habermas, Jürgen. 1984. *The Theory of Communicative Action*, vol. 2, *Lifeworld and System*, translated by Thomas McCarthy. Boston: Beacon Press.

———. 1989 [1962]. *The Structural Transformation of the Public Sphere: An Inquiry into a Category of Bourgeois Society*, translated by Thomas Burger and Frederick Lawrence. Cambridge, MA: MIT Press.

Hains, Rebecca C. 2007. "Inventing the Teenage Girl: The Construction of Female Identity in Nickelodeon's *My Life as a Teenage Robot*." *Popular Communication* 5 (3): 191–213.

Halberstam, Judith. 2005. *In a Queer Time and Place: Transgender Bodies, Subcultural Lives*. New York: New York University Press.

———. 2011. *The Queer Art of Failure*. Durham, NC: Duke University Press.

Hall, Stuart. 1996. "Introduction: Who Needs Identity?" In *Questions of Cultural Identity*, edited by Stuart Hall and Paul du Gay, pp. 1–17. London: SAGE.

Harrison, Blake A. 2006. *The View from Vermont: Tourism and the Making of an American Rural Landscape*. Burlington, VT: UPNE/University of Vermont Press.

Hart, Daniel, and Robert Atkins. 2011. "American Sixteen- and Seventeen-Year-Olds Are Ready to Vote." *Annals of the American Academy of Political and Social Science* 633 (1): 201–22.

Harwood, Eve. 1998. "Learning in Context: A Playground Tale." *Research Studies in Music Education* 11: 52–61.

Hebdige, Dick. 1979. *Subculture: The Meaning of Style*. New York: Routledge.

Hendershot, Heather. 2004. "Nickelodeon's Nautical Nonsense: The Intergenerational Appeal of *Spongebob Squarepants*." In *Nickelodeon Nation: The History, Politics, and Economics of America's Only TV Channel for Kids*, edited by Heather Hendershot, pp. 182–208. New York: New York University Press.

Hennion, Antoine. 2004. "Pragmatics of Taste." In *The Blackwell Companion to the Sociology of Culture*, edited by Mark Jacobs and Nancy Hanrahan, pp. 131–44. Oxford: Blackwell.

Herring, Susan C. 2008. "Questioning the Generational Divide: Technological Exoticism and Adult Constructions of Online Youth Identity." In *Youth, Identity, and Digital Media*, edited by David Buckingham, pp. 72–91. Cambridge, MA: MIT Press.

Hey, Valerie. 2002. "Horizontal Solidarities and Molten Capitalism: The Subject, Intersubjectivity, Self and the Other in Late Modernity." *Discourse: Studies in the Cultural Politics of Education* 23 (2): 227–41.

Higgins, Lee. 2012. "One-to-One Encounters: Facilitators, Participants, and Friendship." *Theory Into Practice* 51 (3): 159–66.

Hijazi-Omari, Hiyam, and Rivka Ribak. 2008. "Playing with Fire: On the Domestication of the Mobile Phone among Palestinian Teenage Girls in Israel." *Information, Communication, and Society* 11 (2): 149–66.

Hirschfeld, Lawrence A. 2002. "Why Don't Anthropologists Like Children?" *American Anthropologist* 104 (2): 611–27.

Hochschild, Arlie Russell, with Anne Machung. 2003 [1989]. *The Second Shift*, 2nd ed. New York: Penguin.

Hoffman, Lee. 2009. "Numbers and Types of Public Elementary and Secondary Schools From the Common Core of Data: School Year 2007–08." Washington, DC: National Center for Education Statistics, US Department of Education, https://nces.ed.gov/pubsearch/pubsinfo.asp?pubid=2010305.

Holland, Sally, and Alexandra Hillman. 2010. "Power, Agency and Participatory Agendas: A Critical Exploration of Young People's Engagement in Participative Qualitative Research." *Childhood* 17 (3): 360–75.

Holt, Douglas B. 1998. "Does Cultural Capital Structure American Consumption?" *Journal of Consumer Research* 25 (1): 1–25.

Holt, John. 1974. *Escape from Childhood: The Needs and Rights of Children*. New York: Dutton.

Hubbard, Ruth. 1988. "Unofficial Literacy in a Sixth-Grade Classroom." *Language Arts* 65 (2): 126–34.

———. 1989. "Notes from the Underground: Unofficial Literacy in One Sixth Grade." *Anthropology and Education Quarterly* 20 (4): 291–307.

Hunter, Erin. 2003. *Into the Wild*. Vol. 1 of *Warriors: The Prophecy Begins*. New York: HarperCollins.

Hutchby, Ian. 2001. "Technologies, Texts, and Affordances." *Sociology* 35 (2): 441–56.

———. 2003. "Affordances and the Analysis of Technologically Mediated Interaction: A Response to Brian Rappert." *Sociology* 37 (3): 581–89.

Hymes, Dell. 1973. "Speech and Language: On the Origins and Foundations of Inequality among Speakers." *Daedalus* 102 (3): 59–85.

Ito, Mizuko. 2005a. "Introduction: Personal, Portable, Pedestrian." In *Personal, Portable, Pedestrian: Mobile Phones in Japanese Life*, edited by Mizuko Ito, Daisuke Okabe, and Misa Matsuda, pp. 1–16. Cambridge, MA: MIT Press.

———. 2005b. "Mobilizing Fun in the Production and Consumption of Children's Software." *Annals of the American Academy of Political and Social Sciences* 597 (1): 82–102.

———. 2007. "Technologies of the Childhood Imagination: *Yu-Gi-Oh!*, Media Mixes, and Everyday Cultural Production." In *Structures of Participation in Digital Culture*, edited by Joe Karaganis, pp. 88–110. New York: Social Science Research Council.

———. 2008a. "Education vs. Entertainment: A Cultural History of Children's Software." In *The Ecology of Games: Connecting Youth, Games, and Learning*, edited by Katie Salen, pp. 89–116. Cambridge, MA: MIT Press.

———. 2008b. "Introduction." In *Networked Publics*, edited by Kazys Varnelis, pp. 1–14. Cambridge, MA: MIT Press.

———. 2009. *Engineering Play: A Cultural History of Children's Software*. Cambridge, MA: MIT Press.

———. 2011. "Machinima in a Fanvid Ecology." *Journal of Visual Culture* 10 (1): 51–54.

Ito, Mizuko, Sonja Baumer, Matteo Bittani, danah boyd, Rachel Cody, Becky Herr-Stephenson, Heather A. Horst, Patricia G. Lange, Dilan Mahendren, Katynka Z. Martinez, C. J. Pascoe, Dan Perkel, Laura Robinson, Christo Sims, Lisa Tripp, Judd Antin, Michael Finn, Arthur Law, Annie Manion, Sarai Mitnick, Dan Schlossberg, and Sarita Yardi. 2010. *Hanging Out, Messing Around, Geeking Out: Living and Learning with New Media.* Cambridge, MA: MIT Press.

Ito, Mizuko, Kris Gutiérrez, Sonia Livingstone, Bill Penuel, Jean Rhodes, Katie Salen, Juliet Schor, Julian Sefton-Green, and S. Craig Watkins. 2013. "Connected Learning: An Agenda for Research and Design." Irvine, CA: Digital Media and Learning Research Hub, http://eprints.lse.ac.uk/48114/.

Ito, Mizuko, Daisuke Okabe, and Ken Anderson. 2008. "Portable Objects in Three Global Cities: The Personalization of Urban Places." In *The Reconstruction of Space and Time: Mobile Communication Practices,* edited by Rich Ling and Scott W. Campbell, pp. 67–87. Piscataway, NJ: Transaction Publishers.

Jacoby, Sally, and Elinor Ochs. 1995. "Co-Construction: An Introduction." *Research on Language and Social Interaction* 28 (3): 171–83.

James, Allison. 1982. "Confections, Concoctions, and Conceptions." In *Popular Culture: Past and Present,* edited by Bernard Waites, Tony Bennett, and Graham Martin, pp. 294–307. Buckingham, UK: Open University Press.

James, Allison, and Alan Prout. 1997. "Re-presenting Childhood: Time and Transition in the Study of Childhood." In *Constructing and Reconstructing Childhood: Contemporary Issues in the Sociological Study of Childhood,* 2nd ed., edited by Alan Prout and Allison James, pp. 227–46. New York: Falmer Press.

James, Allison, Alan Prout, and Chris Jenks. 1998. *Theorizing Childhood.* Cambridge, UK: Polity Press.

Johansson, Barbro. 2012. "Doing Adulthood in Childhood Research." *Childhood* 19 (1): 101–14.

Kafer, Alison. 2013. *Feminist, Queer, Crip.* Bloomington: Indiana University Press.

Keane, Webb. 2003. "Self-Interpretation, Agency, and the Objects of Anthropology: Reflections on a Genealogy." *Comparative Studies in Society and History* 45 (2): 222–48.

———. 2008. "Modes of Objectification in Educational Experience." *Linguistics and Education* 19 (3): 312–18.

Kehily, Mary Jane, Mairtin Mac An Ghaill, Debbie Epstein, and Peter Redman. 2002. "Private Girls and Public Worlds: Producing Femininities in the Primary School." *Discourse: Studies in the Cultural Politics of Education* 23 (2): 167–77.

Kenney, William Howland. 1999. *Recorded Music in American Life: The Phonograph and Popular Memory, 1890–1945.* New York: Oxford University Press.

Kirsch, Max H. 1998. *In the Wake of the Giant: Multinational Restructuring and Uneven Development in a New England Community.* Albany: State University of New York Press.

Kittay, Eva Feder, and Ellen K. Feder, eds. 2002. *The Subject of Care: Feminist Perspectives on Dependency.* Lanham, MD: Rowman and Littlefield.

Kline, Stephen. 1993. *Out of the Garden: Toys, TV, and Children's Culture in the Age of Marketing.* New York: Verso.

Kotval, Zenia, and John Robert Mullin. 1997. "The Closing of the Yankee Rowe Nuclear Power Plant." *Journal of the American Planning Association* 63 (4): 454–68.

Kozlovsky, Roy. 2008. "Adventure Playgrounds and Postwar Reconstruction." In *Designing Modern Childhoods: History, Space, and the Material Culture of Children,* edited by Marta Gutman and Ning de Coninck-Smith, pp. 171–90. New Brunswick, NJ: Rutgers University Press.

Kress, Gunther. 1997. *Before Writing: Rethinking the Paths to Literacy.* New York: Routledge.

Kristeva, Julia. 1982. *Powers of Horror: An Essay on Abjection,* translated by Leon S. Roudiez. New York: Columbia University.

Kromidas, Maria. 2014. "The 'Savage' Child and the Nature of Race: Posthuman Interventions from New York City." *Anthropological Theory* 14 (4): 422–41.

Labov, William. 2001. *Principles of Linguistic Change,* vol. 2, *Social Factors.* Malden, MA: Blackwell.

Ladd, Gary W. 1999. "Peer Relationships and Social Competence During Early and Middle Childhood." *Annual Review of Psychology* 50: 333–59.

Langer, Beryl. 2004. "The Business of Branded Enchantment: Ambivalence and Disjuncture in the Global Children's Culture Industry." *Journal of Consumer Culture* 4 (2): 251–77.

Lave, Jean, and Ray McDermott. 2002. "Estranged (Labor) Learning." *Outlines* 4 (1): 19–48.

Lave, Jean, and Etienne Wenger. 1991. *Situated Learning: Legitimate Peripheral Participation.* New York: Cambridge University Press.

Lefstein, Adam, and Julia Snell. 2011. "Promises and Problems of Teaching With Popular Culture: A Linguistic Ethnographic Analysis of Discourse Genre Mixing in a Literacy Lesson." *Reading Research Quarterly* 46 (1): 40–69.

Lenhart, Amanda, Joseph Kahne, Ellen Middaugh, Alexandra Rankin MacGill, Chris Evans, and Jessica Vitak. 2008. "Teens, Video Games, and Civics." Washington, DC: Pew Internet and American Life Project, http://www.pewinternet.org/Reports/2008/Teens-Video-Games-and-Civics.aspx.

Lenhart, Amanda, Mary Madden, Alexandra Rankin MacGill, and Aaron Smith. 2007. "Teens and Social Media." Washington, DC: Pew Internet and American Life Project, http://www.pewinternet.org/Reports/2007/Teens-and-Social-Media.aspx.

Lesnik-Oberstein, Karin. 2011. "Introduction: Voice, Agency and the Child." In *Children in Culture, Revisited: Further Approaches to Childhood,* edited by Karin Lesnik-Oberstein, pp. 1–17. New York: Palgrave Macmillan.

Levine, Lawrence. 1990. *Highbrow/Lowbrow: The Emergence of Cultural Hierarchy in America.* Cambridge, MA: Harvard University Press.

Levy, Steven. 2006. "Q&A: Jobs on iPod's Cultural Impact." *Newsweek.com,* October 16, https://web.archive.org/web/20070104153310/http://www.msnbc.msn.com/id/15262121/site/newsweek/page/3/.

Lill, Athena. 2014a. "An Analytical Lens for Studying Informal Learning in Music: Subversion, Embodied Learning, and Participatory Performance." *Action, Criticism, and Theory for Music Education* 13 (1): 223–47.

———. 2014b. "From Local to Global: The Evolution of Musical Play in Secondary Schools." *International Journal of Play* 3 (3): 251–66.

———. 2015. "Informal Learnings? Young People's Informal Learning of Music in Australian and British Schools." PhD diss., University of Sydney.

Lowood, Henry. 2006. "High-performance Play: The Making of Machinima." *Journal of Media Practice* 7 (1): 25–42.

Lucas, Gavin. 2002. "Disposability and Dispossession in the Twentieth Century." *Journal of Material Culture* 7 (1): 5–22.

Mahon, Maureen. 2004. *Right to Rock: The Black Rock Coalition and the Cultural Politics of Race.* Durham, NC: Duke University Press.

Mankekar, Purnima. 1999. *Screening Culture, Viewing Politics: An Ethnography of Television, Womanhood, and Nation in Postcolonial India.* Durham, NC: Duke University Press.

Manning, Steven. 1999. "Students for Sale: How Corporations Are Buying Their Way into America's Classrooms." *The Nation* 269 (9) September 27: 11–18.

Marsh, Jackie. 2002. "Colloquium: Electronic Toys: Why Should We Be Concerned? A Response to Levin and Rosenquest." *Contemporary Issues in Early Childhood* 3 (1): 132–38.

———. 2004. "The Techno-Literacy Practices of Young Children." *Journal of Early Childhood Research* 2 (1): 51–66.

———. 2006. "Popular Culture in the Literacy Curriculum: A Bourdieuan Analysis." *Reading Research Quarterly* 41 (2): 160–74.
———. 2007. "New Literacies and Old Pedagogies: Recontextualizing Rules and Practices." *International Journal of Inclusive Education* 11 (3): 267–81.
———. 2010. "Young Children's Play in Virtual Worlds." *Journal of Early Childhood Research* 8 (1): 23–39.
———. 2014. "From the Wild Frontier of Davy Crockett to the Wintery Fiords of Frozen: Changes in Media Consumption, Play and Literacy from the 1950s to the 2010s." *International Journal of Play* 3 (3): 267–79.
Marsh, Jackie, and Julia Bishop. 2012. "Rewind and Replay? Television and Play in the 1950s/1960s and 2010s." *International Journal of Play* 1 (3): 279–91.
Marsh, Jackie, and Elaine Millard. 2001. *Literacy and Popular Culture: Using Children's Culture in the Classroom*. London: Paul Chapman.
Marsh, Kathryn. 1995. "Children's Singing Games: Composition in the Playground?" *Research Studies in Music Education* 4: 2–11.
———. 1999. "Mediated Orality: The Role of Popular Music in the Changing Tradition of Children's Musical Play." *Research Studies in Music Education* 13: 2–12.
———. 2001. "It's Not All Black or White: The Influence of the Media, the Classroom, and Immigrant Groups on Children's Playground Singing Games." In *Play Today in the Primary School Playground*, edited by Julia C. Bishop and Mavis Curtis, pp. 80–97. Buckingham, UK: Open University Press.
———. 2002. "Observations on a Case Study of Song Transmission and Preservation in Two Aboriginal Communities: Dilemmas of a 'Neo-Colonialist' in the Field." *Research Studies in Music Education* 19: 4–13.
———. 2006. "Cycles of Appropriation in Children's Musical Play: Orality in the Age of Reproduction." *World of Music* 48 (1): 9–32.
———. 2008. *The Musical Playground: Global Tradition and Change in Children's Songs and Games*. New York: Oxford University Press.
———. 2009. "Music Education, Ethnographic Research, and Thick Description: A Response." *Research Studies in Music Education* 31 (1): 96–100.
Marshall, Wayne. 2014. "Treble Culture." In *The Oxford Handbook of Mobile Music Studies*, vol. 2, edited by Jason Stanyek and Sumanth Gopinath, pp. 43–76. New York: Oxford University Press.
Massoud, Lindsey A., and Joel Kuipers. 2008. "Objectification and the Inscription of Knowledge in Science Classrooms." *Linguistics and Education* 19 (3): 211–24.
Mauss, Marcel. 1979. "Body Techniques." In *Sociology and Psychology: Essays*, translated by Ben Brewster, pp. 95–123. Boston: Routledge and Kegan Paul.
McCall, Leslie. 2005. "The Complexity of Intersectionality." *Signs: Journal of Women in Culture and Society* 30 (3): 1771–800.
McCarthy, Joseph F., and danah boyd. 2005. "Digital Backchannels in Shared Physical Spaces: Experiences at an Academic Conference." In *CHI '05: Proceedings of the SIGCHI Conference on Human Factors in Computing Systems*, pp. 1641–44. New York: Association for Computing Machinery.
McDermott, Ray. 1988. "Inarticulateness." In *Linguistics in Context: Connecting Observation and Understanding*, edited by Deborah Tannen, pp. 37–68. Norwood, NJ: Ablex Publishing Corp.
———. 2011. "Can We Afford Theories of Learning?" In *Theories of Learning and Studies of Instructional Practice*, edited by Timothy Koschmann, pp. 403–15. New York: Springer.
McDermott, Ray, Shelley Goldman, and Hervé Varenne. 2006. "The Cultural Work of Learning Disabilities." *Educational Researcher* 35 (6): 12–17.

McDermott, Ray, and Hervé Varenne. 1995. "Culture *as* Disability." *Anthropology and Education Quarterly* 26 (3): 324–48.

McDonough, John. 2004. "It's 'Kids First' Philosophy and 'Let Kids Be Kids' Mantra Drive the Mighty Nickelodeon Engine." Special advertising section of *Advertising Age* 75 (11) March 15: N2–N10.

McGillis, Roderick. 2003. "Coprophilia for Kids: The Culture of Grossness." In *Youth Cultures: Texts, Images, and Identities*, edited by Kerry Mallan and Sharyn Pearce, pp. 183–96. Westport, CT: Praeger.

McLeod, Julie. 2002. "Working Out Intimacy: Young People and Friendship in an Age of Reflexivity." *Discourse: Studies in the Cultural Politics of Education* 23 (2): 212–26.

McRuer, Robert. 2006. *Crip Theory: Cultural Signs of Queerness and Disability*. New York: New York University Press.

Mehan, Hugh. 1979. *Learning Lessons: Social Organization in the Classroom*. Cambridge, MA: Harvard University Press.

———. 1986. "'What Time Is It Denise?': Asking Known Information Questions in Classroom Discourse." In *Case Studies in Classroom Research*, edited by M. Hammersley. Milton Keynes, UK: Open University Press.

Melton, Stephanie. 2010. "Food Rules: The Role of Kids' Food in Children's Peer Culture." Paper presented to "Exploring Childhood Studies" conference, Department of Childhood Studies, Rutgers University–Camden, Camden, New Jersey, April 9.

Mertz, Elizabeth. 1996. "Recontextualization as Socialization: Text and Pragmatics in the Law School Classroom." In *Natural Histories of Discourse*, edited by Michael Silverstein and Greg Urban, pp. 229–49. Chicago: University of Chicago Press.

Miller, Daniel. 2008. *The Comfort of Things*. Cambridge, UK: Polity Press.

———. 2010. *Stuff*. Cambridge, UK: Polity Press.

Miller, Kiri. 2012. *Playing Along: Digital Games, YouTube, and Virtual Performance*. New York: Oxford University Press.

Milner, Murray. 2004. *Freaks, Geeks, and Cool Kids: American Teenagers, Schools, and the Culture of Consumption*. New York: Routledge.

Minks, Amanda. 1999. "Growing and Grooving to a Steady Beat: Pop Music in Fifth-Graders' Social Lives." *Yearbook for Traditional Music* 31: 77–101.

———. 2002. "From Children's Song to Expressive Practices: Old and New Directions in the Ethnomusicological Study of Children." *Ethnomusicology* 46 (3): 379–408.

Mintz, Steven. 2015. *The Prime of Life: A History of Modern Adulthood*. Cambridge, MA: Belknap Press.

Mitchell, J. Allen. 2014. *Becoming Human: The Matter of the Medieval Child*. Minneapolis: University of Minnesota Press.

Mitroff, Donna, and Rebecca Herr Stephenson. 2007. "The Television Tug-of-War: A Brief History of Children's Television Programming in the United States." In *The Children's Television Community*, edited by J. Alison Bryant, pp. 3–34. New York: Routledge.

Montgomery, Kathryn C. 2007. *Generation Digital: Politics, Commerce, and Childhood in the Age of the Internet*. Cambridge, MA: MIT Press.

Munster, Anna. 2006. *Materializing New Media: Embodiment in Information Aesthetics*. Hanover, NH: Dartmouth College Press.

National Center for Educational Statistics. 2010. "Common Core of Data Public Elementary/Secondary School Universe Survey: School Year 2007–08, Version 1b." Washington, DC: US Department of Education, http://nces.ed.gov/ccd/pubschuniv.asp.

Nietzsche, Friedrich. 1989 [1887]. "On The Genealogy of Morals." In *On the Genealogy of Morals and Ecce Homo*, translated by Walter Kaufman and R. J. Hollingdale, edited by Walter Kaufman, pp. 15–163. New York: Vintage.

Nodelman, Perry. 1997. "Fear of Children's Literature: What's Left (or Right) After Theory?" In *Reflections of Change: Children's Literature Since 1945*, edited by Sandra Beckett. Westport, CT: Greenwood.

Novak, David. 2013. *Japanoise: Music at the Edge of Circulation*. Durham, NC: Duke University Press.

Nussbaum, Martha C. 2000. *Women and Human Development*. New York: Cambridge University Press.

———. 2006. *Frontiers of Justice: Disability, Nationality, Species Membership*. Cambridge, MA: The Belknap Press of Harvard University Press.

O'Hara, Kenton, and Barry Brown, eds. 2006. *Consuming Music Together: Social and Collaborative Aspects of Music Consumption Technologies*. Dordrecht: Springer.

O'Hara, Kenton, April Slayden, and Alex Vorbau. 2007. "Consuming Video on Mobile Devices." In *CHI '07, Proceedings of the SIGCHI Conference on Human Factors in Computing Systems*, pp. 857–66. New York: Association for Computing Machinery.

O'Kane, Claire. 2000. "The Development of Participatory Techniques: Facilitating Children's Views about Decisions which Affect Them." In *Research with Children: Perspectives and Practices*, edited by Pia Christensen and Allison James, pp. 136–59. London: Falmer.

Oakley, Ann. 1993. "Women and Children First and Last: Parallels and Differences between Children's and Women's Studies." In *Childhood as a Social Phenomenon: Lessons from an International Project*, edited by Jens Qvortrup, pp. 51–69. Vienna: European Centre for Social Welfare Policy and Research.

Opie, Iona. 1994. *The People in the Playground*. New York: Oxford University Press.

Opie, Iona, and Peter Opie. 1960. *The Lore and Language of Schoolchildren*. Oxford: Clarendon Press.

———. 1979. *Children's Games in Street and Playground*. New York: Oxford University Press.

———. 1985. *The Singing Game*. New York: Oxford University Press.

Ortner, Sherry B. 1972. "Is Female to Male as Nature Is to Culture?" *Feminist Studies* 1 (2): 5–31.

Palfrey, John, and Urs Gasser. 2008. *Born Digital: Understanding the First Generation of Digital Natives*. New York: Basic Books.

Palfrey, John, Dena T. Sacco, danah boyd, Laura DeBonis, and Jessica Tatlock. 2008. "Enhancing Child Safety and Online Technologies: Final Report of the Internet Safety Task Force to the Multi-State Working Group on Social Networking of State Attorneys General of the United States." Cambridge, MA: Berkman Center for Internet and Society at Harvard University (December 31), http://cyber.law.harvard.edu/pubrelease/isttf.

Parmentier, Richard J. 1994. *Signs in Society: Studies in Semiotic Anthropology*. Bloomington: Indiana University Press.

Pascoe, C. J. 2007. *"Dude, You're a Fag": Masculinity and Sexuality in High School*. Berkeley: University of California Press.

Pecknold, Diane. 2007. *The Selling Sound: The Rise of the Country Music Industry*. Durham, NC: Duke University Press.

Pecora, Norma. 1995. "Children and Television Advertising from a Social Sciences Perspective." *Critical Studies in Mass Communication* 12 (3): 354–64.

Pelissier, Catherine. 1991. "The Anthropology of Teaching and Learning." *Annual Review of Anthropology* 20: 75–95.

Perlman, Marc. 1993. "Idioculture: De-Massifying the Popular Music Audience." *Postmodern Culture* 4 (1).

Peters, John Durham. 1999. *Speaking Into the Air: A History of the Idea of Communication*. Chicago: University of Chicago Press.

Plowman, Lydia. 2004. "'Hey, Hey, Hey! It's Time to Play': Children's Interactions with Smart Toys." In *Toys, Games, and Media*, edited by Jeffrey Goldstein, David Buckingham, and Gilles Brougère, pp. 207–23. Mahwah, NJ: Lawrence Erlbaum.

Pole, Christopher, Philip Mizen, and Angela Bolton. 1999. "Realizing Children's Agency in Research: Partners and Participants?" *International Journal of Social Research Methodology* 2 (1): 39–54.

Poo, Ai-jen. 2015. *The Age of Dignity: Preparing for the Elder Boom in a Changing America*. New York: New Press.

Poole, Deborah. 2008. "The Messiness of Language Socialization in Reading Groups: Participation in and Resistance to the Values of Essayist Literacy." *Linguistics and Education* 19 (4): 378–403.

Porcello, Thomas. 1998. "'Tails Out': Social Phenomenology and the Ethnographic Representation of Technology in Music-Making." *Ethnomusicology* 42 (3): 485–510.

Portwood-Stacer, Laura. 2012. "Media Refusal and Conspicuous Non-consumption: The Performative and Political Dimensions of Facebook Abstention." *New Media and Society* 15 (7): 1041–57.

Postill, John. 2006. *Media and Nation Building: How the Iban Became Malaysian*. Oxford: Berghahn Books.

Powell, Kathy, Susan Danby, and Ann Farrell. 2006. "Investigating an Account of Children 'Passing Notes' in the Classroom: How Boys and Girls Operate Differently in Relation to an Everyday, Classroom Regulatory Practice." *Journal of Early Childhood Research* 4 (3): 259–75.

Prout, Alan. 2000. "Childhood Bodies: Construction, Agency, and Hybridity." In *The Body, Childhood, and Society*, edited by Alan Prout, pp. 1–18. New York: St. Martin's Press.

Prout, Alan, and Allison James. 1997. "A New Paradigm for the Sociology of Childhood? Provenance, Promise, and Problems." In *Constructing and Reconstructing Childhood: Contemporary Issues in the Sociological Study of Childhood*, 2nd ed., edited by Allison James and Alan Prout, pp. 7–32. New York: Falmer Press.

Quinn, Amy Z. 2008. "How Young Is Too Young for Electronics Presents? For Parents, a New Issue on Gifts." *Philadelphia Inquirer* (December 17): http://articles.philly.com/2008-12-17/living/25243820_1_cell-phone-cell-phone-kids-and-parents.

Qvortrup, Jens. 1994. "Childhood Matters: An Introduction." In *Childhood Matters: Social Theory, Practice, and Politics*, edited by Jens Qvortrup, Marjatta Bardy, Giovanni Sgritta, and Helmut Wintersberge, pp. 1–24. Aldershot: Avebury.

Radano, Ronald. 2003. *Lying Up a Nation: Race and Black Music*. Chicago: University of Chicago Press.

Raffety, Erin L. 2015. "Minimizing Social Distance: Participatory Research with Children." *Childhood* 22 (3): 409–22.

Rampton, Ben. 2006. *Language in Late Modernity: Interaction in an Urban School*. New York: Cambridge University Press.

Rappert, Brian. 2003. "Technologies, Texts, and Possibilities: A Reply to Hutchby." *Sociology* 37 (3): 565–80.

Redman, Peter, Debbie Epstein, Mary Jane Kehily, and Mairtin Mac An Ghaill. 2002. "Boys Bonding: Same-Sex Friendships, the Unconscious, and Heterosexual Discourse." *Discourse: Studies in the Cultural Politics of Education* 23 (2): 179–91.

Rehfel, Andrew. 2011. "The Child as Democratic Citizen." *Annals of the American Academy of Political and Social Science* 633 (1): 141–66.

Reynolds, Jennifer F., and Marjorie Faulstich Orellana. 2009. "New Immigrant Youth Interpreting in White Public Space." *American Anthropologist* 111 (2): 211–23.

Rideout, Victoria J., Ulla G. Foehr, and Donald F. Roberts. 2010. "Generation M2: Media in the Lives of 8- to 18-Year-Olds." Kaiser Family Foundation (January), http://kff.org/other/event/generation-m2-media-in-the-lives-of/.

Roberts, Donald F., Ulla G. Foehr, and Victoria J. Rideout. 2005. "Generation M: Media in the Lives of 8–18 Year-olds." Kaiser Family Foundation (March), http://kff.org/other/generation-m-media-in-the-lives-of/.

Rose, Jacqueline. 1984. *The Case of Peter Pan, or, The Impossibility of Children's Fiction.* London: MacMillan.

Rothenbuhler, Eric W., and John Durham Peters. 1997. "Defining Phonography: An Experiment in Theory." *The Musical Quarterly* 81 (2): 242–64.

Rymes, Betsy. 2003. "Relating Word to World: Indexicality During Literacy Events." In *Linguistic Anthropology of Education,* edited by Stanton Wortham and Betsy Rymes, pp. 121–50. Westport, CT: Praeger.

———. 2004. "Contrasting Zones of Comfortable Competence: Popular Culture in a Phonics Lesson." *Linguistics and Education* 14 (3–4): 321–35.

———. 2008. "The Relationship between Mass Media and Classroom Discourse." *Working Papers in Educational Linguistics* 23 (1): 65–88.

Sanches, Mary, and Barbara Kirshenblatt-Gimblett. 1976. "Children's Traditional Speech Play and Child Language." In *Speech Play,* edited by Barbara Kirshenblatt-Gimblett and Joel Sherzer, pp. 1–18. Philadelphia: University of Pennsylvania Press.

Schapiro, Tamar. 1999. "What Is a Child?" *Ethics* 109 (4): 715–38.

Scheper-Hughes, Nancy, ed. 1989. *Child Survival: Anthropological Perspectives on the Treatment and Maltreatment of Children.* Dordrecht: Reidel.

Schloss, Joseph, and Bill Bahng Boyer. 2014. "Urban Echoes: The Boombox and Sonic Mobility in the 1980s." In *The Oxford Handbook of Mobile Music Studies,* vol. 1, edited by Jason Stanyek and Sumanth Gopinath, pp. 399–412. New York: Oxford University Press.

Schor, Juliet B. 2004. *Born to Buy: The Commercialized Child and the New Consumer Culture.* New York: Scribner.

———. 2006. "When Childhood Gets Commercialized, Can Children Be Protected?" In *Regulation, Awareness, Empowerment: Young People and Harmful Media Content in the Digital Age,* edited by Ulla Carlsson, pp. 101–21. Göteborg: NORDICOM.

Schutz, Alfred. 1977 [1951]. "Making Music Together: A Study in Social Relationships." In *Symbolic Anthropology,* edited by Janet L. Dolgin, David S. Kemnitzer, and David M. Schneider, pp. 106–19. New York: Columbia University Press.

Seiter, Ellen. 1993. *Sold Separately: Children and Parents in Consumer Culture.* New Brunswick, NJ: Rutgers University Press.

Silverstein, Michael. 1976. "Shifters, Linguistic Categories, and Cultural Description." In *Meaning in Anthropology,* edited by Keith Basso and Henry A. Selby, pp. 11–55. Alberquerque: University of New Mexico Press.

Silverstein, Michael, and Greg Urban. 1996. "The Natural History of Discourse." In *Natural Histories of Discourse,* edited by Michael Silverstein and Greg Urban, pp. 1–17. Chicago: University of Chicago Press.

Singer, Peter. 1994. *Rethinking Life and Death: The Collapse of Our Traditional Ethics.* New York: St. Martin's Press.

Skuse, Andrew. 2005. "Enlivened Objects: The Social Life, Death, and Rebirth of Radio as Commodity in Afghanistan." *Journal of Material Culture* 10 (2): 123–37.

Small, Christopher. 1998. *Musicking: The Meaning of Performing and Listening.* Hanover, NH: University Press of New England.

Stallybrass, Peter, and Allon White. 1986. *Politics and Poetics of Transgression*. Ithaca, NY: Cornell University Press.

Stephens, Sharon. 1995. "Children and the Politics of Culture in 'Late Capitalism.'" In *Children and the Politics of Culture*, edited by Sharon Stephens, pp. 3–48. Princeton, NJ: Princeton University Press.

Sterne, Jonathan. 2003. *The Audible Past: Cultural Origins of Sound Reproduction*. Durham, NC: Duke University Press.

———. 2012. *MP3: The Meaning of a Format*. Durham, NC: Duke University Press.

Stevens, Reed, Tom Satwicz, and Laurie McCarthy. 2007. "In-Game, In-Room, In-World: Reconnecting Video Game Play to the Rest of Kids' Lives." In *The Ecology of Games: Connecting Youth, Games, and Learning*, edited by Katie Salen, pp. 41–66. Cambridge, MA: MIT Press.

Suhr, Hiesun Cecilia. 2012. *Social Media and Music: The Digital Field of Cultural Production*. New York: Peter Lang.

Sutton-Smith, Brian. 1959. *The Games of New Zealand Children*. Berkeley: University of California Press.

———. 1982. "Play Theory of the Rich and for the Poor." In *Children In and Out of School: Ethnography and Education*, edited by Perry Gilmore and Allan A. Glatthorn, pp. 187–205. Washington, DC: Center for Applied Linguistics.

———. 1986. *Toys as Culture*. New York: Gardner Press.

———. 1997. *The Ambiguity of Play*. Cambridge, MA: Harvard University Press.

Sutton-Smith, Brian, and David M. Abrams. 1978. "Psychosexual Material in the Stories Told by Children: The Fucker." *Archives of Sexual Behavior* 7 (6): 521–43.

Svitak, Adora. 2010. "What Adults Can Learn from Kids." Talk presented to TED Conference, Long Beach, California, February 13, http://www.ted.com/talks/adora_svitak.html.

Tanaka, Atau, Guillaume Valadon, and Christophe Berger. 2007. "Social Mobile Music Navigation Using The Compass." Paper presented at the Fourth International Mobile Music Workshop, Amsterdam, May 7.

Tannen, Deborah. 1989. *Talking Voices: Repetition, Dialogue, and Imagery in Conversational Discourse*. New York: Cambridge University Press.

Tedlock, Dennis. 1983. "Phonography and the Problem of Time in Oral Narrative Events." In *The Spoken Word and the Work of Interpretation*, pp. 194–215. Philadelphia: University of Pennsylvania Press.

Thorne, Barrie. 1987. "Re-Visioning Women and Social Change: Where are the Children?" *Gender and Society* 1 (1): 85–109.

Thornham, Helen, and Angela McFarlane. 2010. "Discourses of the Digital Native." *Information, Communication, and Society* 14 (2): 258–79.

Tobin, Joseph J., ed. 2004. *Pikachu's Global Adventure: The Rise and Fall of Pokémon*. Durham, NC: Duke University Press.

Tufekci, Zeynep. 2014. "Big Questions for Social Media Big Data: Representativeness, Validity and Other Methodological Pitfalls." In *Proceedings of the Eighth International AAAI Conference on Weblogs and Social Media*, pp. 505–14. Palo Alto, CA: AAAI Press.

Turkle, Sherry. 2011. *Alone Together: Why We Expect More from Technology and Less from Each Other*. New York: Basic Books.

United States Census Bureau/American FactFinder. 2009. "S1901 Income in the Past 12 Months (In 2009 Inflation-Adjusted Dollars)." *2005–2009 American Community Survey*. Washington, DC: United States Census Bureau.

———. 2010. "DP05 ACS Demographic and Housing Estimates." *2006–2010 American Community Survey*. Washington, DC: United States Census Bureau.

Urban, Greg. 1991. *A Discourse-Centered Approach to Language and Culture: Native South American Myths and Rituals*. Austin: University of Texas Press.

Van Bueren, Geraldine. 2011. "Multigenerational Citizenship: The Importance of Recognizing Children as National and International Citizens." *Annals of the American Academy of Political and Social Science* 633 (1): 30–51.

Vannini, Phillip. 2009. "Introduction." In *Material Culture and Technology in Everyday Life: Ethnographic Approaches*, edited by Phillip Vannini, pp. 1–12. New York: Peter Lang.

Varenne, Hervé, Shelley Goldman, and Ray McDermott. 1998. "Racing in Place." In *Successful Failure: The School America Builds*, edited by Hervé Varenne and Ray McDermott, pp. 106–15. Boulder, CO: Westview Press.

Voloshinov, V. N. 1986 [1929]. *Marxism and the Philosophy of Language*, translated by Ladislav Matejka and I. R. Titunik. Cambridge, MA: Harvard University Press.

Wallis, Claudia. 2006. "The Multitasking Generation." *Time* 167 (13) March 19: 48–55.

Warner, Michael. 1990. *The Letters of the Republic: Publication and the Public Sphere in Eighteenth-Century America*. Cambridge, MA: Harvard University Press.

———. 1992. "The Mass Public and the Mass Subject." In *Habermas and the Public Sphere*, edited by Craig Calhoun, pp. 377–401. Cambridge, MA: MIT Press.

———. 2002. "Publics and Counterpublics." *Public Culture* 14 (1): 49–90.

Weheliye, Alexander G. 2005. *Phonographies: Grooves in Sonic Afro-Modernity*. Durham, NC: Duke University Press.

Weikle-Mills, Courtney A. 2008. "'Learn to Love Your Book': The Child Reader and Affectionate Citizenship." *Early American Literature* 43 (1): 35–61.

———. 2013. *Imaginary Citizens: Child Readers and the Limits of American Independence, 1640–1868*. Baltimore: Johns Hopkins University Press.

Weisbard, Eric. 2014. *Top 40 Democracy: The Rival Mainstreams of American Music*. Chicago: University of Chicago Press.

Willett, Rebekah. 2013. "Remixing Children's Culture: Media-Referenced Play on the Playground." In *Children's Games in the New Media Age: Childlore, Media, and the Playground*, edited by Andrew Burn and Chris Richards, pp. 133–51. Burlington, VT: Ashgate.

———. 2014. "Children's Media-referenced Games: The Lived Culture of Consumer Texts on a School Playground." *Children and Society* 29 (5): 410–20.

Willett, Rebekah, Chris Richards, Jackie Marsh, Andrew Burn, and Julia C. Bishop. 2013. *Children, Media, and Playground Cultures: Ethnographic Studies of School Playtimes*. New York: Palgrave Macmillan.

Willis, Ellen. 2014 [1970]. "Women and the Myth of Consumerism." In *The Essential Ellen Willis*, edited by Nona Willis Aronowitz. Minneapolis: University of Minnesota Press.

Willis, Paul. 1981 [1977]. *Learning to Labor: How Working Class Kids Get Working Class Jobs*. New York: Columbia University Press.

Witmore, Christopher L. 2006. "Vision, Media, Noise, and the Percolation of Time: Symmetrical Approaches to the Mediation of the Material World." *Journal of Material Culture* 11 (3): 267–92.

Woodhead, Martin, and Dorothy Faulkner. 2000. "Subjects, Objects, or Participants? Dilemmas of Psychological Research with Children." In *Research with Children: Perspectives and Practices*, edited by Pia Christensen and Allison James, pp. 9–35. London: Falmer.

Woodruff, Jennifer A. 2009. "Learning to Listen, Learning to *Be*: African-American Girls and Hip-Hop in Durham, NC." PhD diss., Duke University.

Woolard, Kathryn A., and Bambi B. Schieffelin. 1994. "Language Ideology." *Annual Review of Anthropology* 23: 55–82.

Yano, Christine R. 2002. *Tears of Longing: Nostalgia and the Nation in Japanese Popular Song.* Cambridge, MA: Harvard University Press.

Yardi, Sarita. 2008. "Whispers in the Classroom." In *Digital Youth, Innovation, and the Unexpected,* edited by Tara McPherson, pp. 143–64. Cambridge, MA: MIT Press.

Young, Susan. 2003. *Music with the Under-Fours.* New York: RoutledgeFalmer.

———. 2008. "Lullaby Light Shows: Everyday Musical Experience among Under-two-year-olds." *International Journal of Music Education* 26 (1): 33–46.

Young, Susan, and Julia Gillen. 2007. "Toward a Revised Understanding of Young Children's Musical Activities: Reflections from the 'Day in the Life' Project." *Current Musicology* 84: 79–99.

Youth Liberation of Ann Arbor. 1972. *Youth Liberation: News, Politics and Survival Information.* Washington, NY: Times Change Press.

Zelizer, Viviana A. 1985. *Pricing the Priceless Child: The Changing Social Value of Children.* Princeton, NJ: Princeton University Press.

INDEX

The manufacturer's authorised representative in the EU for product
safety is Oxford University Press España S.A. of El Parque Empresarial
San Fernando de Henares, Avenida de Castilla, 2 - 28830 Madrid
(www.oup.es/en or product.safety@oup.com). OUP España S.A. also acts
as importer into Spain of products made by the manufacturer.
Printed and bound by CPI Group (UK) Ltd, Croydon, CR0 4YY
14/09/2026
02216308-0017